TRADE PROMOTION COORDINATING COMMITTEE

The 2007
National Export Strategy

The Administration's
Trade Promotion Agenda

UNITED STATES OF AMERICA

Contents

Letter from the Secretary of Commerce

Dear Mr. President and Madam Speaker:

As Chairman of the interagency Trade Promotion Coordinating Committee (TPCC), it is my pleasure to present to you the 2007 National Export Strategy as mandated by the Export Enhancement Act of 1992.

Americans can be proud of the strong performance of the U.S. economy. U.S. gross domestic product (GDP) grew a solid 3.3 percent in 2006—faster than that of any other major industrialized country. High U.S. productivity has helped America lead the world in manufacturing, producing 50 percent more than second-place Japan. The growing U.S. economy has created more than 8 million new jobs since August 2003—more jobs than the European Union and Japan combined. We see continued steady growth of real wages and after-tax income for American workers and families. This performance is a testament to the enterprising spirit and competitiveness of U.S. companies, workers, and farmers.

Americans should also be confident of their ability to compete in the global marketplace. In 2006, U.S. exports grew by 13 percent over 2005 to $1.4 trillion, while imports increased by 10 percent to $2.2 trillion. The United States is the world's largest exporter. U.S. exports to all regions of the world showed significant growth. U.S. exports rose for 29 of our top 30 trading partners and grew at double-digit rates in key markets including South Korea, Malaysia, Singapore, Mexico, India, Brazil, and the European Union. Exports of goods to China, now our fourth-largest export market, expanded 32 percent in 2006, while imports from China increased 18 percent during the same period. Export success has become a major contributor to strong U.S. economic growth. Exports comprised 11.1 percent of U.S. GDP in 2006 compared to 9.6 percent in 2002 and 5.2 percent 50 years ago.

The Bush Administration is committed to keeping our economy strong and vibrant. The President's agenda for a flexible and dynamic U.S. economy includes making tax relief permanent, balancing the budget, reforming our healthcare system, diversifying our energy supply, and strengthening public education. A critical element for sustained growth and for advancing this agenda is extension of Trade Promotion Authority (TPA) to continue opening markets and expand opportunities for American businesses, farmers, and workers.

Trade Promotion Authority has played an important part in the current export boom. Over the last six years, the Administration has put free trade agreements (FTAs) into effect with 10 countries under TPA and expects to seek Congressional approval of FTAs with four more countries—Peru, Colombia, Panama, and South Korea—over the coming months. In addition, the Administration is working to bring FTAs into force with Oman and Costa Rica. American companies have clearly benefited from current agreements in force and from the United States' engagement in the global economy. While our FTA partners make up only 7 percent of the world's GDP (excluding the United States), they account for 43 percent of total U.S. exports.

Congress can help to ensure the continued contribution of American exports to a healthy U.S. economy by renewing TPA this year and approving the agreements with Peru, Colombia, Panama, and South Korea. If these and other pending free trade agreements enter into force, they will provide another major boost to U.S. exports.

With 95 percent of the world's consumers outside the United States, the global trading system under the World Trade Organization also plays a key role in securing new foreign market access for U.S. goods and services. The ongoing negotiations under the WTO Doha Development Agenda hold enormous potential for creating new economic opportunities through a strong market-opening outcome. TPA renewal will ensure U.S. leadership at this critical phase of the negotiations. A successful conclusion of the Doha Round would have a tremendous impact on U.S. exports as well as benefits for the rest of the world, lifting as many as 66 million of the world's poor out of poverty, according to the World Bank.

The Administration is committed to pursuing trade agreements that are fair, and to ensuring that the terms of all agreements are fully enforced and implemented by our trading partners. Moreover, the Administration is committed to ensuring that both large and small companies throughout the United States have opportunities to benefit from these agreements. I commend state and local governments, trade associations, and corporate partners for working with us to introduce more American companies to exporting. This year's National Export Strategy highlights public-private partnerships and the growing power of new services and technologies, such as e-commerce, to make exporting easier than ever.

The Administration looks forward to working with Congress in the coming year. Together, we can pursue a trade agenda that ensures that the global marketplace continues to be a major boon to the U.S. economy, improving the lives of all Americans.

Sincerely,

Carlos M. Gutierrez
Secretary of Commerce and
Chairman of the Trade Promotion
Coordinating Committee

Editor's Note

American companies, and the goods and services that they market, remain among the most competitive in the world. No major country can match the creativity and innovation of U.S. companies or the skill and productivity of U.S. workers and farmers. While the upturn in U.S. exports reflects these strengths, we are only just beginning to see their potential to benefit our country.

The 2007 National Export Strategy examines how the combination of declining trade barriers and advancing technologies has made exporting easier than ever. American businesses should look at the global economy as a major sales opportunity as well as a source of competition. The goals of this report are to raise awareness in the American business community about the advantages of exporting, to convince businesses that are not exporting to consider exporting, and to get those businesses that are exporting to enter more overseas markets.

Let me briefly highlight the themes of each of the chapters, including the major changes we see in the global marketplace and the public and private sector response to these changes.

The State of Trade and U.S. Competitiveness documents the current U.S. export boom by market and sector, reviews the U.S. rankings atop international measures of competitiveness, and looks at global economic growth. Foreign markets have never been more attractive and more open for business with American companies, with healthy economic growth, especially in emerging and developing markets.

■ **Conclusions**: The Commerce Department's Transformational Diplomacy Initiative shifts resources to emerging markets important to future opportunities for U.S. businesses. Commerce's Invest in America Initiative promotes the United States as the best market in the world for investment. And the Federal Government continues to develop new programs and initiatives promoting the services sector.

The Impact of Trade Liberalization looks at the track record of bilateral Free Trade Agreements (FTAs) already in force as of 2006. Market access gains through FTAs with several countries in Central and South America and the Middle East make these regions a priority for our promotion efforts.

■ **Conclusions**: The Federal Government's FTA promotion strategy closely coordinates agencies' activities and ensures that U.S. businesses have access to the tools and opportunities they need to expand into FTA markets. We highlight the Americas Competitiveness Forum where leaders from throughout Latin America met in Atlanta in June. The Overseas Private Investment Corporation held a conference in El Salvador in May focusing on investment opportunities. In the Middle East, TPCC agencies are working to deepen the level of U.S. business involvement in the region, through projects and activities that improve the flow of goods throughout the region.

The Rise of E-Commerce features the transformative power of the Internet and the exponential rise in electronic access to potential buyers outside of the United States, including in emerging markets. While growing Internet access abroad does not automatically translate into new online sales, powerful new online business tools and secure payment mechanisms can represent a cost-effective means for companies to become active exporters. The chapter provides practical information on some of the most attractive foreign markets for e-commerce, and presents steps that companies must take to unleash the export potential of the Internet.

■ **Conclusions**: U.S. SMEs are becoming more adept at using e-commerce tools, and will increasingly use e-commerce to enter new foreign markets. Powerful e-commerce platforms based in the United States are rapidly expanding their foreign presence. The Federal Government and its public and private partners are helping SMEs employ e-commerce strategies to target foreign markets and reach more buyers.

Using Strategic Partnerships to Help Small and Medium-Sized Companies Export presents the Federal Government's action plan for broadening the base of U.S. companies that export—particularly small and medium-sized enterprises (SMEs)—by partnering with state and local governments, trade associations and business groups, and major U.S. corporations and banks. All of these partners have access to large client bases and offer unique services and technologies that make exporting easier. More importantly, they all share a commitment to making export opportunities more available to their clients and constituencies.

▩ **Conclusions**: Federal, state, and local governments, trade associations, and corporate partners are working together to reach more potential exporters. The Strategic Partnership Initiative broadens both the number of stakeholders we partner with and the kinds of activities we jointly pursue. While activities to date have focused on domestic outreach, future cooperation will include more foreign trade missions, conferences, and other events targeting foreign buyers.

Strategic Initiatives in Priority Markets features select markets that companies should consider, as they present either attractive market conditions or significant new market openings. China's economy continues to grow by 9 to 11 percent a year, and we are beginning to see the emergence of a large consumer middle class in that country. Likewise, India's economy has been consistently growing at 8 to 10 percent a year. U.S. exports have benefited from economic reforms in India and a strong bilateral commercial dialogue. In addition, healthy economic growth makes entry into Brazil a priority.

▩ **Conclusions**: Federal, state, and local governments, trade associations, and our corporate partners will focus trade promotion resources and activities in the 2007 priority markets.

☐ In **China**, we are focusing on intellectual property rights, target sectors (e.g., education, energy, and the environment), greater use of our 14 American Trading Centers, and development of opportunities outside of Beijing and Shanghai.

- In **India**, we continue to strengthen the bilateral partnership by combining export promotion and commercial policy activities under the U.S.–India Commercial Dialogue.

- In **Brazil**, we are improving our commercial dialogue and cooperation on commercial issues through the U.S.–Brazil Commercial Dialogue and the new U.S.–Brazil CEO Forum.

Taken together, U.S. export competitiveness, improvements in market access and technology, and strong foreign demand represent a superlative set of conditions for U.S. companies to begin exporting. American companies should feel confident in their ability to grow their bottom line through foreign sales, and they should know that their Federal Government and its public and private partners stand ready to help.

Franklin L. Lavin
Under Secretary of Commerce for International Trade
Editor, 2007 NES

The State of Trade and U.S. Competitiveness

The 2006 trade numbers tell a very positive story about the state of America's trading relationships with the rest of the world. U.S. exports are booming and at an all-time high. International measures of competitiveness tell the same story, with the United States continuing to rank at or near the top for factors such as overall business setting, microeconomic market conditions, ease of doing business, and innovation. Global economic numbers suggest that the world economy is in the midst of one of its longest and broadest periods of growth, with economic expansions in every region and forecasts of the rapid expansion of a global middle class. All of these factors should boost the confidence of the U.S. business community that American companies can thrive in the global marketplace.

AN OVERVIEW OF U.S. TRADE

Trade volume is up and both trade and exports in dollar terms are at all-time highs (*Chart 1*). After growing almost 11 percent from 2004 to 2005, U.S. exports grew 13 percent in 2006. With 22 of our top 30 trading partners, U.S. exports grew by double-digit percentages in 2006. U.S. exports grew faster than imports with 21 of our top 30 trading partners. At $1.4 trillion, U.S. exports were greater than the entire economies of countries such as Canada or Spain.

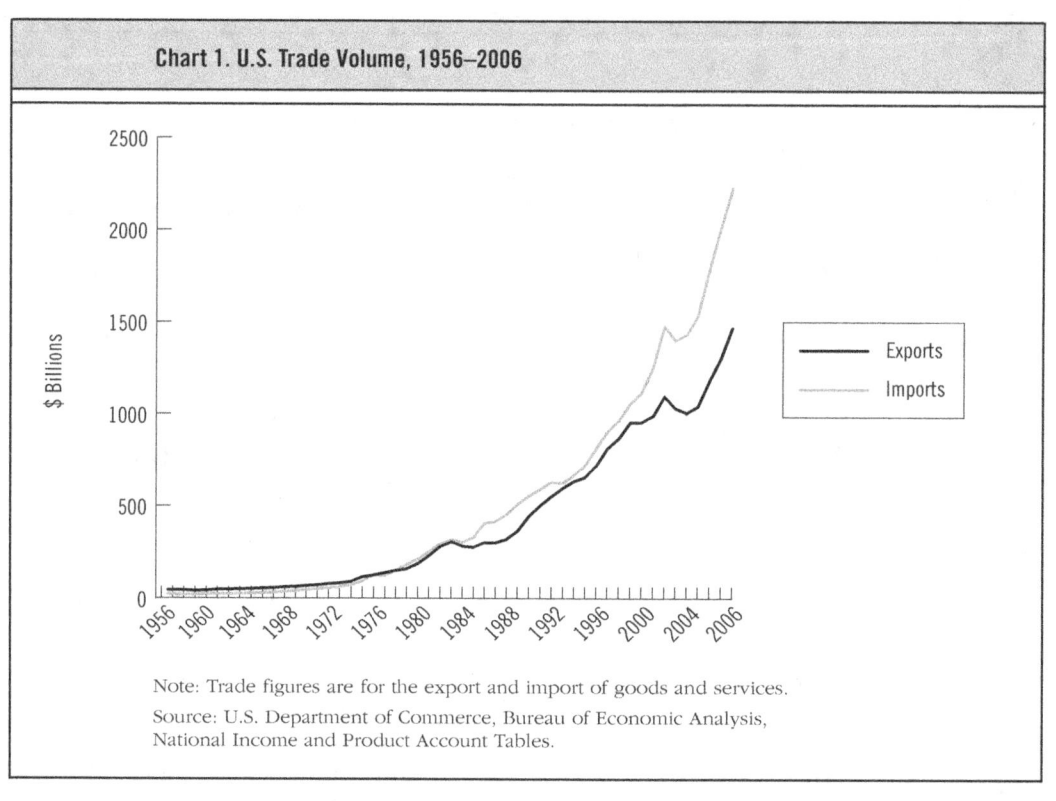

Chart 1. U.S. Trade Volume, 1956–2006

Note: Trade figures are for the export and import of goods and services.

Source: U.S. Department of Commerce, Bureau of Economic Analysis, National Income and Product Account Tables.

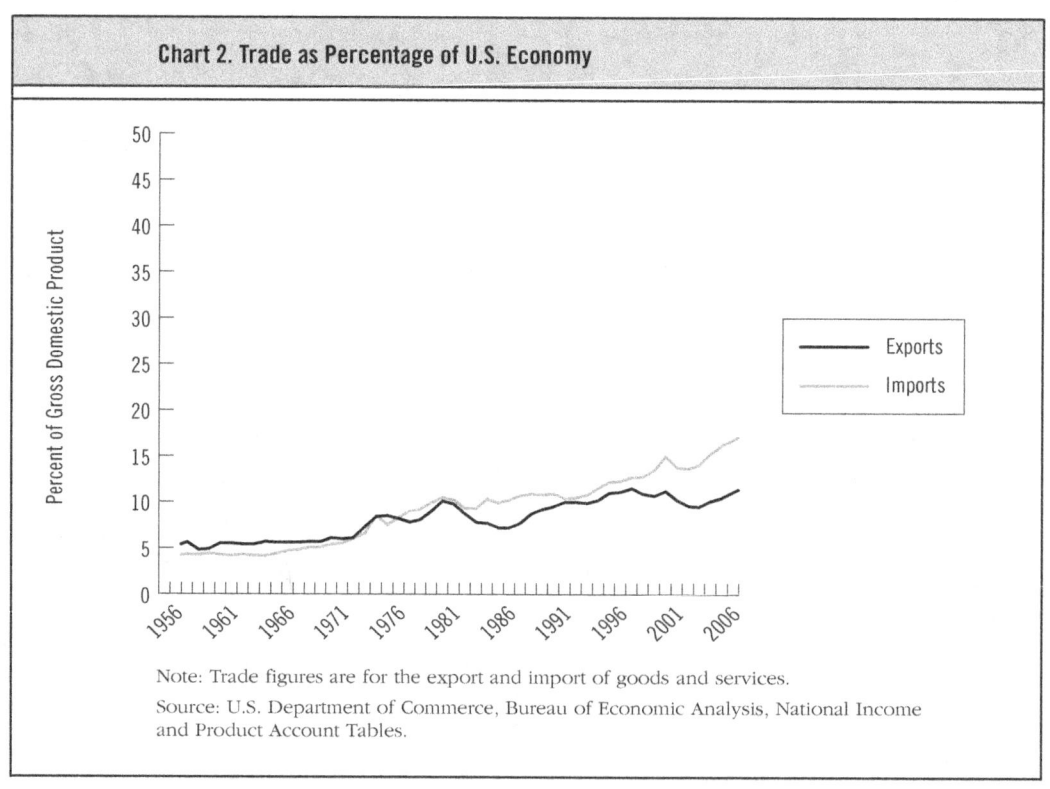

Chart 2. Trade as Percentage of U.S. Economy

Note: Trade figures are for the export and import of goods and services.

Source: U.S. Department of Commerce, Bureau of Economic Analysis, National Income and Product Account Tables.

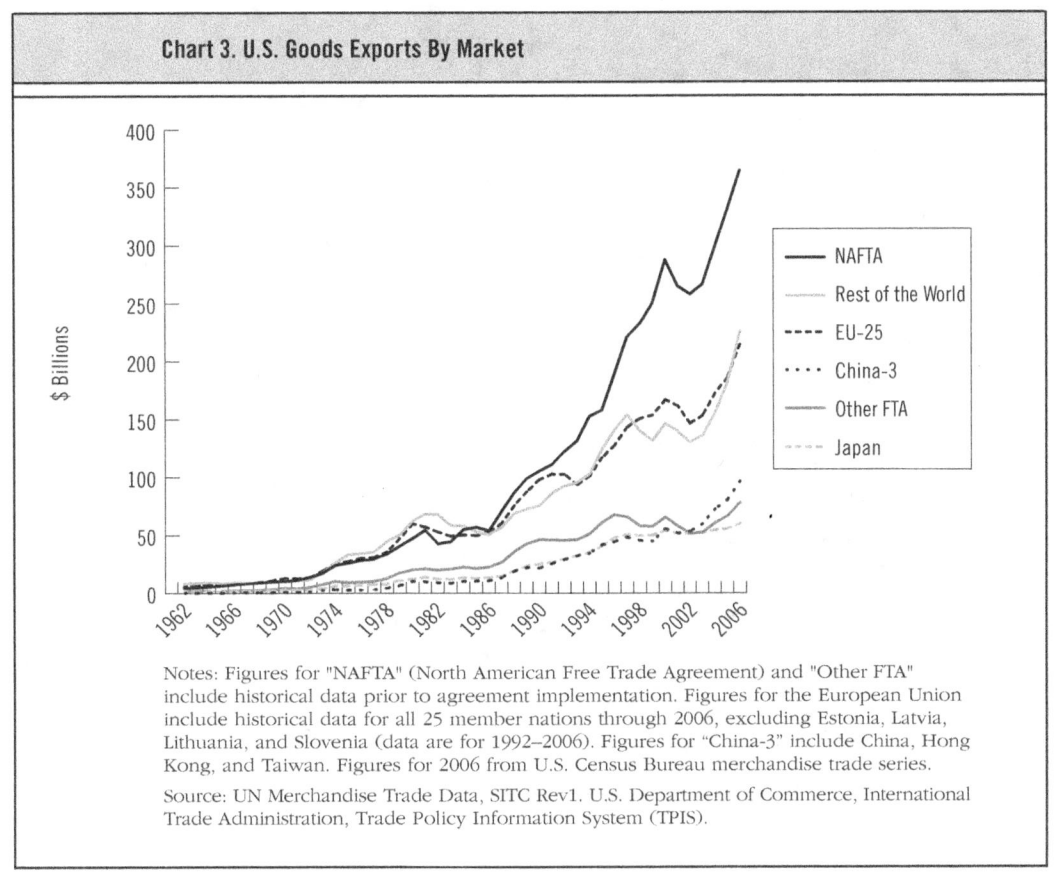

Chart 3. U.S. Goods Exports By Market

Notes: Figures for "NAFTA" (North American Free Trade Agreement) and "Other FTA" include historical data prior to agreement implementation. Figures for the European Union include historical data for all 25 member nations through 2006, excluding Estonia, Latvia, Lithuania, and Slovenia (data are for 1992–2006). Figures for "China-3" include China, Hong Kong, and Taiwan. Figures for 2006 from U.S. Census Bureau merchandise trade series.

Source: UN Merchandise Trade Data, SITC Rev1. U.S. Department of Commerce, International Trade Administration, Trade Policy Information System (TPIS).

In percentage terms, trade makes up a larger share of the U.S. economy than ever before; exports are near an all-time high and will likely continue to be an increasingly important part of the U.S. economy (*Chart 2*).

A look at the most important destinations for U.S. exports shows the rapidly growing importance of emerging markets, as well as the continued importance of Europe and our North American Free Trade Agreement (NAFTA) partners (*Chart 3*).

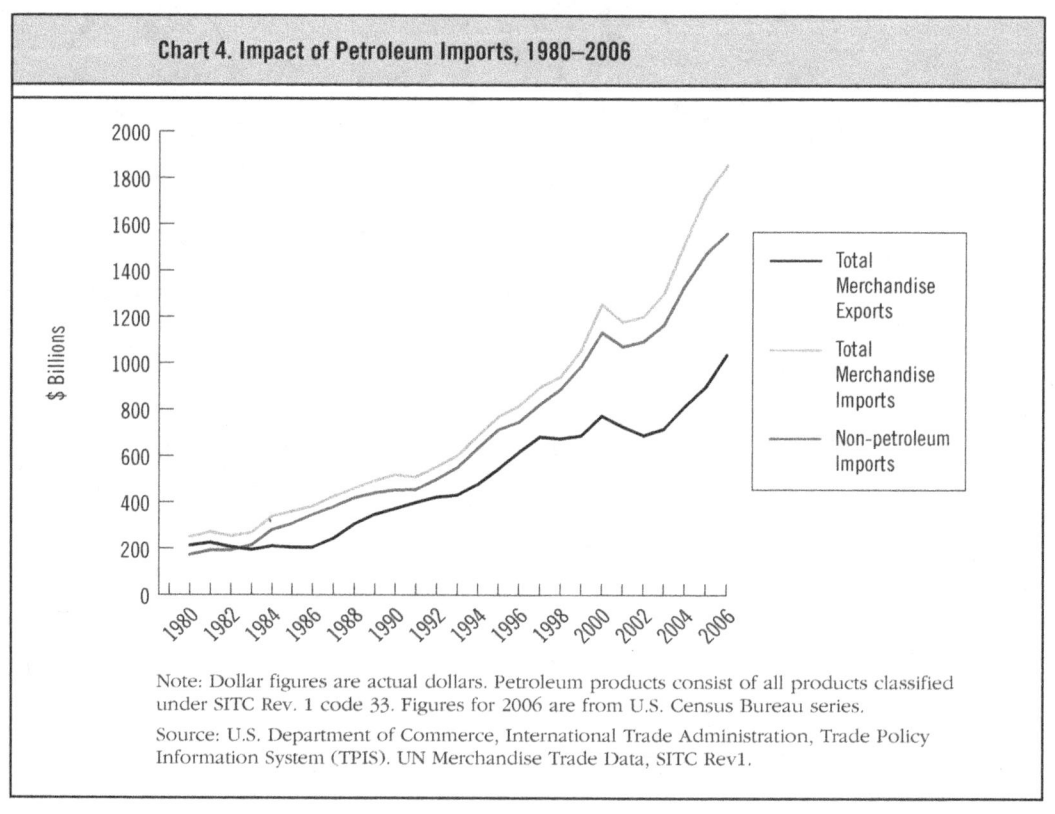

Chart 4. Impact of Petroleum Imports, 1980–2006

Note: Dollar figures are actual dollars. Petroleum products consist of all products classified under SITC Rev. 1 code 33. Figures for 2006 are from U.S. Census Bureau series.

Source: U.S. Department of Commerce, International Trade Administration, Trade Policy Information System (TPIS). UN Merchandise Trade Data, SITC Rev1.

If oil imports are removed from the picture, narrowing of the U.S. trade deficit is apparent in the last half of 2006, as 80 percent of our trade deficit increase resulted from increased prices of petroleum imports (*Chart 4*).

Exports are growing in all areas of the U.S. economy—most rapidly in the manufactured goods industries (*Chart 5a*). Services trade and agricultural trade continue to show a surplus (*Chart 5b*). Manufacturing output continues its steady rise, although manufacturing employment has continued to decline due to productivity gains. Manufacturing employment is reliant on exporting, with one in six manufacturing jobs related to exports. Manufacturing continues to be a significant portion of U.S. exports, in 2006 representing 89 percent of merchandise exports.

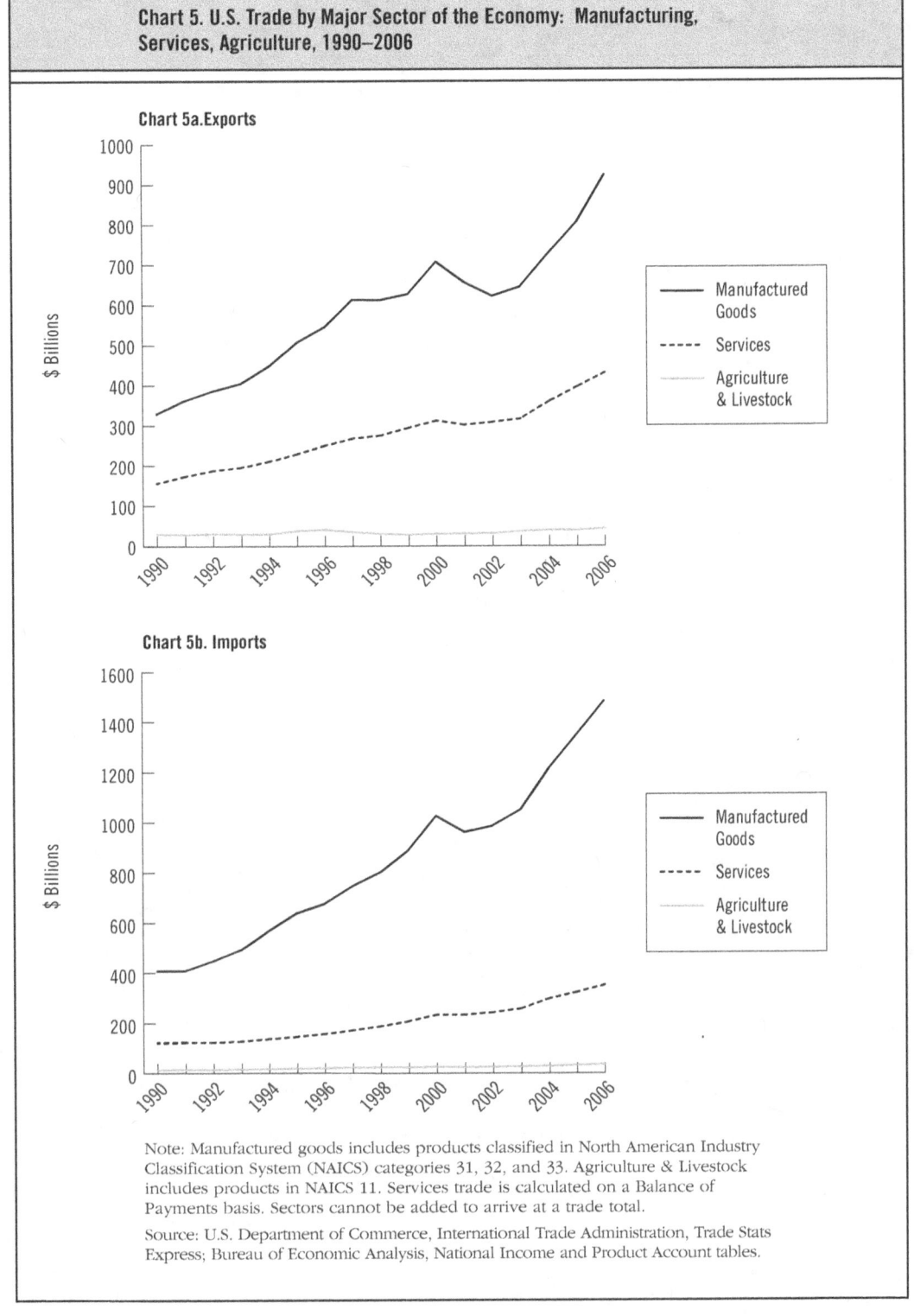

Chart 5. U.S. Trade by Major Sector of the Economy: Manufacturing, Services, Agriculture, 1990–2006

Chart 5a. Exports

$ Billions

Legend:
— Manufactured Goods
--- Services
— Agriculture & Livestock

Chart 5b. Imports

$ Billions

Legend:
— Manufactured Goods
--- Services
— Agriculture & Livestock

Note: Manufactured goods includes products classified in North American Industry Classification System (NAICS) categories 31, 32, and 33. Agriculture & Livestock includes products in NAICS 11. Services trade is calculated on a Balance of Payments basis. Sectors cannot be added to arrive at a trade total.

Source: U.S. Department of Commerce, International Trade Administration, Trade Stats Express; Bureau of Economic Analysis, National Income and Product Account tables.

Chart 6. Top Sectors in U.S. Merchandise Trade, 1996–2006

Chart 6a. Exports

$ Billions

Legend:
- Aerospace Products & Parts
- Semiconductors & Other Electronic Components
- Computer Equipment
- Motor Vehicles
- Motor Vehicle Parts

Chart 6b. Imports

$ Billions

Legend:
- Oil & Gas
- Motor Vehicles
- Computer Equipment
- Semiconductors & Other Electronic Components
- Motor Vehicle Parts

Note: Product categories represent the top five out of all merchandise at a 4-digit NAICS category level.

Source: U.S. Department of Commerce, International Trade Administration, Trade Policy Information System (TPIS).

Our greatest overall strength in manufacturing exports continues to be in the high-tech and high value-added industrial sectors such as aerospace, electronics, and computers (*Chart 6a*).

However, industrial raw materials experienced some of the biggest gains in 2006 in both exports and imports (*Chart 7a, 7b*). It is notable that amongst top import sectors, oil and gas represented both the largest percentage growth (*Chart 6b*) and dollar increase (*Chart 7b*) of any sector from 2005 to 2006.

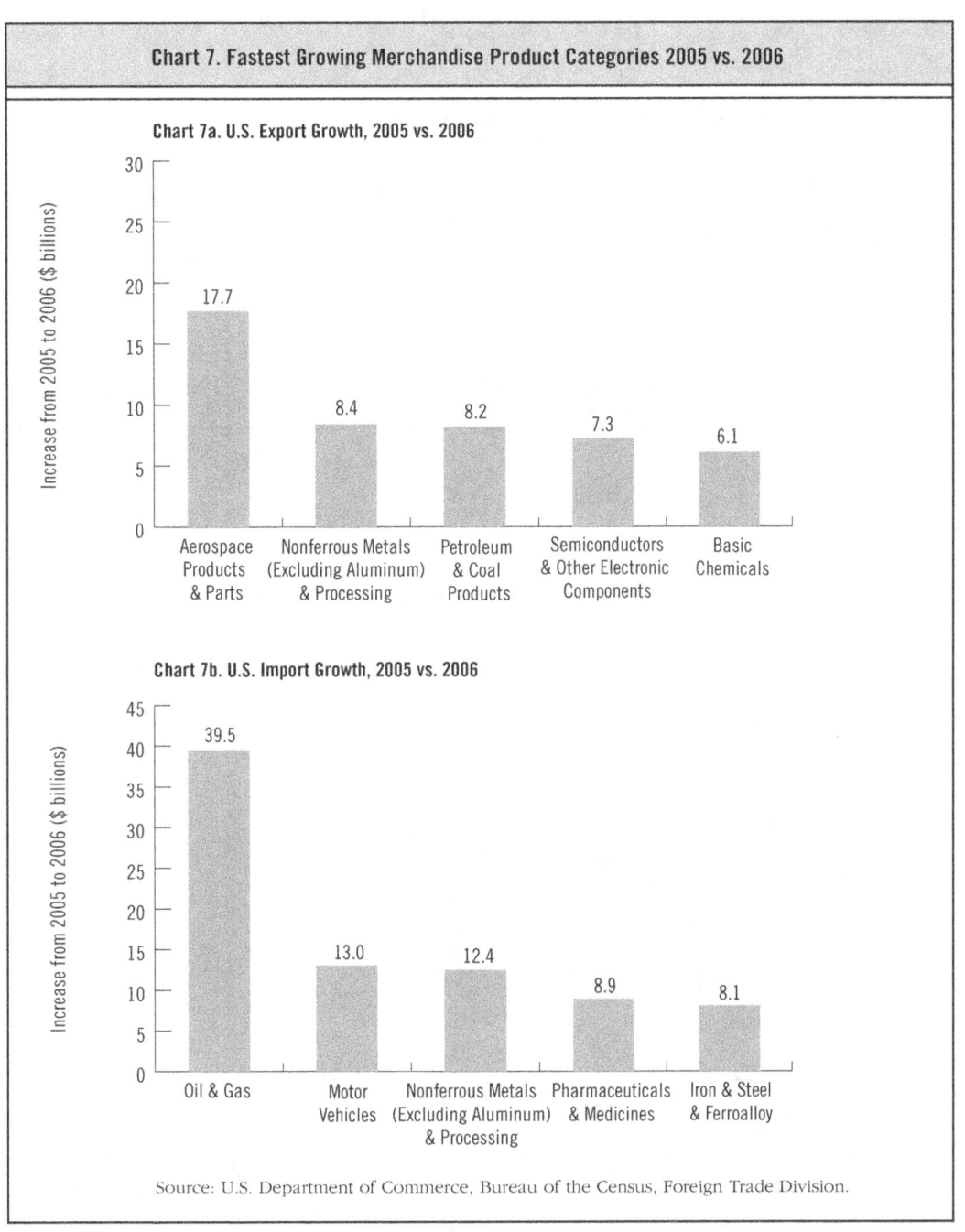

Chart 7. Fastest Growing Merchandise Product Categories 2005 vs. 2006

Chart 7a. U.S. Export Growth, 2005 vs. 2006

Increase from 2005 to 2006 ($ billions)

Aerospace Products & Parts	17.7
Nonferrous Metals (Excluding Aluminum) & Processing	8.4
Petroleum & Coal Products	8.2
Semiconductors & Other Electronic Components	7.3
Basic Chemicals	6.1

Chart 7b. U.S. Import Growth, 2005 vs. 2006

Increase from 2005 to 2006 ($ billions)

Oil & Gas	39.5
Motor Vehicles	13.0
Nonferrous Metals (Excluding Aluminum) & Processing	12.4
Pharmaceuticals & Medicines	8.9
Iron & Steel & Ferroalloy	8.1

Source: U.S. Department of Commerce, Bureau of the Census, Foreign Trade Division.

The United States remains the world's leading exporter of services by a wide margin (*Chart 8*), and we continue to run a sizable surplus in services trade. For 2006, exports of services were $414.1 billion, up $33.5 billion from 2005. Increases occurred in areas such as business, professional, and technical services, insurance services, and financial services ($20.2 billion), freight and port services ($5.9 billion), royalties and license fees ($4.5 billion), travel ($5.1 billion), and passenger fares ($1.1 billion).[1] These are some of the industries where the United States is a global leader and where we have a strong competitive advantage. Technology is changing the nature of trade in services, and services exports are highly reliant on the protection of intellectual property rights for their success. Consequently, one of our highest priorities is to extend that protection wherever possible.

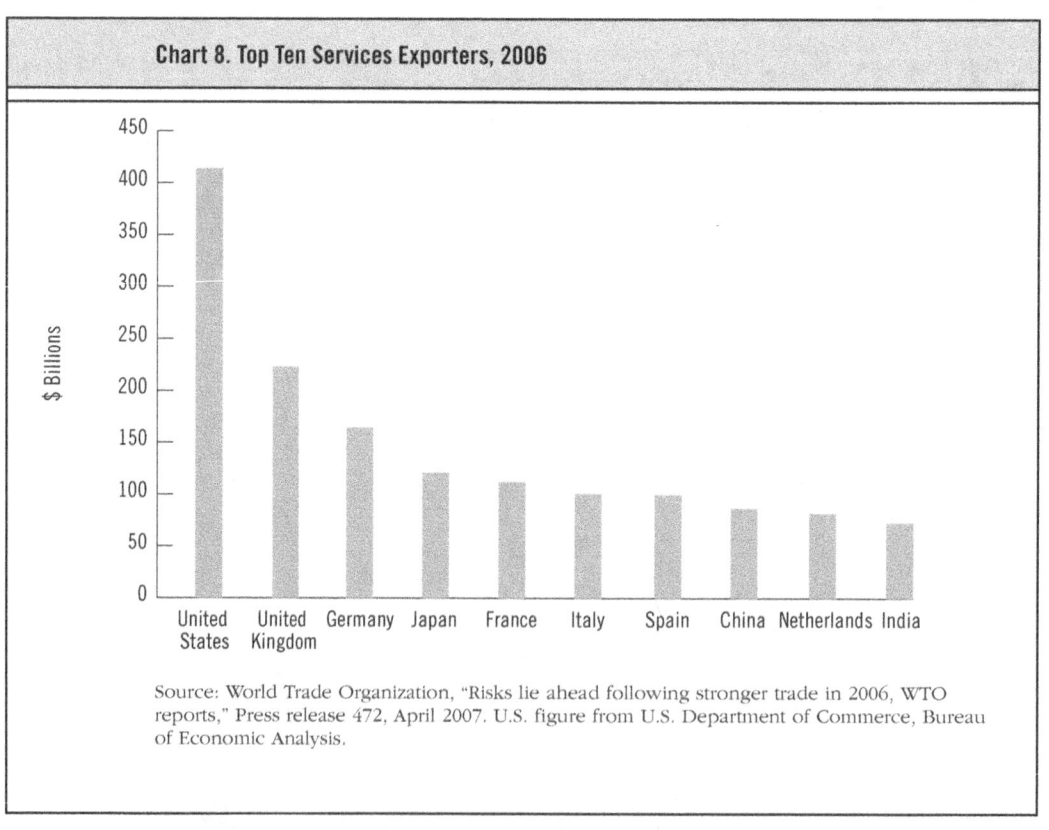

Chart 8. Top Ten Services Exporters, 2006

Source: World Trade Organization, "Risks lie ahead following stronger trade in 2006, WTO reports," Press release 472, April 2007. U.S. figure from U.S. Department of Commerce, Bureau of Economic Analysis.

---

1 U.S. Department of Commerce, Bureau of Economic Analysis, "U.S. International Trade in Goods and Services," news release, February 13, 2007, *http://www.bea.gov/newsreleases/international/trade/2007/trad1206.htm/*.

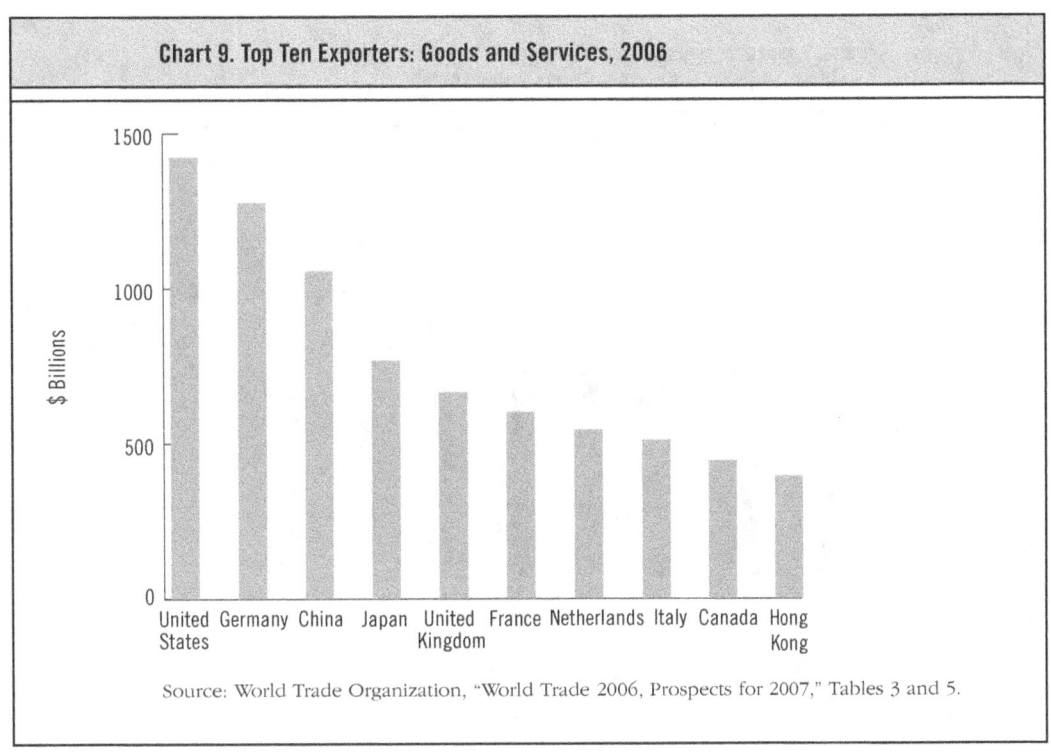

Chart 9. Top Ten Exporters: Goods and Services, 2006

Source: World Trade Organization, "World Trade 2006, Prospects for 2007," Tables 3 and 5.

U.S. COMPETITIVENESS IN THE GLOBAL ECONOMY

Strong services exports and the increasing growth of U.S. goods exports have together kept the United States the world's largest exporter, followed by Germany, China, and Japan (*Chart 9*).

One of the most important factors keeping U.S. exports competitive has been strong U.S. labor productivity growth. Since the early 1990s, the United States has experienced the fastest increase in productivity growth among major developed countries. *Chart 10* shows that, after lagging behind most of the countries in the G7 between 1990 and 1995, the United States became the G7 country with the fastest growth in productivity (measured as growth of GDP per hour worked) between 2000 and 2005. Moreover, only the United States and Japan had faster productivity growth in the most recent period than they did in the early 1990s, and only the United States has shown consistent acceleration over this time period.[2]

---

2 Council of Economic Advisers, *Economic Report of the President*, 2007, (Washington, D.C: GPO, 2007): 58-59, *http://www.whitehouse.gov/cea/2007_erp.pdf*.

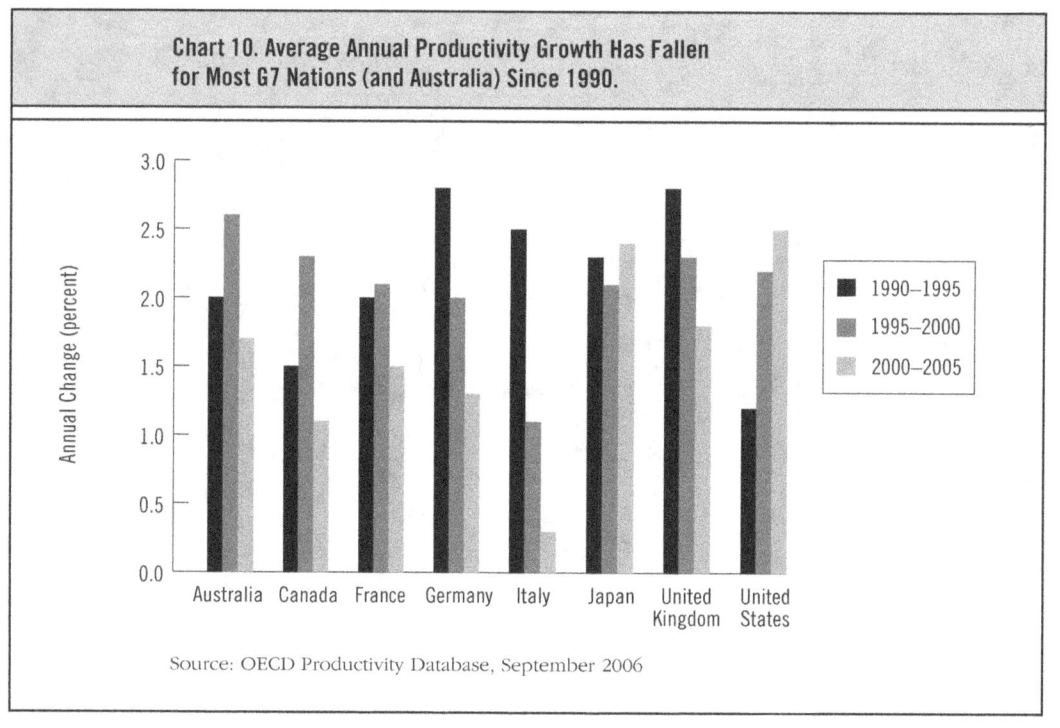

Chart 10. Average Annual Productivity Growth Has Fallen for Most G7 Nations (and Australia) Since 1990.

Source: OECD Productivity Database, September 2006

Citing these trends, the Council of Economic Advisers' 2007 *Economic Report* points to a number of key factors driving strong U.S. productivity, including international openness (e.g., to investment, financial markets, and trade), flexible labor markets, and the low costs of starting a business in the United States.[3] These factors also put the U.S. economy in a position to more quickly take advantage of the rapid advance of information technology.

Other Independent Measures of Global Competitiveness: Several independent international research groups point to many of the same factors when placing the United States at or near the top of their measures of global competitiveness (*Table 1*). While some of these measures look at how connected the United States is to the rest of the world, others focus on macroeconomic and microeconomic efficiencies within the U.S. economy that characterize U.S. companies and the business environment.

---

3 *Ibid.*, 58-61.

Table 1. U.S. Rankings in Global Competitiveness

	U.S. Ranking	Countries Ahead of the U.S.	Countries Behind the U.S.
Globalization Index 2006 (A.T. Kearney/Foreign Policy)	3	Singapore (1) Switzerland (2)	Ireland (4) Denmark (5) Canada (6) Netherlands (7) Australia (8)
Global Competitiveness Index (World Economic Forum)	6	Switzerland (1) Finland (2) Sweden (3) Denmark (4) Singapore (5)	Japan (7) Germany (8) Netherlands (9) United Kingdom (10) Hong Kong, SAR (11)
Business Competitiveness Index 2006 (World Economic Forum)	1		Germany (2) Finland (3) Switzerland (4) Denmark (5) Netherlands (6)
Ease of Doing Business 2006 (World Bank)	3	Singapore (1) New Zealand (2)	Canada (4) Hong Kong, SAR (5) United Kingdom (6) Denmark (7) Australia (8)
Global Innovation Index 2007 (World Business/INSEAD)	1		Germany (2) United Kingdom (3) Japan (4) France (5) Switzerland (6)

The **2006 Globalization Index** of *Foreign Policy* magazine looks at whether countries are becoming more or less globally connected. The index examines underlying international trends such as economic integration, personal contact, technological connectivity, and political engagement.

- By this measure, the United States ranked third, behind only Singapore and Switzerland. The United States moved up one place from fourth in 2005 due to an "off-the-charts" technology score.[4] The United States had more Internet users, more Internet hosts, and more secure servers per capita than any other country. In the previous year, the Index had moved the United States up three places, making the United States the first large country to enter the top five. Other factors boosting the United States were more inward foreign investment and stronger engagement with international organizations, and a greater financial commitment to U.N. peacekeeping. Holding back the U.S. ranking was its last-place rating (among the 62 countries ranked) for economic integration, based on the low number of treaties or trade agreements ratified by the United States.

The **Global Competitiveness Index (GCI)** published by the World Economic Forum (WEF) is a broad measure of a country's overall competitiveness, with the United States remaining a world leader in a number of key areas such as market efficiency, technological innovation, higher education and training, and business sophistication.

- The GCI's 2006/2007 measure ranked the United States as the world's most competitive large economy, placing sixth overall behind five smaller countries (Switzerland, Finland, Sweden, Denmark, and Singapore). The United States previously ranked in first place (2005), but the WEF cited large macroeconomic imbalances (particularly public indebtedness associated with repeated fiscal deficits and historically high trade deficits) as the main reason for lowering the U.S. ranking in 2006. Additional factors counted against the United States were the levels of efficiency and transparency of public institutions relative to those of most developed industrial countries.[5]

Of greater significance to individual U.S. companies considering their own global competitiveness is the WEF's **Business Competitiveness Index (BCI)**, which ranks 121 countries by their microeconomic competitiveness in terms

---

4 *Foreign Policy*, "The Globalization Index," November/December 2006, 74–81.

5 World Economic Forum, *Global Competitiveness Report*, 2006–2007 (Geneva: WEF, 2007), xv.

of business environment and company operations and strategies. This measure, in turn, provides an assessment of the sustainability of a country's level of prosperity.

■ According to the BCI rankings, the United States remains first, ahead of Germany and Finland. Key factors keeping the United States at the top include measures of domestic rivalry (intensity of local competition and effectiveness of antitrust policy), financial markets (venture capital availability, local equity market access, and financial market sophistication), and innovative capacity (company R&D spending, local availability of specialized research and training services, and quality of scientific research institutions).[6]

The World Bank's **Ease of Doing Business** is an aggregate ranking based on ten factors such as ease of starting a business, employing workers, and getting credit.

■ By this measure, the United States ranks third behind Singapore and New Zealand, indicating that the U.S. regulatory environment is more conducive to the operation of business than any other major economy.[7]

A new measure, the **Global Innovation Index (GII)** was developed by INSEAD[8] to help show the degree to which individual nations and regions respond to the challenge of innovation.

■ The GII puts the United States in first place, well ahead of second-place Germany.[9] The GII credits the United States with having a better environment for innovation and with being more effective in exploiting innovation. U.S. universities attract the brightest minds from around the world. Efficient U.S.

---

6 *Ibid.*, xxiv.

7 Doing Business: Economy Rankings, *http://worldbank.org/EconomyRankings/Default. aspx?direction=asc&sort=1*

8 Note: INSEAD was originally founded as the "Institut Européen d'Administration des Affaires" (European Institute for Business Administration). However, having extended its roots to Asia, it is now known as INSEAD (pronounced IN-SEE-ADD).

9 Sumitra Dutta and Simon Caulkin, "The World's Top Innovators," *World Business*, January 17, 2007. *www.worldbusinesslive.com/article/625441*

markets and capital flows support innovation, and U.S. companies effectively apply new technology and processes in innovations. With the emergence of new competitors such as China and India, the GII raised questions about the United States' continued ability to draw overseas talent, directing attention to our primary and secondary education and to the need to produce more scientists and engineers from within. The GII also noted the United States' need to improve aging communications and transportation infrastructure.

Another possible indicator of competitiveness is the ability to attract inward foreign direct investment (FDI). The United Nations Conference on Trade and Development (UNCTAD) has developed two measures of this ability. The **Inward Foreign Direct Investment (FDI) Performance Index**[10] ranks 141 countries by the FDI they receive relative to their economic size. While frequent changes occur in the rankings of the Performance Index, there are few changes from year to year in the rankings of the **Inward FDI Potential Index**,[11] a reflection of the stability of the structural variables measured. This index is based on 12 economic and structural variables—an unweighted average of scores on factors ranging from GDP per capita and GDP growth to telecommunications infrastructure, education, country risk, exports of natural resources and services as a percentage of the world total, and inward FDI stock as a percentage of the world total.

■ The Performance Index shows the United States in decline since 1990 (from 43 in 1990, to 76 in 2000, to 120 in 2005), a trend driven largely by investments in extractive industries (especially oil and gas) in smaller countries, but also by the rise of new competition for FDI from emerging markets. By this

---

10 United Nations Conference on Trade and Development, *World Investment Report 2006*, *www.unctad.org/Templates/Page.asp?intItemID=3198&lang=1* (Country fact sheet: United States).

11 United Nations Conference on Trade and Development, Inward Foreign Direct Investment Potential Index, *www.unctad.org/Templates/WebFlyer.asp?intItemID=2472&lang=1*.

measure, 12 of the top performers in 2005 were developing countries and three were transition economies. By region, the largest declines were in the EU. The highest regional index was that of Southeast Asia, while the sharpest rises were for North Africa and West Asia.

☐ In contrast, the Potential Index has had the United States dominating the top position since it was first published in 1991, with the United Kingdom ranking second in 2005. Developed countries accounted for 15 of the top 20 economies. Singapore, Qatar, Hong Kong, South Korea, and Taiwan, in that order, were the developing economies featured among the top 20.[12]

GLOBAL ECONOMY AND TRADE

While U.S. competitiveness is "pushing" more exports to foreign markets, the rest of the world is "pulling" more U.S. goods and services exports abroad with growing economies, consumption, and demand for imports. An in-depth look at global economic growth and import consumption numbers shows an important shift of activity to emerging markets.

Global Economic Growth: The global economy is enjoying one of its longest periods of sustained growth in decades. Through the first half of 2006, global expansion has been buoyant, exceeding expectations in most regions.[13] In addition to strong growth in the United States, economic expansions continued in both Europe and Japan. Emerging markets, like China, are growing rapidly, and many low-income countries have been growing well due to strong commodity prices.

---

12 United Nations Conference on Trade and Development, *World Investment Report 2006*, *www.unctad.org/Templates/Page.asp?intItemID=3198&lang=1* (Country fact sheet: United States).

13 International Monetary Fund, *World Economic Outlook*, (Washington D.C: September 2006), xiii.

As a result, global GDP is likely to sustain about a 5 percent growth rate through 2008, following a steep increase from 2001 to 2004 (*Chart 11*).

Looking ahead, the World Bank predicts the global economy could expand from $35 trillion in 2005 to $72 trillion in 2030. While this would represent only a slight increase in global growth rates relative to the last 25 years, a growing share of that growth would come from developing countries. Such growth would result in a substantial reduction in poverty. The number of people living on less than $1 a day would be cut in half, from 1.1 billion today, to 550 million in 2030. Forecast growth in the emerging markets of the developing world would also result in the rapid expansion of the global middle class. According to the World Bank, the ranks of the world's middle class will triple

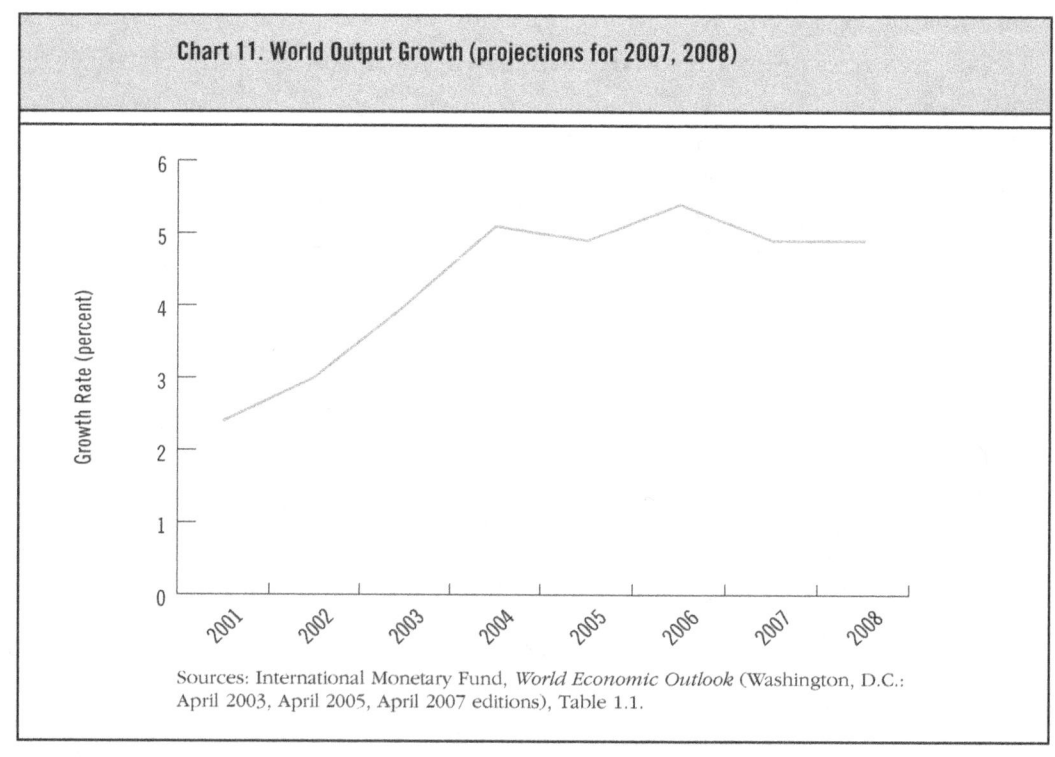

Chart 11. World Output Growth (projections for 2007, 2008)

Sources: International Monetary Fund, *World Economic Outlook* (Washington, D.C.: April 2003, April 2005, April 2007 editions), Table 1.1.

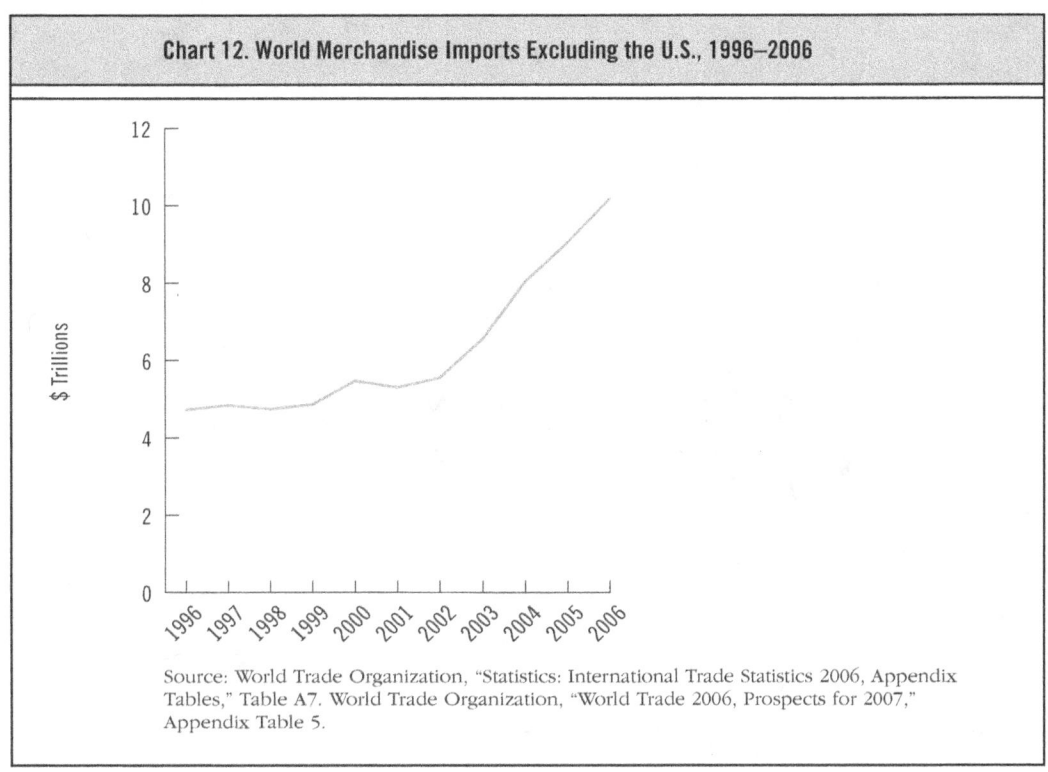

Chart 12. World Merchandise Imports Excluding the U.S., 1996–2006

Source: World Trade Organization, "Statistics: International Trade Statistics 2006, Appendix Tables," Table A7. World Trade Organization, "World Trade 2006, Prospects for 2007," Appendix Table 5.

from 400 million today to 1.2 billion in 2030 if developing country growth continues. While about half of middle-class consumers currently reside in developing countries, by 2030, 92 percent will.[14]

Global Import Demand: Strong global economic growth has fueled the strong growth of world imports. World imports exclusive of the United States more than doubled from 1996 to 2006, reaching more than $10 trillion in 2006—with the most rapid growth occurring since 2002 (*Chart 12*).

Shift to Emerging Markets: While imports are growing in all regions, imports have in recent years consistently grown more rapidly in developing countries than in developed countries (*Chart 13*). Especially in key emerging markets, growing consumption and productive investment are fueling import demand.

---

14 World Bank, "Growth Prospects Are Strong, But Social, Environmental Pressures from Globalization Need More Attention," Press Release 2007/159/DEC, December 13, 2006.

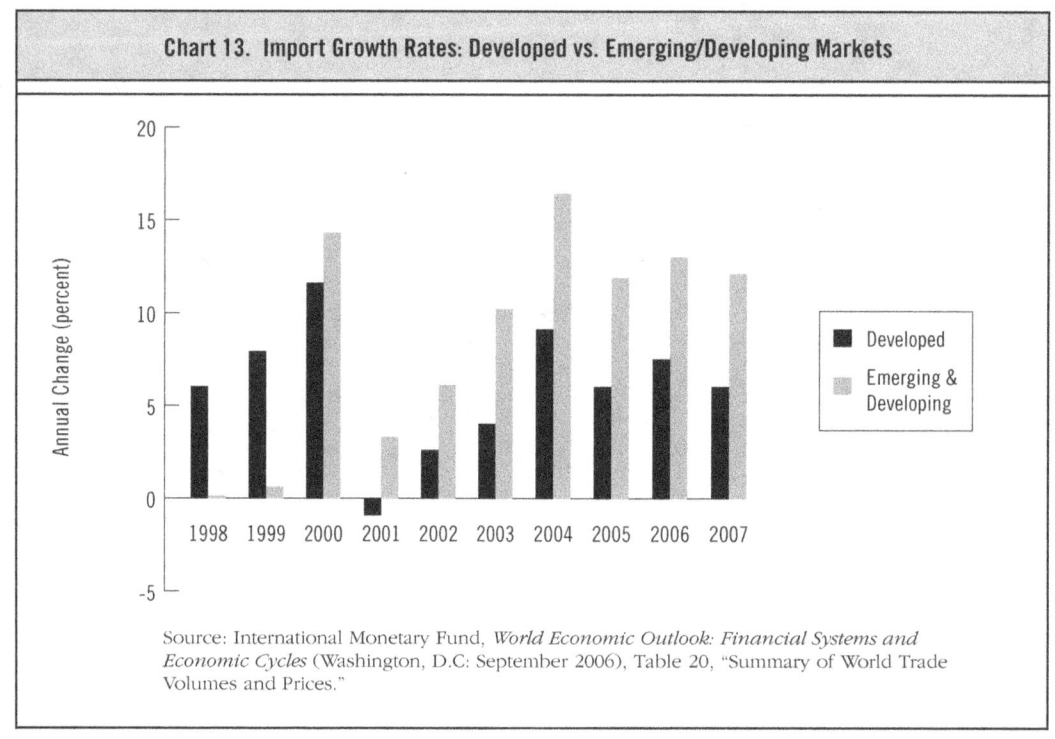

Chart 13. Import Growth Rates: Developed vs. Emerging/Developing Markets

Source: International Monetary Fund, *World Economic Outlook: Financial Systems and Economic Cycles* (Washington, D.C: September 2006), Table 20, "Summary of World Trade Volumes and Prices."

Shift to Emerging Markets: Over time, these trends have resulted in an important shift of global import consumption. Since 1988, the developed countries' share of global imports (excluding the United States) has declined by 11 percent, from 65 percent in 1988 to 54 percent in 2005 (*Chart 14*). Conversely, the developing countries' share of imports has grown 11 percent. While developing countries accounted for only 35 percent of global imports (excluding the United States) in 1988, they accounted for 46 percent in 2005.

The World Bank forecasts that trade, as a share of the global economy, will rise from about one-quarter today to more than one-third by 2030 resulting in more than a tripling of global trade in goods and services to $27 trillion by 2030.[15]

---

15 *Ibid.*, xxiv.

This projected growth in world trade has major implications for U.S. exporters as import demand from developing countries becomes ever more an engine of the global economy. U.S. multinational corporations are well aware of these trends, and project that their overseas sales, particularly in emerging markets, will account for a growing share of their bottom line—already over 50 percent for many. Future U.S. export growth potential will depend on the extent to which other U.S. businesses, particularly small and medium-sized enterprises, become aware of these trends and respond.

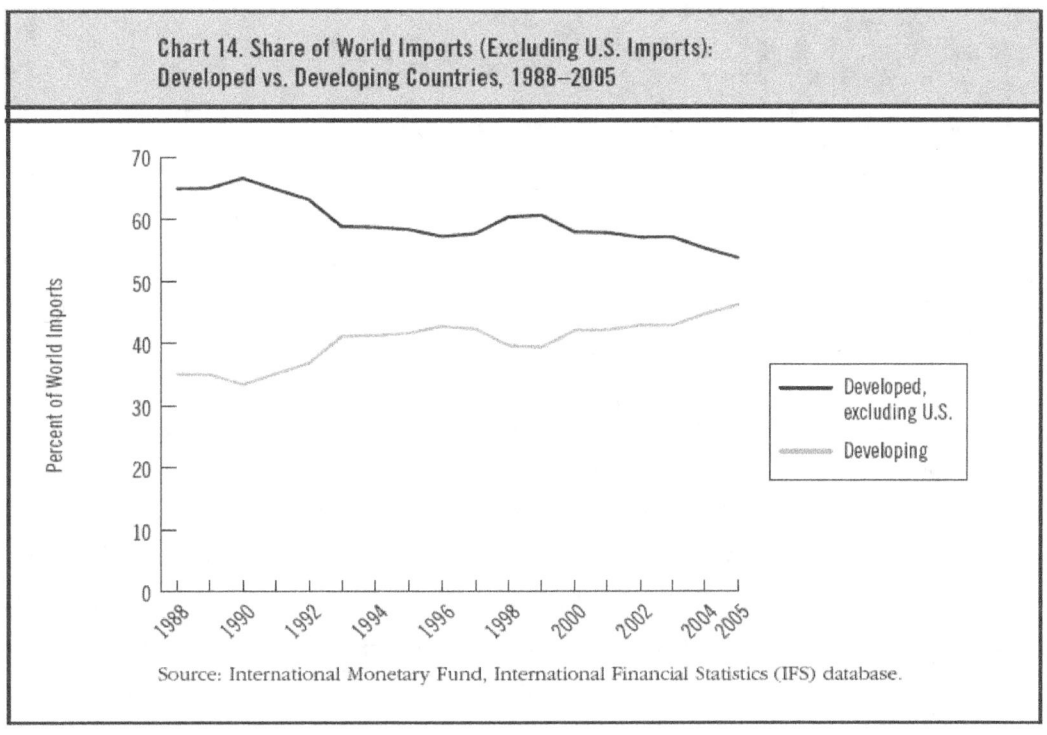

Chart 14. Share of World Imports (Excluding U.S. Imports): Developed vs. Developing Countries, 1988–2005

Source: International Monetary Fund, International Financial Statistics (IFS) database.

American competitiveness in the global marketplace is due in large part to an economy and culture that welcome and encourage innovation and flexible, open markets. The Administration is committed to maintaining this economic environment through sound economic policy based on free-market principles. The February 2007 *Economic Report of the President* points to several Administration priorities for maintaining a strong and dynamic U.S. economy, including: keeping taxes low, breaking down barriers to trade, making private-sector health insurance affordable, diversifying our energy supply, maintaining a strong and vibrant education system, and pursuing a variety of other pro-growth policies that promote strong productivity growth.[16]

Building on this agenda, the trade promotion agencies of the Federal Government are pursuing a number of initiatives to ensure that American companies can take advantage of growing emerging markets, to acknowledge the importance to our economy of inward foreign direct investment and services sector exports, and to facilitate travel to the United States as an activity critical to all of these business endeavors.

Transformational Commercial Diplomacy and Repositioning: While most global output and growth are still accounted for by the developed countries, developing countries account for a growing share of global growth–led by several key emerging markets. In the emerging markets, we see burgeoning middle classes, economic reform, and new industrial competition. The Commercial Service's on-the-ground contributions to shaping the commercial environment are critical to the long-term success of U.S. business interests in these markets.

---

16 Council of Economic Advisers, *Economic Report of the President, 2007*, (Washington, D.C: GPO, 2007): 58–59, *www.whitehouse.gov/cea/2007_erp.pdf*.

The Commercial Service, therefore, has submitted a transformational commercial diplomacy proposal to the Congress to shift resources and enhance its diplomatic and program support in emerging markets. Similar to the State Department's Transformational Diplomacy Initiative, this proposal responds to a changing global marketplace in which emerging markets are of increasing importance to future opportunities for U.S. business.

The Commercial Service proposal will close a number of small satellite offices in well-developed markets or in small markets with limited commercial potential. These resources will be used to open offices in new emerging markets and to augment Commercial Service staff in existing markets with greater commercial potential, such as China and India.

The Joint Commercial Service–State Partner Post Program is intended to provide the best possible service to American companies seeking assistance in countries where the Commercial Service has no presence (non-Commercial Service). Partnership Programs operate at more than 75 U.S. Embassies, where the State Department Economic Sections draw on the specialized advice and experience of nearby Commercial Service offices to provide a higher level of support worldwide for U.S. business. We continue to seek ways to strengthen these partnerships; these efforts include training and regional strategic planning programs, IT improvements, and enhanced cooperation between the two Departments. To date, 40 non-Commercial Service embassies have participated in the Joint Commercial Service–State Training Program launched in 2006.

Investment In America Initiative: Foreign direct investors employ 5.1 million Americans, pay on average 32 percent higher wages than the national average, account for 19 percent of U.S. exports, and in 2005 reinvested $59 billion in profits back into the U.S. economy. Although the United States has historically been the world's largest recipient of inward investment with 16 percent of the global share, in recent years competition for inward investment has intensified. With the emergence of new industrial competitors, we must ensure that we continue to attract such investment.

In March, the International Trade Administration (ITA) launched the Invest in America Initiative to use ITA's global resources to promote the United States as the best market in the world for investment. The initiative will focus on:

- **Outreach to Foreign Governments and Investors**: We will engage foreign governments and major investors abroad, with particular attention to countries that invest heavily in the United States and those with concerns about investing in the United States. This outreach could also highlight opportunities in the Gulf Coast recovery efforts.

- **Outreach to State and Local Governments**: We will bring state and local groups together to discuss best practices, highlight successes, and coordinate messaging. Importantly, ITA will remain neutral in decisions affecting the location of inward investment.

- **Address Business Climate Concerns**: We will stress the need for further action on issues that would improve the business climate (e.g., tax reduction, healthcare cost reduction, litigation reform, faster visa processing, and reform of the Committee on Foreign Investment in the United States).

These efforts will help ensure that the United States maintains its reputation as having the most open investment climate in the world and partially offset concerns about outsourcing and the migration of businesses overseas.

Service Sector Export Promotion: The United States has a global comparative advantage in services, yet significant barriers to trade remain abroad. Services such as financial services, insurance, transportation and storage, telecommunications, express delivery, and business services generate 68 percent of world GDP but account for just 20 percent of global trade. While global advances in information and communications technology are making services increasingly tradable, the trade barriers are significant. In addition to increasing its focus on services trade barriers in current trade negotiations, the Federal Government continues to develop new programs and initiatives for strengthening the services sector:

- **Travel and Tourism Promotion**: International travel is one of the largest exports of the United States, accounting for 7 percent of all U.S. exports and 26 percent of services exports. In 2006, international visitors spent a record

$107.8 billion in travel receipts.[17] Travel and tourism exports have increased by 20 percent since the lows after September 11, 2001, and now exceed the peak in 2000. The 51.1-million total of international travelers hosted by the United States in 2006 is expected to grow by 21 percent in the next five years, reaching about 62 million visitors in 2011. Recent public–private promotional initiatives are contributing to this growth:

☐ Since December 2004, the Commerce Department has had great success with its U.S. Tourism Promotion Campaign in the United Kingdom, with at least 362,500 U.K. travelers visiting the United States as a direct result of seeing the advertising from this campaign. While traveling in the United States, these visitors spent an estimated $481 million, yielding $117 in additional visitor spending for every $1 spent on advertising. In 2005 and 2006, the campaign was expanded to Japan and featured television, underground, cinema, and department store advertising.

☐ In February 2007, the Travel and Tourism Advisory Board announced a $3.9-million cooperative agreement with the Travel Industry Association (TIA) to create and market a destination Web site for the United States. The multi-language Web site will target Canada, Germany, Japan, Mexico, and the United Kingdom.

Franchising: The 767,000 franchised small businesses in the United States generate more than 18 million jobs and $1.53 trillion in economic activity, according to "The Economic Impact of Franchised Businesses," a study performed by PricewaterhouseCoopers for the International Franchise Association (IFA) Educational Foundation and released in 2004.[18] Franchising, as a method of doing business, is increasing worldwide. Rapidly growing markets now include the Pacific Rim (especially Singapore, Taiwan, and Malaysia), the Middle East Gulf States, South America, Eastern

---

17 U.S. Department of Commerce, Bureau of Economic Analysis, News Release, "U.S. International Transactions: Fourth Quarter and Year 2006" (March 14, 2007).

18 International Franchise Association, "The Economic Impact of Franchised Businesses," (Washington, D.C.: IFA Educational Foundation), *www.franchise.org/impactstudy.aspx*.

and Western Europe, and recently China and the countries of the former Soviet Union. In addition to promotion of key trade shows and missions, we will rely increasingly on public–private partnerships:

☐ In September 2006, Secretary Carlos Gutierrez addressed 450 members of the franchise community at the Annual Franchise Appreciation Day sponsored by the IFA in Washington, D.C., highlighting a landmark agreement between the Commercial Service and the IFA to promote U.S. franchise systems. The Commercial Service is promoting the Virtual Franchise Opportunities Mall on IFA's website and the International Franchise Expo, the world's largest franchise show, which attracts franchisors and potential franchisees from around the world.

☐ The International Franchise Association has teamed with the Department of Commerce to bring trade and economic development to Southern Africa and led a mission of six U.S. franchisors to Johannesburg, South Africa, to participate in a regional forum on "Franchise as an Engine of Economic Development" on May 2. This event was held in conjunction with the Franchise Association of Southern Africa's International Franchise Exhibition. The U.S. Agency for International Development (USAID) and the State Department are supporting the participation of government regulators and e ntrepreneurs from 10 other countries in the Southern Africa Development Community. Another highly successful program was held in 2006 in Dakar, Senegal, promoting franchise opportunities in West Africa. The exchange between American franchisors, African government regulators, and indigenous entrepreneurs focuses on the practical challenges of realizing the potential of franchise to contribute to economic development. Specifically, in an enabling environment, franchise offers African countries entrepreneurship, capital formation, technology transfer, and skills development.

▪ **Education Promotion**: Education services are one of America's most visible exports around the globe. International receipts for education increased 4 percent in 2005 to $14.1 billion. This increase was due to tuition increases as the number of foreign student enrollments decreased 1 percent in 2005 and 2 percent in 2004.

☐ The Commerce Department in partnership with the Department of State (and with the support of the Department of Education), has led an effort to develop a promotion strategy for American higher education. This effort has been dubbed the Electronic Education Fair Initiative. A pilot project in China reached over 180 million people through an innovative multimedia campaign which let Chinese students studying in the United States tell America's education story to their peers back home through television programs and the Internet. Secretary Gutierrez, during his February 2007 visit to New Delhi, announced that the initiative will expand to India in the fall of 2007.

Facilitating Business Travel to the United States: Business travel to the United States by foreign employees, customers, and potential clients of U.S. firms is critical to the success of U.S. businesses. Over the past few years, numerous improvements were made to facilitate and, when necessary, expedite travel for business travelers of interest to U.S. companies.

To address rising passport and visa demands, the State Department has added 570 consular positions worldwide since 2001. Visa applicants use an electronic application form, which reduces data entry errors and increases efficiency. All consular offices post their visa appointment wait times online. All visa-issuing U.S. embassies and consulates around the world have put in place special procedures to facilitate the processing of business visas for urgent business travelers at the request of U.S. companies. In 2006, the State Department's Business Visa Center fielded over 5,000 inquiries from U.S. firms, assisting 311,531 prospective travelers in navigating the business visa application process. As a result, the speed with which visas, especially business visas, were processed improved between fiscal year 2002 and fiscal year 2006:

▪ Total visa issuance up 8 percent worldwide

▪ Business/tourist visa issuance up 12 percent

▪ Wait for a temporary business/tourist visa appointment (April 2007): 30 days or less, 90 percent of posts; 15 days or less, 78 percent of posts; seven days or less, 62 percent of posts

- Visa issuance following interview within two days: 97 percent of visas

- Over 18,000 visas processed in Beijing, Shanghai, and Guangzhou through the American Chamber of Commerce Business Facilitation program in China.

The U.S. Government took a number of other initiatives recently to improve travel to the United States. The State Department's budget includes $1.3 billion for the Border Security Program, to facilitate the lawful entry of legitimate foreign visitors, while protecting against illegal entry. A Private Sector Advisory Committee comprised of representatives from academia, business, and the travel and tourism sector is working on recommendations for how the U.S. Government can improve travel security and facilitation. Pilot programs at the Washington Dulles and Houston Intercontinental airports have been launched to make traveler processing at our airports quicker and more pleasant.

The Impact of Trade Liberalization

American companies, farmers, workers, and consumers benefit significantly from liberalized trade. Free markets and open trade play an important role in the growth of the U.S. economy and spur economic growth throughout the world.

Over the past 60 years, eight rounds of multilateral trade negotiations have brought the tariffs of industrial countries down from an average of 38.5 percent to 4 percent. As global economic growth strengthens in new emerging markets, it is important that tariffs also come down in developing countries. China, for example, has reduced tariff rates from an average of 25 percent in 1997 (before China joined the World Trade Organization (WTO)) to under 10 percent by the end of 2005. While the ultimate outcome of the current round of WTO talks, the Doha Development Round, is unknown, an agreement would further liberalize trade among the WTO's 150 members. If Doha were to achieve even a one-third cut in global tariff barriers to trade in goods and services, it is estimated that the real income gain to a U.S. family of four could be around $2,500 annually.[1]

---

1 Council of Economic Advisers, *Trade and the American Economy: The Case for Trade Promotion Authority*, *www.whitehouse.gov/cea/pubs/html*. D. Brown, A. Deardorff, and R. Stern, "Impacts on NAFTA Members of Multilateral and Regional Trading Arrangements and Initiatives and Harmonization of NAFTA's External Tariffs," University of Michigan, Research Seminar in International Economics Discussion Paper 471, June 2001. (Population Data from Department of Commerce, U.S. Census Bureau, and family gains calculations by Council of Economic Advisers.)

In addition to multilateral negotiations, another effective tool for increasing U.S. market access and expanding trade has been Free Trade Agreements (FTAs). FTAs are comprehensive trade agreements that address tariffs and non-tariff barriers to trade in goods and services, government procurement opportunities, and investment. FTAs also promote the rule of law and encourage transparent and enforceable regulatory practices in the areas of competition, intellectual property, labor, and the environment. Currently the United States has a total of ten[2] FTAs in force with 14 countries.

Since 2001, the Administration has implemented seven of these FTAs with 11 countries, working with Congressional guidance on what types of trade and investment practices should be addressed in a trade agreement. Looking at the most recent year-over-year data (2005 to 2006), we can see that the growth rate of U.S. exports in seven of 10 countries with FTAs in force at the end of 2006 outpaced the growth rate of U.S. exports to the world (*Chart 15*).[3]

The 13 countries with which America implemented FTAs through 2006, including our NAFTA partners and Israel, account for 7.3 percent of world GDP (excluding the United States), but account for 42.1 percent of U.S. exports (*Charts 16a, 16b*).

---

2 Agreements in effect are the Israel FTA, NAFTA, CAFTA–DR (other than Costa Rica), and FTAs with Jordan, Singapore, Chile, Australia, Morocco, and Bahrain. The U.S.–Canada FTA has been suspended since the entry into force of NAFTA.

3 Excludes Dominican Republic, for which CAFTA–DR entered into force on March 1, 2007.

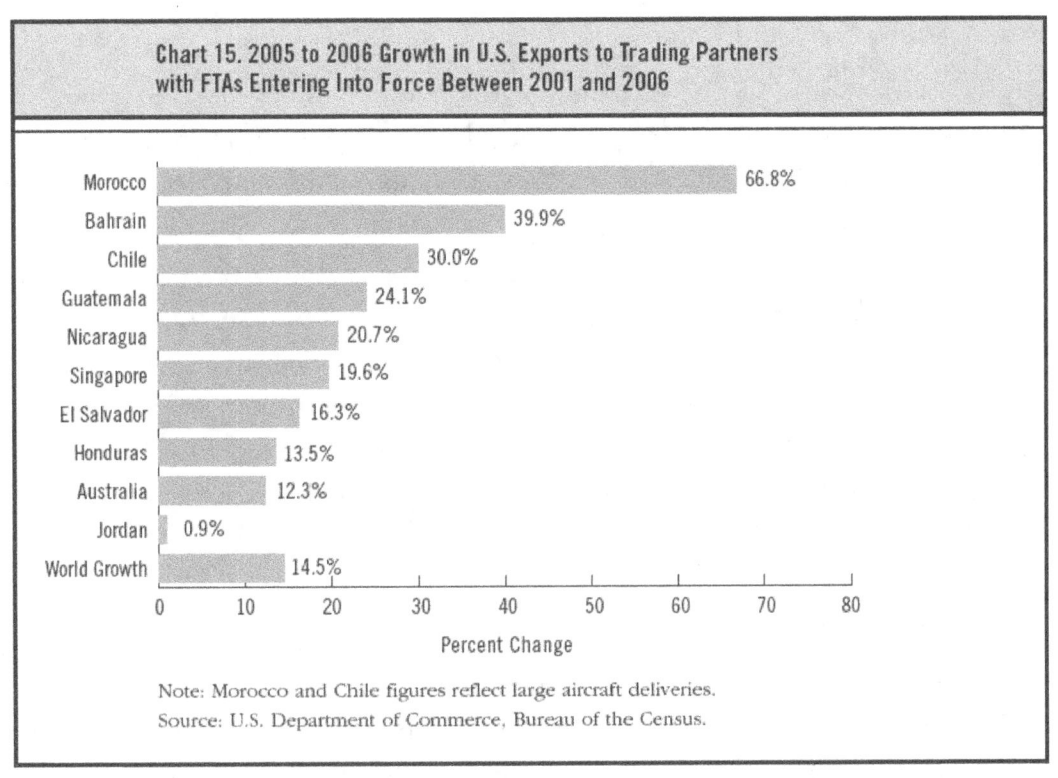

Chart 15. 2005 to 2006 Growth in U.S. Exports to Trading Partners with FTAs Entering Into Force Between 2001 and 2006

Country	Percent Change
Morocco	66.8%
Bahrain	39.9%
Chile	30.0%
Guatemala	24.1%
Nicaragua	20.7%
Singapore	19.6%
El Salvador	16.3%
Honduras	13.5%
Australia	12.3%
Jordan	0.9%
World Growth	14.5%

Note: Morocco and Chile figures reflect large aircraft deliveries.
Source: U.S. Department of Commerce, Bureau of the Census.

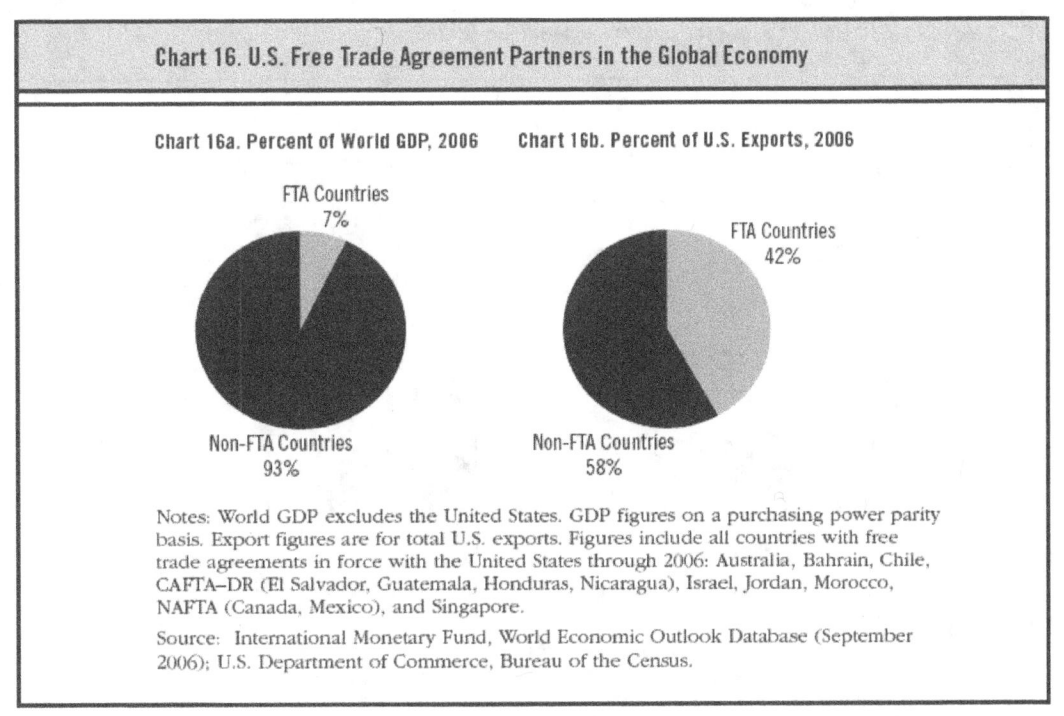

Chart 16. U.S. Free Trade Agreement Partners in the Global Economy

Chart 16a. Percent of World GDP, 2006

FTA Countries 7%
Non-FTA Countries 93%

Chart 16b. Percent of U.S. Exports, 2006

FTA Countries 42%
Non-FTA Countries 58%

Notes: World GDP excludes the United States. GDP figures on a purchasing power parity basis. Export figures are for total U.S. exports. Figures include all countries with free trade agreements in force with the United States through 2006: Australia, Bahrain, Chile, CAFTA–DR (El Salvador, Guatemala, Honduras, Nicaragua), Israel, Jordan, Morocco, NAFTA (Canada, Mexico), and Singapore.

Source: International Monetary Fund, World Economic Outlook Database (September 2006); U.S. Department of Commerce, Bureau of the Census.

FREE TRADE AGREEMENTS AND THE TRADE BALANCE

Trade barriers are just one of many factors that can affect the U.S. trade deficit, and eliminating trade barriers would by no means result in a disappearance of the trade deficit. Nevertheless, it is noteworthy that our combined trade deficit with FTA partner countries is smaller than with non-FTA countries. In fact, 16 percent of our overall trade deficit results from trade with FTA trading partners, while 84 percent is attributable to non-FTA trading partners (*Chart 17*). Prior to the implementation of a free trade agreement, U.S. producers face higher barriers to trade in foreign markets than foreign producers face in the United States. This is especially true with regard to developing countries, which maintain foreign import duties much higher than in developed countries.

IMPORTANCE OF COMPREHENSIVE FREE TRADE AGREEMENTS

U.S. FTAs have a successful track record because they are comprehensive, cutting-edge, and tailored to today's high-tech world. Such agreements are difficult to negotiate, but the United States has always held out for high-quality

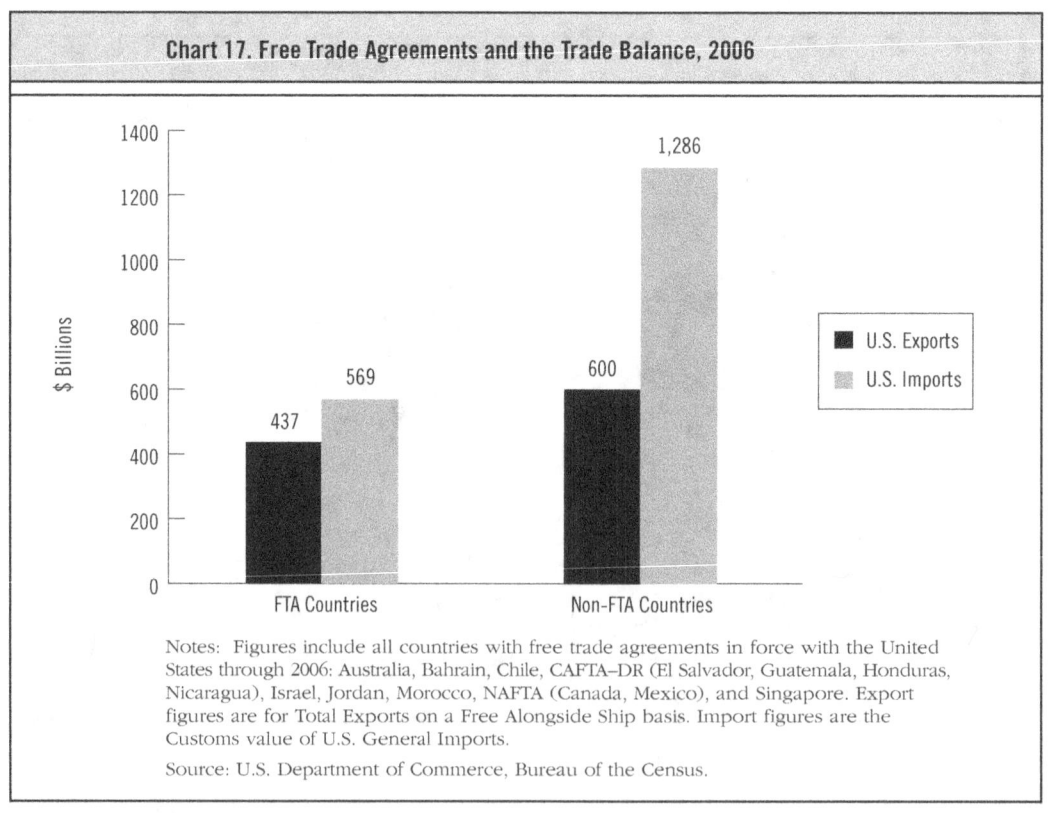

Chart 17. Free Trade Agreements and the Trade Balance, 2006

Notes: Figures include all countries with free trade agreements in force with the United States through 2006: Australia, Bahrain, Chile, CAFTA–DR (El Salvador, Guatemala, Honduras, Nicaragua), Israel, Jordan, Morocco, NAFTA (Canada, Mexico), and Singapore. Export figures are for Total Exports on a Free Alongside Ship basis. Import figures are the Customs value of U.S. General Imports.

Source: U.S. Department of Commerce, Bureau of the Census.

FTAs, with benefits for both the United States and our trading partners. The FTAs negotiated by the United States are comprehensive, addressing many other issues besides tariff reductions important to U.S. businesses, workers, farmers, and investors. For both parties to an agreement, these issues are fundamental to enhancing efficiency, lowering the cost of capital, and creating the economic conditions for businesses to compete effectively. These issues include:

- Improved operation through trade facilitation measures that lower barriers to trade (such as customs administration)

- Encouragement of innovation through protection of intellectual property rights and promotion of e-commerce and telecommunications

- Market access for services and financial services

- Promotion and protection of investment

- Transparency and fairness of procurements

- Regulatory improvements:

  □ Labor

  □ Environment

  □ Transparency and anti-corruption measures

- Compliance tools for rules clarification and establishment of dispute resolution processes

- Adoption of international standards to address sanitary and phytosanitary barriers to trade

IMPORTANCE OF FREE TRADE AGREEMENTS TO SME EXPORTERS

U.S. small and medium-sized enterprises (SMEs) are a significant source of innovation and jobs for the U.S. economy, and free trade agreements expand markets for SMEs. FTAs lower foreign market tariffs, thus reducing SMEs' to-market costs. FTA transparency obligations are also very important to SMEs, which may not have the resources to cut through customs and regulatory red tape. In 2005 (latest data available), U.S. merchandise exports from SME exporters to our FTA partners totaled $82.1 billion. Similarly, over 90 percent of U.S. companies exporting to Canada, Mexico, and Australia are SMEs. At least 70 percent of all U.S. companies that exported to Chile, Morocco, and the individual Central America–Dominican Republic FTA (CAFTA–DR) countries are SMEs. SMEs accounted, by value, for 29 percent of all U.S. exports to the world in 2005 (latest available). In comparison, the SME share of U.S. exports exceeded 30 percent in eight of our 14 current FTA partners (*Table 2*).

Table 2. U.S. SME Exports to FTA Trading Partners, 2005

Country	SME Export Value ($ millions)	SME Share of Total Exports (percent)
Australia	3,618	25.9
Bahrain	65	27.0
Canada	33,355	21.2
Chile	1,430	31.2
Dominican Republic	2,264	53.5
El Salvador	841	52.8
Guatemala	1,268	50.9
Honduras	1,173	40.6
Israel	3,196	45.2
Jordan	221	42.9
Mexico	30,614	29.0
Morocco	129	26.2
Nicaragua	403	73.5
Singapore	3,550	18.5

Source: U.S. Department of Commerce, Exporter Database.

Chart 18 shows the aggregate leading sectors in 2006 for the seven FTAs with 10 countries that came into force between 2001 and 2006.

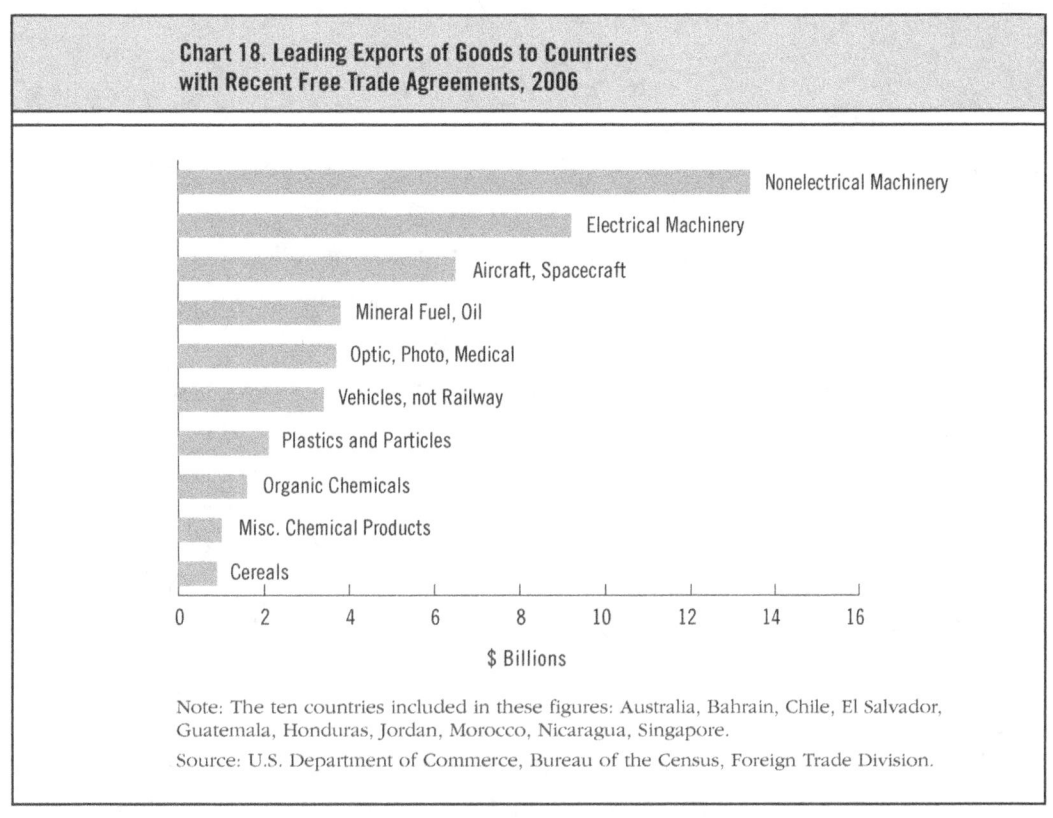

Chart 18. Leading Exports of Goods to Countries with Recent Free Trade Agreements, 2006

$ Billions

Note: The ten countries included in these figures: Australia, Bahrain, Chile, El Salvador, Guatemala, Honduras, Jordan, Morocco, Nicaragua, Singapore.

Source: U.S. Department of Commerce, Bureau of the Census, Foreign Trade Division.

A more detailed look at the four FTAs implemented since 2001 that have been in force the longest (the Jordan, Singapore, Chile, and Australia FTAs) shows that U.S. exports in certain sectors have experienced incredibly rapid growth, often as a direct result of particular market access gains included in the FTA.

Jordan: Since the implementation of the United States–Jordan FTA in 2001, U.S. exports to Jordan have risen 92 percent. Immediately prior to the FTA, the United States' annual exports of goods to Jordan were $339 million. In 2006, exports were $650 million. U.S. agricultural exports accounted for $142 million of this amount, representing a 60 percent increase in agricultural exports to Jordan since 2005. Among the biggest growth sectors between 2001 and 2006:

- Vehicle (not railway) exports rose 1,573 percent to $133 million.

- Aluminum exports rose 610 percent to $20 million.

- Books, newspapers, and manuscripts exports rose 360 percent to $5 million.

Singapore: Building on an already strong trade relationship, U.S. exports to Singapore have risen by 49 percent since the entry into force of the United States–Singapore FTA in 2004. In 2003, prior to the FTA, the United States exported $16.6 billion in goods to Singapore. In 2006, U.S. merchandise exports totaled $24.7 billion and resulted in a $6.9 billion trade surplus with Singapore. The biggest dollar gains were in established export sectors. Between 2003 and 2006:

- Tools and cutlery of base metals exports rose 143 percent to $110 million.

- Mineral fuels and oil exports rose 136 percent to $1.1 billion.

- Organic chemicals exports rose 128 percent to $1.1 billion.

- Precious stones and metals exports rose 71 percent to $122 million.

Chile: Exports to Chile from the United States rose by over 150 percent, from $2.7 billion in 2003 prior to implementation of the United States–Chile FTA, to $6.8 billion in 2006. Among the strong performers between 2003 and 2006:

- Aircraft and spacecraft exports rose 2,968 percent to $916 million. 2006 exports in this sector were double the previous all-time high of $455 million in 1998:

- Mineral fuels and oil exports rose 1,615 percent to $1.1 billion.

- Vehicles (other than railway) exports rose 182 percent to $629 million.

- U.S. financial services firms may now offer financial services to participants in Chile's highly successful privatized pension system.

While U.S. exports to Chile constituted 25 percent of the Chilean import market in 1995, that share consistently dropped in subsequent years as other trading partners, including the EU, Mexico, and Canada, all negotiated FTAs with Chile. U.S. import share reached a low of 14.5 percent in 2003. With the implementation of the FTA in January 2004, U.S. import share in Chile has begun to climb again, reaching 16 percent in 2006.

Australia: The United States has significantly strengthened and diversified its exports to Australia. U.S. exports to Australia in 2006 totaled $17.8 billion, having grown 12.3 percent since the United States–Australia FTA was implemented in January 2005. This agreement has already eliminated tariffs on over 99 percent of lines for exports of U.S. industrial and consumer goods. As a result, the execution of this FTA has contributed to a $9.6 billion U.S. trade surplus in 2006. In 2004, prior to the implementation of the agreement, the United States had exports of $500 million or greater in two categories. One year later, in 2005, the United States had five categories over $500 million, and in 2006, the number of categories valued over $500 million grew to seven. Significant gains between 2004 and 2006 include:

- Rubber and rubber products exports rose 69 percent to $249 million.

- Precious stones and metals exports rose 52 percent to $249 million.

- Perfumery and cosmetics exports rose 39 percent to $272 million.

- Total U.S. agricultural exports to Australia were a record $520 million in 2006. Exports of pork totaled $47.0 million and exports of fresh fruit reached a record $48.6 million.

RECENT AND FUTURE FTAS

Morocco: The United States–Morocco FTA entered into force on January 1, 2006. In the last full year prior to entry into force (2005), the United States exported $525 million in goods to Morocco. In 2006, U.S. exports increased to over $876 million, bringing total bilateral trade to almost $1.4 billion. U.S. agricultural exports were $294 million, representing a 79 percent increase in U.S. agricultural exports to Morocco since 2005. The market liberalization under the FTA includes preferential market access for all agricultural products in accordance with negotiated schedules. In addition, the FTA provides preferential duty treatment for textile and apparel products that meet the FTA's rule of origin requirements. Under the FTA, all remaining tariffs on consumer and industrial products will be eliminated by 2015.

Bahrain: The free trade agreement with Bahrain took effect August 1, 2006. In the last full year prior to entry into force of the FTA (2005), the United States exported $351 million in goods to Bahrain. In 2006, U.S. exports totaled $491 million, a 40 percent increase.

CAFTA–DR: The United States, five countries of Central America (Costa Rica, El Salvador, Guatemala, Honduras, and Nicaragua), and the Dominican Republic signed the Dominican Republic–Central America–United States Free Trade Agreement (CAFTA–DR) on August 5, 2004. Since March 2006, CAFTA–DR has entered into force with respect to five countries: El Salvador, Honduras, Nicaragua, Guatemala, and the Dominican Republic. Entry into force for Costa Rica is expected to follow a public referendum and completion of its implementation process during 2007.

- **El Salvador**: CAFTA–DR entered into force with El Salvador on March 1, 2006, and expanded market access opportunities in El Salvador for U.S. companies (about 7 million consumers and $17 billion in GDP). In the last full year prior to entry into force of the FTA (2005), the United States exported $1.9 billion in goods to El Salvador. In 2006, U.S. exports totaled $2.2 billion—a 16.3 percent increase.

- **Honduras**: CAFTA–DR entered into force with Honduras on April 1, 2006, and expanded market access opportunities in Honduras for U.S. companies (over 7 million consumers and $8 billion in GDP). In the last full year prior to entry into force (2005), the United States exported $3.3 billion in goods to Honduras. In 2006, U.S. exports totaled $3.7 billion—a 13.5 percent increase.

- **Nicaragua**: CAFTA–DR entered into force with Nicaragua on April 1, 2006, and expanded market access opportunities in Nicaragua for U.S. companies (about 6 million consumers and $5 billion in GDP). In the last full year prior to entry into force (2005), the United States exported $625 million in goods to Nicaragua. In 2006, U.S. exports totaled $755 million—a 20.8 percent increase.

- **Guatemala**: CAFTA–DR entered into force with Guatemala on July 1, 2006, and expanded market access opportunities in Guatemala for U.S. companies (about 13 million consumers and $32 billion in GDP). In the last full year prior to entry into force of the FTA (2005), the United States exported $2.8 billion in goods to Guatemala. In 2006, U.S. exports totaled $3.5 billion—a 24.1 percent increase.

- **Dominican Republic**: CAFTA–DR entered into force with the Dominican Republic on March 1, 2007, and expanded market access opportunities in the Dominican Republic for U.S. companies (about 9 million consumers and $28 billion in GDP). In 2006, U.S. exports totaled $5.4 billion.

Reopening of Guatemalan Beef Market

Following the detection of Bovine Spongiform Encephalopathy (BSE) in the United States in 2003, most countries banned imports of live U.S. cattle. In early 2006, U.S. Livestock Genetics Export, Inc. (USLGE), the Texas Department of Agriculture (USDA), and the Foreign Agricultural Service (FAS) jointly arranged for Guatemala's Vice Minister of Agriculture to visit Texas and meet with livestock contacts for advice on establishing a beef genetics improvement center in Guatemala. Soon after, USDA was able to renegotiate Guatemala's bovine health protocol and, in March 2006, Guatemala announced the reopening of its borders to live U.S. cattle and bone-in beef. USLGE representatives visited Guatemala in May 2006 to offer technical advice to the Guatemalan Agriculture Ministry. In July 2006, U.S. beef cattle arrived in Guatemala for the first time since 2003, a direct result of the successful matching of Market Access Program, industry funds, and close coordination between FAS, USLGE, and the Texas Department of Agriculture.

Oman: The United States signed a free trade agreement with Oman on January 19, 2006. President Bush signed the agreement into law, following Congressional approval, on September 26, 2006. Oman is working on the necessary implementing legislation. Oman accounts for approximately 3.2 million consumers and a GDP of over $43 billion. In 2006, U.S. goods exported to Oman totaled $853 million.

Panama: In December 2006, the United States and Panama announced completion of negotiations on a free trade agreement, with the understanding that it is subject to further discussions regarding labor. The Administration notified Congress on March 30, 2007, of its intent to sign the agreement following a 90-day waiting period, after which it would be subject to Congressional consideration.

Panama Canal Expansion

In 2008, the Panama Canal will undergo its first major expansion at an estimated cost of $5.25 billion, representing one of the largest infrastructure project in the Western Hemisphere. TPCC agencies, including Ex-Im Bank, the Departments of Commerce, State, and Transportation, U.S. Trade and Development Agency (USTDA), Overseas Private Investment Corporation(OPIC), and other TPCC agencies are working together to increase awareness of U.S. Government financing and other support available. The goal is to assist U.S. engineering, project management, construction, and equipment firms seeking to participate in Canal contract awards.

- During its April 2007 Annual Conference, Ex-Im Bank organized a roundtable discussion on the expansion project. Ricaurte Vásquez, Chairman of the Panama Canal Authority, the institution directly responsible for overseeing the project, briefed U.S. exporters, lenders, and brokers interested in participating in the project. Through similar outreach activities, Ex-Im Bank will continue to work within the TPCC to advance U.S. participation in the project.

- Representatives from the Commerce Department's Advocacy Center attended the Panama Canal Authority's conference in March and are working with U.S. companies interested in bidding on each of the individual tenders.

- U.S. Transportation Secretary Mary E. Peters traveled to Panama in May to meet with interested U.S. companies and representatives of the Canal Authority.

Peru and Colombia: The United States signed a free trade agreement with Peru on April 12, 2006, and a free trade agreement with Colombia on November 22, 2006. The Administration is working towards securing Congressional approval of both agreements. Together, Peru and Colombia account for approximately 72 million consumers and a combined GDP of almost $550 billion, representing a substantial market for U.S. businesses, farmers, and workers. In 2006, U.S. goods exports to Peru totaled $2.9 billion and our exports to Colombia totaled $6.7 billion. Colombia is currently the largest market for U.S. agricultural exports in South America.

South Korea: On April 1, 2007, President Bush notified Congress of the intent to sign a free trade agreement with the Republic of Korea. South Korea accounts for approximately 48 million consumers and a GDP of over $897 billion. In 2006, U.S. goods exported to South Korea totaled $32.5 billion.

CONCLUSIONS

Together with pre-existing FTA partners Israel, Canada, and Mexico, these new free trade alliances are beginning to form a critical mass for the stimulation of trade-led growth. Collectively, new and pending FTA partners would constitute America's third-largest export market and the third-largest economy in the world. In countries and regions throughout the world, the United States is achieving market gains for U.S. exporters, economic growth and development opportunities for our free trade partners, and enhanced leadership stature for the United States in the global economy.

A priority of the trade promotion agencies is sustained follow-up in FTA markets, ensuring that U.S. businesses are aware of new market openings and have access to the tools and opportunities they need to expand their exports to these markets. Whether a new FTA trading partner represents a large or small market, the U.S. Government must ensure that all U.S. businesses are informed and enabled to take advantage of negotiated market openings. Our strategy is to increase U.S. companies' activities in all of these markets so that citizens in the FTA partner countries and in the United States see the benefits of increased trade. We will work with all of our partners (corporate, U.S. States, and trade and industry associations) to broaden U.S. business awareness of opportunities. Highlights of our trade promotion activities in recent FTA markets include:

CAFTA–DR: All of the core TPCC agencies are engaged in the CAFTA–DR markets. Commerce Secretary Gutierrez's TPCC CAFTA–DR Mission in October 2005 helped to advance close interagency coordination of activities.

- **The Overseas Private Investment Corporation**: The countries of Central America are a top priority for OPIC, which is focused on investment initiatives in sectors that represent dynamic catalytic growth. These initiatives include access to credit for SMEs and support for housing. OPIC President and CEO Robert Mosbacher, Jr., has visited the region five times in less than two years and has announced over $300 million in new project support for Central America. Projects include: $149 million in financing for three new OPIC-supported investment funds (including the housing and renewable energy sectors)—as well as power generation, microfinance housing construction, and mortgage financing projects.

  The highlight this year was "Access to Opportunity in Central America and the Caribbean." The conference was held May 15–17 in San Salvador, and involved participants from the Departments of State and Commerce, and U.S. Trade and Development Agency (USTDA). Conference sessions with government officials and businesses from each partner country focused on investment opportunities in sectors such as infrastructure, energy, tourism, franchising, financial services, and housing. The conference was, in part, based on Federal Government efforts to identify projects of potential interest to U.S. exporters and investors.

- **The U.S. Trade and Development Agency**: USTDA has provided over $5 million in support of CAFTA–DR in response to priorities identified by Central American countries. USTDA's CAFTA–DR Trade Integration Initiative improves CAFTA–DR implementation by supporting projects that result in increased trade and economic development in the region. The initiative targets projects in the transportation, energy, and information and communications technology sectors. Two recent examples in Nicaragua include improvements to the Port of Corinto and modernization of Managua International Airport. In Honduras, a USTDA grant will assist the National Port Authority in the development of a new dry bulk terminal at Port of Cortés.[4]

---

4 Note: For more detail on these projects see USTDA press release, "USTDA Grants Support CAFTA-DR Implementation." September 1, 2006, *http://www.ustda.gov.*

■ **Export-Import Bank**: In fiscal year 2006, Ex-Im Bank provided support in excess of $88 million for exports to the CAFTA–DR countries, representing more than 75 individual export sales. Ex-Im Bank total current exposure in these markets is in excess of $790 million.

The Dominican Republic is Ex-Im Bank's most active market within the CAFTA–DR region with exposure of $633 million. Of this, approximately 70 percent is sovereign. In March 2006, Vice Chair Linda Conlin met with leading Dominican and regional banks and CEI–RD, the Export and Investment Center of the Dominican Republic. In cooperation with the Commercial Service, banks, and CEI–RD, Ex-Im is seeking to provide training to prospective partner banks and Dominican buyers interested in accessing financing for U.S. exports. Ex-Im Bank hopes that this kind of business development model, linking financial institutions, local business organizations, buyers, and exporters, can be used as a model to further trade for the CAFTA–DR region.

Ex-Im Bank has also been working with the Department of Commerce to identify and train groups that are planning export missions to the CAFTA–DR region. These groups represent the states of Mississippi and South Carolina, as well as Enterprise Florida. Providing these delegations with information regarding Ex-Im Bank financing will complement Ex-Im Bank's ongoing business development efforts in these markets and expand Ex-Im Bank financing opportunities.

■ **U.S. Department of Agriculture, Foreign Agricultural Service**: USDA provided critical input and support during 2006 relating to the implementation of the CAFTA–DR agreement. USDA worked extensively with the Governments of El Salvador, Guatemala, Honduras, and Nicaragua to obtain their recognition that the U.S. food safety inspection systems for red meats and poultry are equivalent to their domestic systems. This recognition eliminated the need for officials from these countries to inspect each U.S. establishment, ensuring that USDA-approved facilities can export to the region with minimal cost and reasonable regulatory burdens. The CAFTA–DR countries already represent important markets for the United States, with the combined value of agricultural exports totaling over $2.2 billion in 2006 compared to $1.8 billion in 2005.

- **Department of Commerce**: Commerce Department efforts have focused on supporting the other TPCC agencies' events and programs in the region, several state trade missions, and domestic outreach to ensure that U.S. companies are aware of opportunities and able to follow up with exports.

- **Small Business Administration**: Through the SME Congress of the Americas on International Trade, SBA has taken the discussion of small business trade to a regional level and is working to use these partnerships to promote and facilitate small-business trade throughout the Western Hemisphere.

Inter-American Development Bank (IDB)

The Advocacy Center is working in tandem with the Inter-American Development Bank (IDB) to highlight its partnership with commercial banks, institutional investors, co-guarantors and other co-lenders to provide private sector companies with the financing needed to meet the region's growing demand for infrastructure and enhanced financial markets capacity. The IDB is constantly seeking to develop new and better options for private financing tailored to the needs of clients investing in its member countries. Together, the Advocacy Center and the IDB are hosting a series of informational sessions with the U.S. banking community to educate them about the risk mitigation options offered by the IDB.

MEFTA Region (Jordan, Morocco, Bahrain, and Oman): The TPCC agencies are working to deepen U.S. commercial ties with MEFTA countries. This means focusing on projects and activities that make trade easier, increase economic activity, and improve the lives of citizens in these countries.

- **USTDA** is funding a grant to the Jordanian Ministry of Transport to fund a National Freight Information and Transportation Hub pilot and feasibility study. This will help promote trade efficiency, security, and global competitiveness through market-oriented reforms. In Morocco, USTDA is funding technical assistance in port security and safety related to Morocco's major port authority, Tangier–Med.

- **OPIC** recently announced three funds that support U.S. commercial interests in Jordan. One of the funds, the Jordan Fund II, will commit $150 million for investments in small and medium-sized Jordanian firms. The fund will be multi-sectoral but will emphasize promising sectors in Jordan, such as telecommunications, information technology, financial services, aviation, education, and health care. The two other funds will dedicate a percentage of their total capitalization to investments in Jordan. The $113 million EuroMENA Fund, 30 percent of which will target investments in Jordan, will invest in the regional expansion of middle-market companies in the Middle East and North Africa (MENA), with a primary focus on Jordan, Egypt, Lebanon, and Morocco. The $300 million Emerging Markets Housing Fund, established to invest in markets that are experiencing rapid growth in housing demand, will focus on Jordan and South Africa.

- **Ex-Im Bank** has $740 million in total exposure in the MEFTA region.

Morocco: In 2006, Ex-Im Bank Chairman James Lambright visited Morocco to further Ex-Im Bank participation in the market and overall trade between Morocco and the United States. In July 2006, Ex-Im Bank and Attijariwafa Bank of Casablanca, the largest private-sector bank in Morocco, signed a Memorandum of Understanding (MOU) to explore coordinated marketing efforts with an emphasis on SMEs, and to develop a future regional infrastructure project conference. The MOU referenced the parties' strong desire to build upon the United States–Morocco FTA and increase bilateral trade.

During 2006, Ex-Im Bank financed the sale of four Boeing 737-800 aircraft to Royal Air Maroc. Ex-Im Bank expects to continue its financing support of Royal Air Maroc's acquisition of additional Boeing aircraft during 2007 and 2008.

Jordan: During 2006, Ex-Im Bank conducted two business development visits to Jordan. Industry segments of interest included energy, power, telecommunications, and food processing. It is also anticipated that Ex-Im Bank will receive a request to support the sales of Boeing Aircraft to Royal Jordanian Airlines for its order of the new Boeing 787.

Oman: Ex-Im Bank has supported sales of Boeing aircraft to Oman Air in the recent past with the prospect of assisting sales to this market in the near future.

- **U.S. Department of Commerce**: The Secretary of Commerce will participate in an economic development conference within the next 12 months in Jordan to highlight opportunities throughout the Middle East. In addition, the Department of Commerce will conduct a Healthcare Technologies Trade Mission to Istanbul, Turkey; Amman, Jordan; and Cairo, Egypt, between October 24 and November 1, 2007. This mission will focus on helping small companies evaluate these markets and make important business contacts to increase export sales.

- **U.S. Department of State**: The Middle East Free Trade and Investment Conference is a unique forum in which U.S. and Arab business leaders can identify strategic business opportunities and partnerships in some of the most rapidly growing economies in the Middle East and North Africa. The March 29, 2007, Conference was a resounding success in demonstrating the concrete benefits of FTAs for both U.S. companies and our FTA partner countries. Approximately 200 private-sector participants attended the event, including upper-tier multinationals, many CEOs of SME firms, and some executives of firms with no prior international experience. A number of firms announced new or increased investments. The presentations by the Prime Minister of Morocco, the Deputy Prime Minister of Jordan, and senior officials from Bahrain and Oman lauded the Administration for the FTAs and the potential commercial benefits. The Tunisian Minister of International Cooperation and Development also attended and observed the benefits of having a closer economic and commercial relationship with the United States.

- **U.S. Department of Agriculture, Foreign Agricultural Service**: The FAS led a team of USDA experts for three back-to-back workshops in Yemen, Bahrain, and the United Arab Emirates on national Sanitary and Phytosanitary Enquiry Points. Host-government officials learned about the U.S. system of interagency coordination and communication with the private sector. Establishment of fully functioning national Inquiry Point authority is required for all WTO member countries, as it is an important administrative tool that encourages transparency and supports free trade.

**Promotional Efforts in More Developed FTA Markets
(Australia, Chile, Singapore):**

▩ **Ex-Im Bank**:

Australia: Ex-Im Bank has over $1 billion in exposure in this market. Ex-Im Bank has supported aircraft exports to Australia in the recent past (e.g., Qantas and Virgin Blue in Australia), and anticipates receiving a request for financing from Qantas to support its order of new Boeing 787 aircraft.

Chile: During 2006, Ex-Im Bank financed the export of four Boeing 767-300 aircraft (three passenger aircraft and one cargo aircraft) to LAN Airlines in Santiago. Target sectors in the coming year include mining and agricultural goods. Ex-Im Bank total exposure in this market is in excess of $800 million.

Singapore: During 2006, Ex-Im Bank financed one Boeing 747-400F cargo aircraft (the largest cargo aircraft available) for Singapore Airlines Cargo Ltd. Ex-Im Bank currently has more than $1 billion in exposure in Singapore.

▩ **U.S. Trade and Development Agency**:

Chile: USTDA has undertaken two projects identified as priorities for the Chilean Government through the FTA and Environmental Cooperation Agreement that are aimed at strengthening Chile's environmental regulatory regimes. USTDA supported a recently concluded technical assistance project aimed at establishing a regulatory regime for remediating environmental contamination related to mining. USTDA also supported a reverse trade mission for senior Chilean officials to meet their counterparts in the United States to learn about the United States' efforts in environmentally clean production.

The Rise of E-commerce

Since the rise of the Internet in the 1990s, there have been many ups and downs in expectations about the growth of e-commerce. Early hopes were tempered by public concerns over issues like privacy and the security of online payment systems. As new strategies and technologies addressed these concerns, e-commerce began to catch up with earlier predictions of its promise. Private-sector estimates of the current and projected value of e-commerce vary widely. A recent study by the Organization for Economic Cooperation and Development (OECD)[1] finds that business-to-consumer (B2C) sales are growing at around 25 percent per year, with international transactions increasingly important.

Census Bureau statistics reflect similar trends in the United States, with B2C e-commerce growing at a 23.5 percent rate in 2006, while total retail sales increased only 5.8 percent. While B2C's share of total retail sales is still small, high growth rates have increased that share from 0.6 percent in 2000 to 2.8 percent in 2006. Though B2C e-commerce is growing at a much faster rate, it is still dwarfed by business-to-business (B2B) e-commerce, which represented 93 percent of all U.S. e-commerce in 2004. Of the $1.951 trillion in total U.S. e-commerce in 2004, $1.821 trillion was accounted for by B2B.

---

1 Organization for Economic Cooperation and Development, "Online Payment Systems and E-Commerce," Report DSTI/ICCP/IE (2004)18/FINAL (Paris, Organization for Economic Cooperation and Development: 2006), 12, *http://www.oecd.org/dataoecd/37/19/36736056.pdf*.

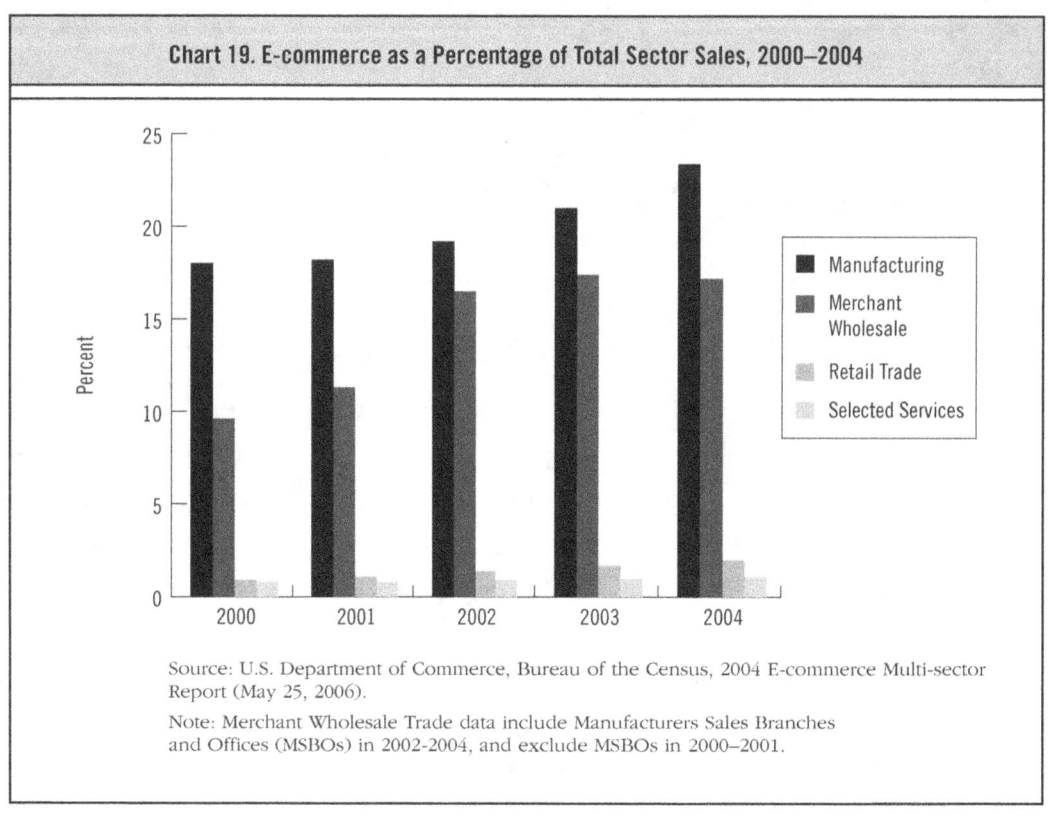

Chart 19. E-commerce as a Percentage of Total Sector Sales, 2000–2004

Source: U.S. Department of Commerce, Bureau of the Census, 2004 E-commerce Multi-sector Report (May 25, 2006).

Note: Merchant Wholesale Trade data include Manufacturers Sales Branches and Offices (MSBOs) in 2002-2004, and exclude MSBOs in 2000–2001.

Manufacturing led all industry sectors in 2004, with e-commerce accounting for 23.4 percent ($996 billion) of all manufacturing shipments in the economy, up substantially for the third straight year (*Chart 19*). While total manufacturing shipments increased by an average annual rate of only 0.4 percent from 2000 to 2004, e-shipments over the same period were up an average annual rate of 7.5 percent over the same period. The biggest e-commerce users by industry sector were transportation equipment and chemicals. The fastest-growing e-commerce sectors from 2003 to 2004 were primary metals, printing, petroleum and coal products, and machinery.

Outside of the United States, e-commerce is expanding at a similarly rapid pace in major markets around the world. In Europe, for example, Forrester Research estimates that the number of Europeans shopping online will grow from 100 million people in 2006 to 174 million in 20112, with a corresponding increase in European online retail sales from €102.6 billion to €263 billion in 2011.[2] Other advanced markets such as Australia, Canada, Japan, and South Korea expect to show similar growth.

We are beginning to see e-commerce grow rapidly in major emerging markets as well. For example, it has been growing by 50 percent a year in China. In Brazil, e-commerce use has doubled in only two years, now accounting for nearly 20 percent of all B2B and more than 7 percent of retail sales. In India, estimates are that e-commerce sales will have grown 300 percent from 2005 to 2007.

All indications are that e-commerce will become an increasingly powerful tool for marketing products and services around the world. For small and medium-sized firms, especially, e-commerce represents a cost-effective means to become an active exporter. For the experienced exporter, e-commerce is a means to expand business in high-growth emerging markets. When a U.S. company opens its Web site for business, it can expect a large percentage of its Web traffic to originate from overseas. In time, the company can expect a growing share of its order inquiries to come from abroad. Many companies, however, are unprepared to respond to international orders, and leave them unfilled. Therefore, the Federal Government, together with its private-sector partners, will focus in the coming year on putting e-business tools in the hands of more U.S. companies.

THE GLOBAL INTERNET REVOLUTION

In less than a decade, the number of Internet users worldwide has grown from 147 million in 1998 to more than one billion in 2006. The United States leads the world in Internet connectivity with 210 million Internet users and per-capita penetration of 70 percent. As growth rates of Internet use in the United States and other advanced markets begin to level off, the spread of Internet access to the rest of the world is accelerating (*Chart 20*). According to the International Telecommunication Union, the world added over 100 million (101.5 million) Internet users in just one year (2004–2005), growing 12 percent

---

2   Jaap Favier, "Europe's eCommerce Forecast: 2005 to 2011," Forrester Research, June 29, 2006, *http://www.forrester.com/Research/Document/Excerpt/o,7211,38297,00.html*

to nearly one billion total (964.3 million). While per-capita penetration rates are still much higher in developed countries, these trends are shrinking the digital divide between the developed and the developing world.

As a result, U.S. companies with a robust Internet presence have exposure online to an exponentially growing global audience. Already, most of the traffic on the United States' top Web properties is generated from outside the United States. The Web usage tracking firm comScore Networks reports that 14 of the top 25 U.S. Web properties generate more traffic from outside the United States than from within. More than 70 percent of unique visitors to Google, Yahoo!, Microsoft sites, and eBay come from outside the United States.[3]

United States is Home to the World's Top E-Commerce Platforms

Google:

- The number-one search engine in Argentina, Australia, Belgium, Brazil, Canada, Denmark, France, Germany, India, Italy, Mexico, Spain, Switzerland, the United Kingdom, and the United States.

- One of the five most popular sites on the Internet used around the world by millions of people.

- More than 50 percent of Google.com traffic is from outside the United States. Google has operations in more than 37 countries and serves more than 100 countries.

eBay:

- Over 233 million registered users worldwide with a global presence in 36 markets.

- Approximately 1.3 million sellers around the world use eBay as their primary or secondary source of income (Source: ACNielson International Research, June 2006).

continued next page

---

3 comScore, "More than Half of Top 25 Web Properties Generate More Traffic from Outside the U.S. than from Within," Press Release, November 9, 2006, *http://www.comscore.com/press/release.asp?press=1057*

■ Roughly 15 percent of its users are either actively participating in export activity or are potential exporters.

■ 15 percent of companies' trade volume is export/import.

PayPal (owned by eBay):

■ Has over 143 million accounts and is available in 103 countries and regions.

■ Accepts payments in several currencies.

Chart 20. Internet Users By Region, 2000–2007

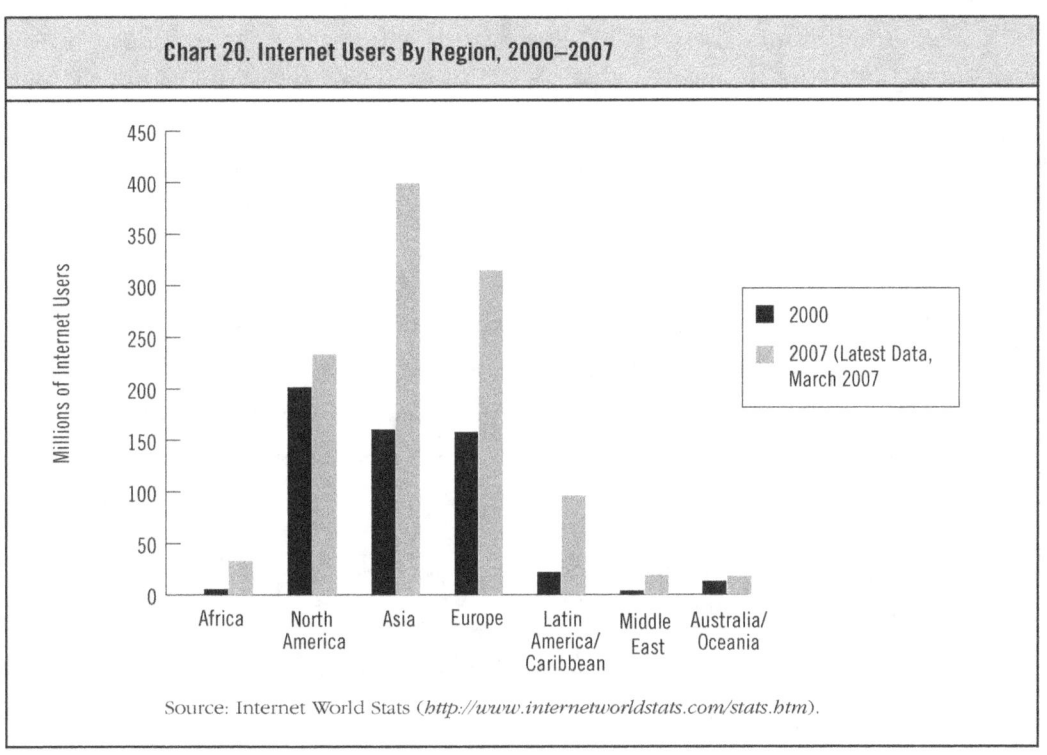

Source: Internet World Stats (*http://www.internetworldstats.com/stats.htm*).

According to the United Nations Conference on Trade and Development (UNCTAD) *Information Economy Report 2006*:

- Asia accounted for nearly 40 percent of all Internet users worldwide. While China represents almost a third of Asia, per-capita penetration is 10.5 percent (China Internet Information Center). South Korea has the highest penetration rate in the region, at 69 percent, followed by Japan with 67 percent.

- 59 percent of European Internet users are in four countries: Germany, the United Kingdom, Italy, and France. Europe has a high overall penetration rate of 66.1 percent.

- In Latin America and the Caribbean, Brazil and Mexico account for over 60 percent of all Internet users. Argentina, Chile, Colombia, Peru, and Venezuela account for another 25 percent. Brazil has a penetration rate of 19.5 percent, the highest among the larger countries in the region.

- Africa has the lowest penetration rate in the world, but had the highest growth rates in terms of numbers of new Internet users.[4]

UNCTAD singles out enterprise access to the Internet as a key developmental factor. Internet access by enterprises is nearly universal (90+ percent) in developed countries. In developing countries, enterprise access is less uniform, but there is a strong correlation between companies having both Internet access and their own Web sites (54 percent)—a good sign of information technology capabilities in the business communities of these countries.

Broadband access to the Internet is of growing importance to e-commerce, particularly for enterprises in developed countries. While the United States has the largest total number of broadband subscribers, at 49 million, several European countries, South Korea, Japan, and Canada have as high, or higher,

---

4 United Nations Conference on Trade and Development, *Information Economy Report 2006*, (New York: United Nations, 2006), 5–10.

per-capita penetration rates, ranging from 16 to 27 percent.[5] Penetration rates are much higher in the business sector than in the overall population. In the EU, for example, 63 percent of enterprises have broadband access.[6]

TARGET E-COMMERCE MARKETS FOR U.S. EXPORTERS

In addition to Internet and broadband penetration, there are several critical elements that determine a country's readiness for e-commerce. Important information technology factors include security of Internet servers, the availability of online payment processing, and the ability to resolve disputes and validate the legitimacy of buyers and sellers. There may also be important legal, regulatory, and cultural issues to consider in a target country, including local language use and advertising rules, especially if a U.S. exporter wants to submit its Web site to the most popular local search engines.

E-commerce Markets for New Exporters

The Economist Intelligence Unit (EIU) has used elements such as these to score and rank the "e-readiness" of countries around the world.[7] A combined look at the EIU rankings alongside an assessment of overall market size and potential points to a short list of geographical markets that are the likely best bets for small and medium-sized companies.

Canada: Canada is frequently the first export market for new U.S. exporters, given several obvious factors that make it easy for U.S. companies to transact business there. Some of these factors, such as similar language, payment preferences, and shipping options also make e-commerce an attractive tool for exporting to Canada. Online shopping in Canada is popular from both

---

5   Organization for Economic Cooperation and Development, OECD Broadband Statistics to June 2006, *http://www.oecd.org/sti/ict/broadband*.

6   United Nations Conference on Trade and Development, *Information Economy Report 2006*, (New York: United Nations, 2006), 10.

7   The Economist Intelligence Unit, "The 2006 E-Readiness Rankings," *http://www.eiu.com/site_info.asp?info_name=eiu_2006_e_readiness_rankings*.

domestic and foreign vendors. In 2005, Canadians placed about 50 million orders online for about $8 billion worth of goods and services. While almost 7 million Canadians placed orders online, another 9 million logged on to window shop.[8]

- **Most popular search engines**: *google.ca, msn.com, yahoo.com, google.com, live.com.*

- **Most popular online marketplaces**: ebay.com, ebay.ca, craigslist.org. About 57 percent of orders (63 percent of total value) for goods and services in Canada in 2005 were placed with a Canadian vendor.

- **Payment preferences**: Three-quarters of Canadians ordering online pay directly over the Internet with a credit or debit card for some or all of their purchases. A majority of Canadians remain concerned about Internet privacy and credit card use.

- **Special considerations**: An estimated 9.2 million adult Canadians used the Internet to window shop for goods and services in 2005, accounting for 55 percent of all Internet users. Six out of ten of these window shoppers ultimately made purchases directly from the retailer (not online). The most popular items for these window shoppers were consumer electronics, housewares, clothing, jewelry, and travel arrangements.

Western Europe: About half of the top 25 countries in the EIU's e-readiness index are Western European countries. While smaller countries like Denmark, Switzerland, Sweden, the Netherlands, Finland, and Norway outrank the larger European economies on the EIU index (and therefore should also be considered), the larger European markets, also in the top 25, are Germany, the United Kingdom, Italy, and France. These countries have well developed e-commerce marketplaces, but there are important differences to consider in terms of payment preferences and regulatory issues.

---

8 Statistics Canada, The Daily, "E-Commerce: Shopping on the Internet," November 2006, *http://www.statcan.ca/Daily/English/061101/d061101a.htm.*

Germany: Germany is the European leader in Internet commerce and is among the world's most sophisticated markets, totaling €320 billion in 2005. Internet commerce is expected to grow to €694 billion by 2009. The use of the Internet by individuals and businesses in Germany continues to expand. About 63 percent, or 51.9 million Germans, were online in 2005, and this percentage is expected to grow to 79.7 percent by the end of 2007. The number of Germans accessing the Internet via broadband is expected to increase from 12.6 million subscribers in June 2006 to 22.4 million in 2010.

Germany holds the highest market share for both B2B and B2C e-commerce in Europe. B2B e-commerce accounted for €289 billion in 2005 and is projected to grow to €580 billion by 2009. Almost all small and medium-sized German businesses have Internet access. Online transactions such as e-procurement are increasing. Revenues of industry- or company-specific marketplaces, such as SupplyOn in the automotive industry, are growing. Major users of B2B solutions are the automotive, retail, energy, and pharmaceutical and chemical production industries.

B2C commerce accounted for €32 billion in 2005 and forecasts expect it to reach €114 billion in 2009. Only about 3 percent of German retail transactions were online sales in 2005. Fifty percent of German adults realized at least one shopping transaction via the Internet in 2005. Favorite B2C products are books, tickets for airlines and trains, hotel reservations, and music. Growing online sales are expected for consumer electronics, pharmaceuticals, and package tours.

- **Most popular search engines**: Google (*google.de* and *google.com*) is by far the most popular search engine in Germany with a market share of almost 90 percent in early 2007. Yahoo! and MSN are ranked second and third respectively. There is no need for a U.S. company to separately submit its site for Germany if the site is already listed in the American search results. Google, Yahoo!, and MSN use slightly different ranking algorithms for their international search engines.

- **Most popular online marketplaces**: *amazon.de* and *ebay.de* are very popular in Germany. eBay is the market leader for online auctions. There are thousands of other marketplaces and online shops.

- **Payment preferences**: Many forms of e-commerce payment are available. Credit cards, pay-upon-delivery, and billing are more popular for bigger payments, as additional fees or administrative obstacles do not make these methods economical for small amounts. Online money transfers, debit cards, mobile phone payments, prepaid money cards, or online money-transfer services such as PayPal are most commonly used for smaller payments. The more payment forms available, the more comfortable a German client will feel about finding a suitable online payment form.

- **Special considerations**: Retailers without "physical" retail stores, or those lacking brand recognition, sometimes encounter difficulties when trying to win the trust of German customers. Besides trust, price and product diversity are the most important competitive factors.

United Kingdom: The United Kingdom is Europe's second biggest e-commerce market. Forrester Research forecasts that by 2011, 32 million UK consumers will be shopping online, purchasing nearly €76 billion in goods over the Internet. The fastest growing retail categories are expected to be alcohol and clothing.[9]

- **Most popular search engines**: The top five search destinations in the United Kingdom are *google.co.uk, yahoo.co.uk, msn.co.uk, google.com,* and *live. com.* Submitting a site to a search engine is exactly the same process as in the United States. Generally, search engine Web sites have an "About us" section that will include details about how to submit a site or add a URL.

- **Most popular online marketplaces**: There are many UK auction sites. A selection of the most visited includes: *ebay.co.uk, cqout.com, ebid.co.uk, amazon. co.uk, qxl.com, bidoutlet.co.uk.*

- **Payment preferences**: Almost all UK-based online businesses allow the customer to use a credit or debit card. Visa and MasterCard are almost universally accepted. American Express, Diners Club, and JCB less so. Discover is not accepted by UK clearing houses. Many Web sites use PayPal or other similar services. UK consumers are becoming much more aware of the issue of online identity theft and will generally conduct financial transactions only on secure Web sites (https).

Italy: Although lower than the European average, e-commerce use in Italy is developing rapidly and appears poised to continue its upward trend in the next few years. The number of business and home Internet users reached 30 million people in 2006, out of a population of 58 million. The Internet penetration rate among Italian enterprises with over 10 employees is close to 95 percent, one of the highest in Europe. Broadband access is developing very rapidly, with over 8 million users in 2006.

---

9 Jaap Favier and Michèle Bouquet, "UK eCommerce Forecast: 2006 to 2011," Forrester Research, August 2, 2006, *http://www.forrester.com/Research/Document/ Excerpt/0,7211,39977,00.html.*

Preliminary estimates value B2B e-commerce transactions in Italy in 2006 at approximately $138 billion. The most active sectors are automotive, pharmaceutical, grocery, information technology, and telecommunications. B2B transactions are expected to register an annual increase of 10 to 20 percent over the next three years. Virtually all major Italian industrial groups and major companies are planning to move to e-procurement. It is predicted that in the next two years over half of all company purchases will be via e-procurement.

B2C e-commerce is growing rapidly as well, but still represents only 1 percent of total retail transactions. Recent studies estimate that in 2006 the Italian B2C e-commerce market exceeded $5 billion, an increase of 45 percent over 2005 and, for the sixth consecutive year, an annual rate of growth higher than 40 percent. The best performing sectors are travel and tourism, IT and consumer electronics, insurance (mostly auto insurance), apparel, and the books, music and video sector. The highest growth rate—approximately 80 percent—was registered by direct consumer-to-consumer sales on eBay.

- **Most popular search engines**: *Google.com, google.it, yahoo.it, alice.it* (controlled by Virgilio/Telecom Italia), *www.libero.it* (controlled by Weather Investments/Infostrada and using the search engine "Arianna"), and *www.msn.it.* Other popular search engines are *www.tiscali.it* (powered by Google), and *www.altavista.it* (powered by Yahoo!). U.S. manufacturers can contact each search engine to submit their sites free of charge, but can also subscribe to special advertising services for a fee. U.S. companies may also decide to hire local firms that specialize in "Web positioning" and search engine marketing services for Web site optimization.

- **Most popular online marketplaces**: *www.ebay.it* is Italy's number-one e-commerce site, with approximately 6.5 million visitors each month. It is also being used by an increasing number of small and medium-sized Italian companies for their e-commerce activities. Italy's leading publisher of free classified advertisements, *www.secondamano.it*, has 800,000 visitors each year. Other popular marketplaces, offering a large range of products, include *www.dmail.it, www.a-more.it, www.comproedono.it, www.costameno.it.*

■ **Payment preferences**: Italy lags behind several European countries in the use of credit cards. Although Italian users are insured against fraudulent use of their credit cards, security is one of their major concerns for e-commerce transactions. Prepaid cards issued by major banking institutions are experiencing success and are becoming the most frequently used type of payment card in Italy for online transactions. The Milan Polytechnic estimates that credit cards and prepaid cards were used for 70 percent of B2C online purchases in 2006, followed by PayPal (10 percent), bank transfer payments (9 percent), and payments upon receipt (8 percent).

■ **Special considerations**: Mobile phone diffusion in Italy is among the highest in the world. This could have an impact on e-commerce in Italy as Web-enabled, new-generation mobile phones become widespread.

Asia: The most developed large markets in Asia in terms of e-readiness are Australia, Japan, and South Korea. Smaller Asian markets in the EIU's top 25 e-readiness rankings include Hong Kong, Singapore, and Taiwan. While Australia's e-commerce is similar to that of the United States, e-commerce in South Korea and Japan presents some additional challenges, including language and different payment preferences.

Australia: B2B e-commerce in Australia was A$33 billion for 2003–2004, and was expected to rise to A$87 billion in 2006. Fifty-three percent of Australian SMEs placed e-commerce orders in 2005 (up from 17 percent in 2000) and 62 percent made online payments (up from 11 percent in 2000).[10]

■ **Most popular search engines**: *google.com.au, msn.com, yahoo.com, google.com, live.com.*

■ **Most popular online marketplaces**: *ebay.com.au, ebay.com, amazon.com.*

---

10 Australian Government, *Invest Australia, http://www.investaustralia.gov.au/index. cfm?id=21283E5A9E40-FF8C-7E3EBD4B86FFD3BD.*

■ **Payment preferences**: Australia shows positive trends in online payments usage and familiarity with online payment systems for e-commerce. Fifty-two percent of Australian Internet users were registered for online banking services and 59 percent of Internet users made online consumer purchases.[11]

South Korea: South Korea ranks among the top countries in the world in terms of Internet usage and broadband penetration. South Korea's aggressive pursuit of IT and networks development has created a world-class IT infrastructure and a growing number of South Korean companies engaging in e-commerce. Total e-commerce in 2005 was $358 billion, up from $235 billion in 2003.[12] By the third quarter of 2006, e-commerce reached $291 billion. Of this total, B2B e-commerce accounted for 88 percent, of which buyer-initiated transactions represented 72 percent—an indication that South Korean buyers see more convenience and benefits from e-commerce than sellers do. Manufacturing accounted for 66 percent of South Korean B2B, followed by wholesale and retail (19 percent) and construction (7.5 percent).[13] South Korean companies of all sizes are engaged in e-commerce; of those surveyed with at least 10 employees, 35.5 percent engaged in e-commerce.

Business-to-government (B2G) e-commerce totaled $29.03 billion in 2005 (up from $16.4 billion in 2003), with construction work accounting for 55 percent and purchases of goods and services accounting for 45 percent.[14]

B2C is also growing at a rapid pace. In 2006, 33.6 million South Koreans (73.5 percent) aged six and older were using the Internet, one million more than in 2005, and the number continues to rise.[15] According to an October 2006 survey, there are 4,518 cyber-shopping malls in South Korea, of which over 94 percent

---

11 Australian Government, *Invest Australia*, *http://www.investaustralia.gov.au/index. cfm?id=A33EC3CC-0631-BB7F-27A238827D2B69BE*.

12 Ministry of Commerce, Industry, and Energy, Republic of Korea, "e-Business in Korea 2006," p.3, *http://www.asemec.org/uploadFolder/key_content/2.pdf*.

13 *Ibid.*, p. 5.

14 *Ibid.*, p. 7.

15 *Ibid.*, p. 10.

were specialized and about 6 percent (or 251) were general. Sales on these Web sites through October 2006, at $10.9 billion, were already topping total sales for 2005 ($10.7 billion).

Mobile Internet is a growing factor in South Korean e-commerce. By September 2006, 45 percent of mobile phone users 12 and older had used the wireless Internet at least once in the previous six months, compared to 32 percent in 2002.

- **Most popular search engines**: Naver (www.naver.com) is the most popular portal that offers a search engine in South Korea. Daum, Yahoo!, Empas, and Google are also among the top five search engines.

- **Most popular online marketplaces**: GS Homeshopping (*www.gseshop.co.kr*), Interpark (*www.interpark.com*), CJ mall (*www.cjmall.com*), and Samsung mall (*www.samsungmall.co.kr*) are well-known online marketplaces primarily dealing with online products. Also, Auction eBay company (*www.auction.co.kr*), which was acquired by eBay is famous for online auctioning. The most popular computer shopping mall site is Danawa Corp. (*www.danawa.co.kr*). For purchasing books on the Internet, Kyobo Bookstore (*www.kyobobook.co.kr*) and Youngpoong Bookstore (*www.ypbooks.co.kr*) are popular. Both bookstores are based offline, whereas Aladdin (*www.aladdin.co.kr*) and Yes24 (*www.yes24.com*) are popular online bookstore companies, which also sell CDs, DVDs, etc.

- **Payment preferences**: Online banking is common in South Korea and continues to grow. In 2006, South Korean financial institutions had 35 million Internet banking customers, of which 33 million were retail customers and about 2 million were corporate customers.[16] Using credit cards, real-time cash transfers, Internet Security Payment, or mobile phones, it is possible to buy or sell through the South Korean Internet. Credit cards are taking an increasing share of online transactions as the use of wire transfers declines.[17]

---

16 *Ibid.*, p. 12.

17 Organization for Economic Cooperation and Development, "Online Payment Systems and E-Commerce," Report DSTI/ICCP/IE (2004)18/FINAL (Paris, Organization for Economic Cooperation and Development: 2006), 14, *http://www.oecd.org/dataoecd/37/19/36736056.pdf.*

One can also use financing vehicles, including PAYplus, GlobalPay, Billgate, etc., real-time cash transfers, Internet Security Payment, or mobile phones to buy or sell through the South Korean Internet.

- **Special considerations**: It is not necessary for the Web site to have a South Korean domain name; however, those individuals or organizations who have a local presence within South Korea are eligible to register for a ".kr" domain name. Transactions over the Internet are recognized as legal sales contracts. With regard to advertising, there are regulations preventing youth-harmful media; the Youth Protection Act declares that youth-harmful advertisements or promotion of music, video, and game content must not be distributed or posted.

Japan: Japan's Ministry of Economy, Trade, and Industry estimates that the Japanese B2B e-commerce market in 2005 was worth between $835 billion (¥92 trillion at ¥110.2 /$1) via Internet only and $1.7 trillion (¥189 trillion) via Internet and other computer network systems.[18] E-commerce accounted for over 20 percent of all B2B sales in Japan and nearly 33 percent of all manufacturing sales. Within the manufacturing sector, automotive equipment and electronics/IT equipment were the largest drivers of e-commerce, with the Internet accounting for 35 percent of all automotive equipment sales and 28 percent of all electronic/IT equipment sales. Other drivers of B2B e-commerce were chemicals, metals, and food.

B2C e-commerce in Japan in 2005 was $31.8 billion (¥3.5 trillion), representing 1.2 percent of all retail sales in Japan. E-commerce is most common in the information and communications (e.g., digital content distribution and software), electric products, and hotel and travel sectors.

- **Most popular search engines**: *yahoo.co.jp, google.co.jp, infoseek.co.jp*

- **Most popular online marketplaces**: *rakuten.co.jp, amazon.co.jp*

---

18 Ministry of Economy, Trade, and Industry, "Announcement of the Results of the 2005 E-Commerce Market Survey," press release, June 6, 2006, *http://www.meti.go.jp/english/ information/downloadfiles/PressRelease/060626eCommerceSurvey.pdf.*

- **Payment preferences**: Japan is one of the few countries where mobile phones are used more frequently for payment than personal computers.[19]

E-commerce Strategies for Priority Emerging Markets

U.S. companies that have more export experience and that have already established an e-commerce track record may be ready to take on more challenging, high-growth emerging markets. In markets like China, Brazil, Mexico, and India, e-commerce is growing from a much smaller base. Given the rapid proliferation of personal computers, Internet use (including broadband), and payment options (including credit cards), along with the emergence of new businesses and middle-class consumers, e-commerce is emerging as a cost-effective strategy for entering these markets.

While these markets offer attractive prospects, they also carry more risk and challenges, and therefore, rank much lower than the markets listed above in terms of their e-readiness. Nevertheless, e-commerce may be a cost-effective strategy for companies ready to invest the time and resources.

Brazil: In Brazil, a study by the Getulio Vargas Foundation (Fundação Getulio Vargas—FGV) shows that e-commerce B2B sales have more than doubled within two years, with electronic B2B growing from 9 percent of sales in 2004 to 19.6 percent in March 2006, and electronic B2C growing from 2.9 percent in March 2004 to 7.45 percent in March 2006.[20]

- **Most popular search engines**: Google, UOL, Terra, AOL, Yahoo!. According to the Brazilian Association of Internet Service Providers (ABRANET), there are currently more than 1,000 ISPs in Brazil, but only five large companies hold 50 percent of market share.

---

19 Organization for Economic Cooperation and Development, "Online Payment Systems and E-Commerce," Report DSTI/ICCP/IE (2004)18/FINAL (Paris: Organization for Economic Cooperation and Development, 2006), 12, *http://www.oecd.org/dataoecd/37/19/36736056.pdf*.

20 Economist Intelligence Unit, Global Technology Forum, "Brazil: Overview of E-commerce," September 2006, *http://globaltechforum.eiu.com*.

- **Most popular online marketplaces**: *americanas.com.br, livrariasaraiva. com.br, webmotors.com/,* and *marketplace.com.br/.* The equivalent to eBay in Brazil is *http://www.mercadolivre.com.br*

- **Payment preferences**: A buyer is free to purchase products over the Internet. The Brazilian Central Bank is trying to track Internet transactions in order to control the remittance of money to other countries, but these new rules are still not in place. Internet transactions as well as digital signatures are recognized as legal operations, but it is strongly suggested that U.S. companies consult with an in-country law firm to avoid legal problems.

- **Special considerations**: Licensing agreements are common means of accessing the Brazilian market. Use of a competent local attorney in structuring such an arrangement is advised. All licensing and technical assistance agreements, including trademark licenses, must be registered with the Brazilian Industrial Property Institute (INPI) at *http://www.inpi.gov.br.*

Mexico: Mexico has relatively low Internet penetration, yet e-commerce in Mexico has grown significantly over the past two years. Internet service is now widely available in the country, and it is estimated that there were about 17 million regular users in 2005, an increase of 7 million from 2002. E-commerce has evolved from a B2B application into a B2C application. B2C e-commerce sales totaled over $221 million in 2004. Travel services ($88 million) and specialty stores ($62 million) register the most online sales. Future e-commerce growth will likely be aided by reduced Internet fees, Internet availability in major cities, increased familiarity and confidence of people, increased adoption by retailers of e-commerce platforms, and increased number of bank accounts and credit/debit cards among the population. In 2004, the most purchased items online were plane tickets, computers, food, console games, show tickets, and car accessories.

- **Most popular search engines**: Google Mexico, Yahoo! Mexico, and Terra Networks. A cost-effective method for American companies to enter the Mexican e-commerce market is to advertise through the search engines' "Sponsored Sites" sections, which list a company's Web site at the top of any list of relevant search results. Currently, the Mexican market is evenly divided between the advertising services offered by Yahoo!'s TeRespondo and Google's AdWord.

- **Most popular online marketplaces**: *www.mercadolibre.com.mx*, *www. todito.com.mx*, *www.esmas.com.mx*

- **Payment preferences**: The most popular way to make purchases online in Mexico is with a credit or debit card: online consumers enter their details directly in the payment form on the retailer's Web site. In far second place is direct bank deposit or wire transfer, with 20 percent of use, and C.O.D. or cash are also used. Credit/debit card payments grew steadily during 2004. Card payments registered 38 percent growth from just the first to the fourth quarters in 2004, with total credit/debit card sales in 2004 of about $83 million.

- **Special considerations**: For software sales, there are special considerations of double taxation and royalty payments to avoid overpaying taxes (see "Software: Retention and Double Taxation" at *www.buyusa.gov/mexico/en/telecom.html*).

India: In India, falling prices of hardware and mobile phones, the growing penetration of the Internet (40 million Internet users), and bandwidth availability have created promising opportunities for e-commerce business models. Internet companies are gearing up to serve the e-commerce market in India. While $135 million worth of business was conducted online in India during 2004–2005, that number is expected to reach $530 million by April 2007, a growth of 300 percent from 2005. The industry feels that e-commerce is slowly, but surely, coming of age. According to a recent study, 55 percent of online shoppers in India have shopped online more than once. Books were the top product sold online, followed by electronics, railway tickets, accessories and apparel, gifts, computers, and airline tickets. Over 80 percent of online shoppers were highly satisfied with online shopping, according to the study.

- **Most popular search engines**: Google, Yahoo!, and MSN are the most popular search engines in India. Indian mirror sites, hosted in India, exist for each of these sites. U.S. exporters can contact these search engines directly for submission.

- **Most popular online marketplaces**: The most popular online marketplace is *Bazee.com* which is an affiliate of eBay. In addition, there are popular consumer portals, such as *sify.com*, *rediff.com*, and *indiatimes.com*. For B2B transactions, there are sector-specific portals.

- **Payment preferences**: Credit cards, domestic and international, are accepted, subject to the merchant's affiliations.

- **Special considerations**: It is prudent for exporters to partner with an Indian merchant and route the transaction through the merchant.

China: Most sources show e-commerce in China growing by about 50 percent a year, with total e-commerce (B2C and B2B) reaching as much as $92.5 billion in 2005.[21] According to *CCNID.net*, the B2B market dominates e-commerce in China with 95 percent ($81.3 billion) of the total e-commerce market in 2005. It is estimated that B2B will reach $180.88 billion by 2010. After years of development, the number of B2C Web sites is also growing significantly. Statistics from the Ministry of Information Industry show that the number of retail Web sites in 2004 was 2,219, making up 49.5 percent of total e-commerce Web sites. From 2004 to 2005, the transaction volume of China B2C shopping grew from $52 to $70 million, a growth rate of 33 percent. With the further improvement of the online shopping environment, the compound annual growth rate in 2005 to 2010 should reach 52 percent.

- **Most popular search engines**: *http://www.baidu.com* is the most popular search engine in China. In addition, Google (which has a Chinese-language version: *www.google.com/intl/zh-CN/*) is also a popular search engine.

- **Most popular online marketplaces**: *Taobao.com* is China's most popular e-marketplace, with 50 million hits per day and about 3.3 million product listings, according to Taobao. *Taobao.com* users pay and receive cash through local banks. eBay recently bought Eachnet (a Chinese online auction site) and now operates as eBay Eachnet, based in Shanghai. Other examples include *www.dangdang.com* and *www.joyo.com*, two online bookstores. Dangdang.com is the largest online book retailer in mainland China. These transactions are C.O.D purchases, and goods are delivered within 48 hours of ordering.

---

21 Organization for Economic Cooperation and Development, p.169, *OECD Information Technology Outlook 2006*, (Paris: OECD).

- **Payment preferences**: The biggest hurdle to conducting e-commerce in China is the fact that Internet transactions are still predominantly paid for either by C.O.D. or through local banks. China is primarily a cash-based society where the use of credit cards is very limited. While more and more affluent Chinese are obtaining credit cards, most vendors, other than Western-oriented outlets and Five-Star hotels and restaurants, do not accept credit cards. Most people with credit cards use extreme caution when providing card information for domestic Internet transactions. Not even eBay Eachnet uses Paypal in China. For international transactions (for instance, a buyer in China purchasing from an overseas site), there are fewer problems and security concerns.

- **Special considerations**: There is a law covering advertising in China that forbids "unfair competition" when carrying out advertising activities. There is no nationwide law for ads targeting children, but in some provinces, local governments have issued rules on ads targeting children.

STEPS FOR MAKING E-COMMERCE A COST-EFFECTIVE TOOL FOR SME EXPORTERS

While any company with a Web site has potential access to foreign buyers overseas, e-commerce does not happen on its own. Companies must become familiar with the steps necessary to make their Web sites e-export-capable and must adopt certain electronic business practices that employ tools available from the private and public sectors.

Companies that have decided how to portray their business online must assess whether they have the most efficient IT solutions to execute their online exporting programs. IT embodies a range of computer systems and software applications for managing a firm's Web site, as well as personnel records, back-end databases, etc. With more and more cyber-attacks on government and corporate sites, companies should invest in security technologies to protect themselves and their customers from identity theft and denial of service.

Companies can then follow a step-by-step approach to creating a Web site and marketing themselves overseas using the Internet and key service providers:

- **Register a Domain Name**: Companies that already have a domain name in the United States may want to register a domain name in key foreign markets even if they are not yet ready to pursue those markets, in order to secure their brand name or company name Web site in that domain.

- **Choose a Web Host**: There are a number of Web hosting services and Internet service providers who offer value-added services such as search engine optimization, site creation, and maintenance.

- **Create Web Content**: If you are having an outside firm create your Web site, submit a request for proposal to several firms: supply information on your product or service, who your target market is, what image you want to portray to visitors, and what you think is important to your potential customers. You will want to decide whether you want localized pages on your U.S. site or whether you want to create a unique localized site for each language version, perhaps located in that country. Another option is allowing your distributors to localize and mirror your U.S. site in their own country. In all cases, a clear understanding of who creates and maintains the localized versions is necessary and may involve a contract. Help is available on cultural issues for design and layout. Always include an address, internationally accessible phone number, and email address for inquiries.

- **Register Your Site With Foreign Search Engines**: By registering with foreign search engines overseas, even if you only have a U.S. site, you will increase the probability of attracting foreign visitors. Some search engines require that only localized versions be registered, or that the sites must be located geographically in the region. So be sure to check this information first.

- **Create Your Privacy Policy for Visitors**: Around the world, privacy issues for visitors are of increasing concern. Develop your privacy policy and have it accessible from your home page. This will increase the likelihood of other sites being willing to link to your site.

- **Be Aware of Internet Legal Issues**: Besides privacy issues, there are a number of issues regarding the content of your site, your advertising claims, consumer protection, and intellectual property. Be sure to check local laws regarding protection of your intellectual property, as well as if and how you are allowed to advertise your product or service, before completing your Web site design.

- **Set Up Payment Processing**: You will need to decide whether you will make use of any of the shopping cart software options available or have a third-party provider do the order processing for your site. You will want to be sure to choose an option that allows several payment options, and may include processing orders in foreign currencies. However you process orders, you should have a form of fraud protection in place. There are many third-party fraud protection providers available for your own site or those that process orders for you.

- **Provide Security**: You will want to be sure that your visitors feel that their payment information and personal data are secure. Many shopping-cart software providers include this in their offering, as do third-party payment processors.

- **Define Order Fulfillment Policies**: Be clear on your ordering information in defining what responsibilities buyers will have when it comes to taxes, duties, and freight charges for their orders. State the expected shipping time on order acknowledgements.

- **State Return or Repair Policy**: Potential customers (or distributors) need to know what your return or repair policy is for products. If you will require a Material Return Authorization for products to be returned, include the blank form on your Web site and state where the request should be sent, as well as your policy for returns.

- **Gather Market Data**: Once your site is created, you will want to track the success of this marketing tool. Web analytic software can collect data on visitors, such as what country they are coming from, what language they use, what search engines and what search words they used to find your site, what pages on your Web site they visited, and even how long they stayed on that page. Many Web hosts offer this additional feature. If you are managing your own site, you will want to be sure to install this type of market intelligence application. It can provide valuable insights as to what languages you may want to localize on your site first, and what products or services to give priority.

While these steps require the investment of time and money, they can prove to be a cost-effective means for small and medium-sized U.S. companies to enter the world's fastest growing Internet markets.

CONCLUSIONS

As noted frequently in the step-by-step approach above, the driving force of e-commerce is private-sector innovation and technology—much of it American. The e-commerce marketplace has responded to early customer concerns over privacy and transaction security. Sophisticated new e-business applications can now help companies market their goods and services to buyers across the world. In the coming year, the Federal Government will work with private e-business providers, including corporate partners eBay and Google, to present new training opportunities to U.S. businesses on the tremendous business facilitation tools now available for making e-commerce an effective gateway to foreign markets.

Featured U.S. Exporters Program: The Commerce Department will expand the Featured U.S. Exporters (FUSE) program (see *http://www.buyusa.gov/home/fuse.html*) to leverage its global network of offices and Web sites. FUSE is a directory of U.S. products featured on Commercial Service Web sites around the world. It gives U.S. companies an opportunity to target specific markets in the local language of business. Currently, listings are offered to qualified U.S. exporters seeking trade leads or representation in over 50 markets around the world. The nominal participation fee for one year (minimum $25) is based on the number of markets selected and on translation requirements. There are about 30 markets offering English listings (at $5 per market) and about another 30 offering local language listings (most ranging from $30 to $50 including translation). Companies renewing their listings pay a reduced fee.

Ex-Im Online: Ex-Im Bank has developed and implemented "Ex-Im Online," an online system for processing and issuing credit insurance and guarantees. These programs support export sales by U.S. companies to overseas corporate customers who require short-term credit or medium-term financing in connection with their purchases of products and services. Ex-Im's short-term credit insurance program is heavily focused on providing support to small and medium-sized businesses; Ex-Im Online is designed to expand and improve services to this segment of the U.S. exporting community. As it evolves, Ex-Im Bank's online system may provide U.S. exporters, particularly SMEs, with greater opportunities to make the extension of short-term trade credit a more customary and widely available e-commerce payment option.

The Digital Freedom Initiative: The Digital Freedom Initiative (DFI) was launched on March 4, 2003, at the White House, where the Governments of Senegal and the United States agreed to pilot the DFI. Since 2003, the DFI has grown to encompass programs in many countries using information and communication technologies (ICT) to help spur economic growth and policy reform. The DFI approach leverages the leadership of the U.S. Government with both the creativity and resources of American business and the vision and energy of local partners throughout the developing world. Current efforts include:

- DFI in Senegal: Over 100 private entities in Senegal have benefited from the entrepreneurial and information and communication technology skill training provided during the first years of the effort.

- DFI in Peru: The U.S. Government, working with Intel, Cisco, Motorola, Voxiva and Hewlett-Packard, is helping to support the Government of Peru's efforts to promote the spread of the Internet to more than 1,000 rural locations. (see *http://www.dfiperu.org*).

- DFI in Jordan: U.S. business volunteers have been assisting the U.S. Agency for International Development and other government efforts to provide technical assistance, encourage innovative uses of ICT, and support policy reform.

For 2007, the DFI seeks to increase connectivity in the developing world in the service of economic development:

- Increasing connectivity in rural areas and across regions;

- Encouraging regulatory reform and technical assistance to support infrastructure investment, including broadband and wireless;

- Showing best practices using universal service funds, in countries where they exist, to expand connectivity; and

- Promoting development through greater use of ICT: delivering health and educational services via ICT and expanding use of the Internet to help share information on government services (e-government).

In addition to several events still being planned, the DFI Calendar in 2007 includes:

- January 2007: East Asia Pacific Workshops—Topics include expanding ICT Infrastructure in Remote Communities, Universal Service Funding, and Local Broadband Wireless Initiatives. Locations: Vietnam and the Philippines.

- February 20, 2007: DFI Roundtable—A forum for the U.S. Government, private, academic, and NGO participants to exchange views and program ideas on using ICTs to aid development. Location: State Department, Washington, D.C.

- March 15, 2007: Celebrating the U.S.–African Partnership in Connecting Africa via IT, Telecommunications, and the Internet. Location: Washington, D.C.

- March 19–21, 2007: USTDA ICT in Africa Conference. Location: San Francisco, C.A.

- April 2–5, 2007: USTDA Central Asia ICT Conference.
  Location: Almaty, Kazakhstan

- June–July 2007: West Africa Regional Connectivity Workshop.

Improvement of the Commerce Department's Selling Online Service: In keeping with its mandate to assist export-ready companies with the tools to export, the Commerce Department will continue to improve its online e-commerce Toolbox at *http://www.export.gov/sellingonline/*. The e-commerce Toolbox has information to get U.S. companies started on the right path. In addition to more detailed information on each of the "Steps" above, the e-commerce Toolbox has guidance on:

- Deciding what type of Web site is most appropriate to the needs and goals of the company, for example, transactional site, information delivery site, or e-marketplace;

- Deciding which markets to target, including tailoring marketing efforts to regional tastes;

- Pursuing market development on the Web, including advertising messages, advertising on search engines, advertising networks, and direct e-mail;

- Processing orders and accepting payment via credit card payments, account-to-account transfers, and person-to-person transfers;

- Determining appropriate pricing, tariff rates, and ideal methods of shipping product; and

- Developing an effective customer service program, including Web design and overall e-commerce business strategy.

The Toolbox also offers detailed Frequently Asked Questions on target e-commerce markets.

Web Applications for Business: Besides teaching U.S. exporters how to use e-commerce, the Federal Government and its public and private partners will explore ways to better inform companies of Web-based services that make them faster, more efficient, and more economical. There is now available a host of new Web applications that allow companies to reduce costs and facilitate not only their online business, but also their traditional sales and marketing efforts. An illustrative example is just-in-time printing. Just-in-time printing allows U.S. clients to upload their marketing materials to a secure Web site, where the service provider localizes the materials and posts them for the client. The client can then request small orders of their product literature in the local language. The literature is printed in the foreign country where it is to be delivered to the client's subsidiary or distributor within a few days. This process cuts down immensely on shipping costs and on overage of out-dated datasheets for products that become obsolete every few months. It also provides a higher level of service.

Using Strategic Partnerships to Help Small and Medium-Sized Companies Export

U.S. industry, workers, and farmers have responded well to export opportunities created by new market access and growing foreign markets. American exporters are once again proving to the world that U.S. goods and services are the most competitive in the world. Yet the United States has only just begun to realize its full export potential. *Chart 21* shows that while the percentage of U.S. Gross Domestic Product (GDP) accounted for by exports has begun to climb in recent years, it has remained near 10 percent over the past 25 years. At the same time, exports play a significantly larger role in the economies of our G7 competitors.

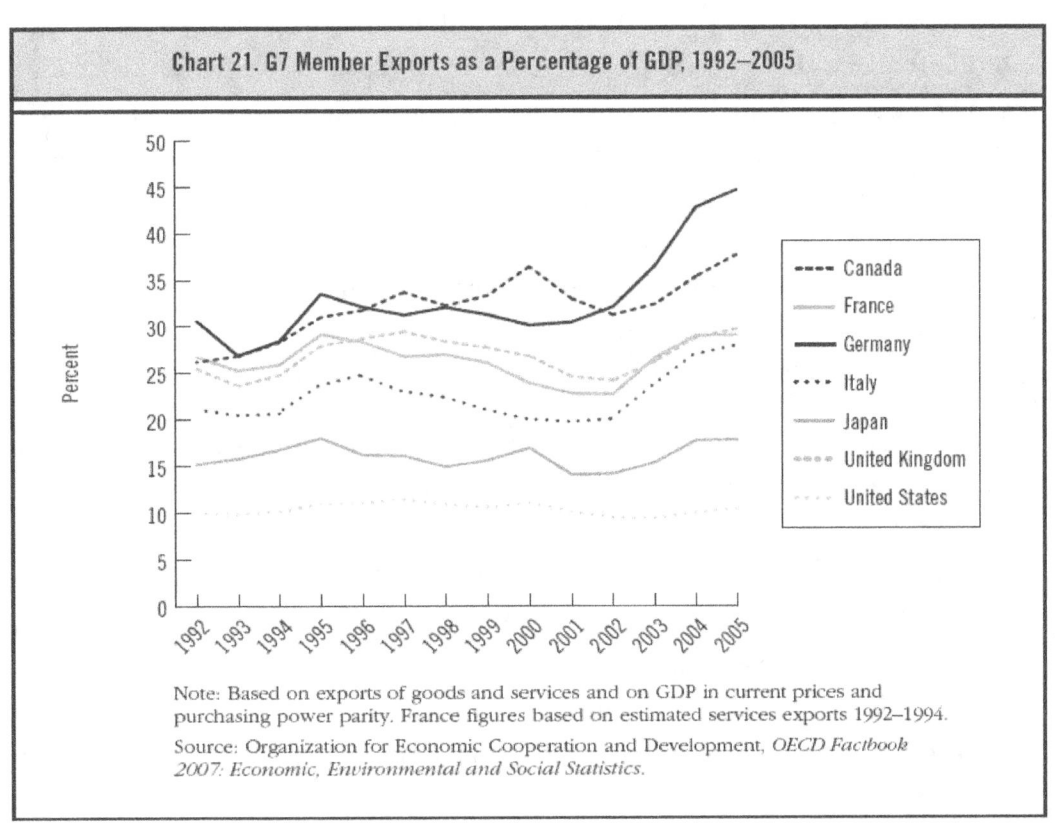

Chart 21. G7 Member Exports as a Percentage of GDP, 1992–2005

Note: Based on exports of goods and services and on GDP in current prices and purchasing power parity. France figures based on estimated services exports 1992–1994.

Source: Organization for Economic Cooperation and Development, *OECD Factbook 2007: Economic, Environmental and Social Statistics.*

Thousands of U.S. companies have competitive products and services and the potential to export, but remain focused only on the domestic market. Thousands more occasionally fill foreign orders, but have not developed a proactive business plan for targeting markets and going after foreign sales. Many companies are not fully aware of the opportunities that await them in growing foreign markets. Just as importantly, many hold outdated perceptions about the difficulties of exporting, and do not realize that exporting has become easier than ever as a result of lower trade barriers, new technology, and the availability of new business services.

Raising awareness of exporting opportunities and putting the tools of the trade in the hands of more potential exporters is no small challenge. There are 24.4 million companies in the United States, of which 5.7 million have employees on the payroll. Our goal, therefore, is to identify and reach out to all potential exporters in the business community by encouraging all stakeholders to become more involved in trade promotion.

The Federal Government is just one of many stakeholders that can do more to encourage and assist U.S. companies in entering foreign markets. State and local governments, trade associations and other business groups, and corporations that provide international business services have large client bases or constituencies that would also benefit from greater awareness of exporting opportunities. Given the combination of both the immense opportunities abroad and the thousands of non-exporting companies at home, all such stakeholders should work together to engage more clients, on more fronts to take advantage of trade promotion information, assistance, and opportunities.

Strategic Partnership Initiative

Our Strategic Partnership Initiative seeks to foster more cooperation between stakeholders and improve our ability to leverage each other's unique capabilities. Building the base of exporters requires more skills and resources than any one stakeholder can bring to bear—more business contacts, more industry expertise, more foreign market expertise, more logistical capabilities, and more cutting-edge marketing, financing, and technology know-how. For example, the Federal Government provides foreign market expertise and matchmaking and problem-solving services that exporters need. But the Federal Government simply lacks the resources, marketing channels, and points of contact with businesses to reach most companies. In the coming year, the Strategic Partnership Initiative will both broaden the number of stakeholders we partner with and deepen our commitment to current partners. Along the way, we are discovering that together we can accomplish things on behalf of our clients that separately we could not even consider.

On the other hand, as public and private partners grow more capable of delivering export services, we also encourage all parties to do more, with or without Federal Government involvement. For example, we are asking governors, trade associations, and business groups to organize more trade missions and events. Together, we will pursue a number of shared goals, including: identifying and serving more small and medium-sized U.S. exporters, increasing awareness of the importance of international trade, delivering higher customer satisfaction, and achieving greater U.S. market penetration in key emerging markets. The bottom line is that all stakeholders—public or private—have an interest and a responsibility to more directly and actively promote exports.

Profile of Small and Medium-Sized Exporters

A major challenge the United States faces in realizing the nation's full export potential is low participation rates among the general business community (*Chart 22*). In 2005, only 239,094 firms were identified as exporters—about 4 percent of companies with payroll. After a period of rapid growth in the late 1980s and early 1990s, participation of U.S. companies in the global economy became fairly flat. In recent years, there has been a steady growth in the number of U.S. exporters, an overall increase of about 7 percent since 2002. This may point to a new trend, reflective of record exports in 2006 and an increased percentage of GDP attributed to exports. In 2005:

■ Small and medium-sized exporters (those employing fewer than 500 workers) comprised over 97 percent of all identified exporters and accounted for 29 percent of the known export value.

■ The number of identified exporting companies increased by 6,266 or almost 3 percent. The number of small and medium-sized companies increased by almost 3 percent from 226,200 in 2004 to 232,600 in 2005, while the number of large companies decreased by over 2 percent from 6,628 to 6,482.

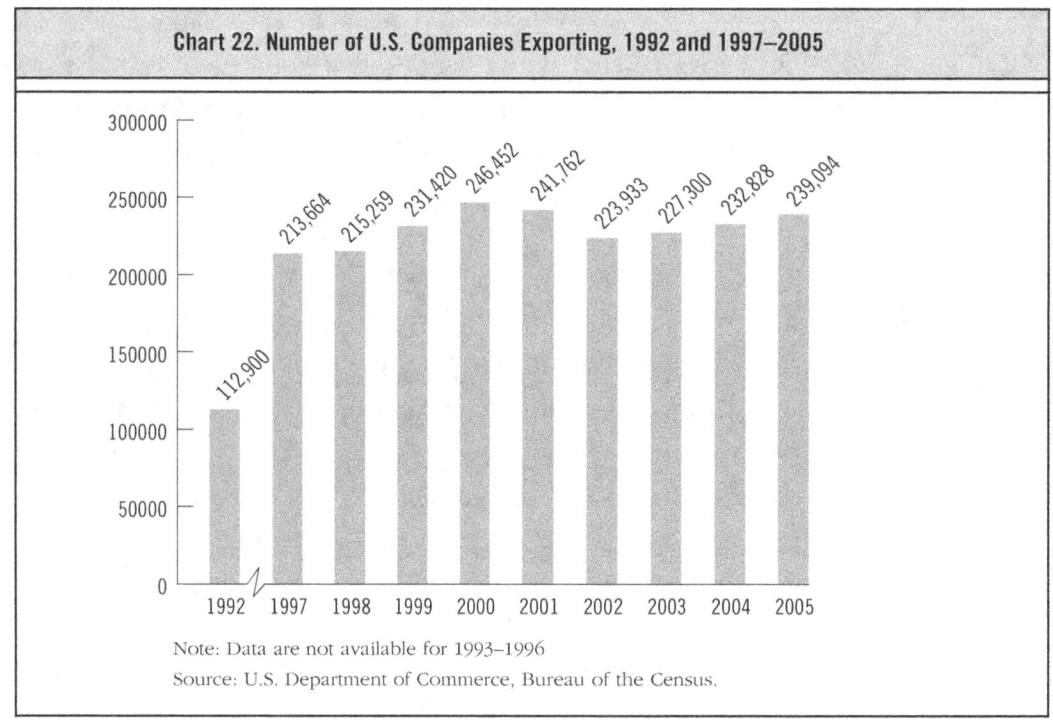

Chart 22. Number of U.S. Companies Exporting, 1992 and 1997–2005

Note: Data are not available for 1993–1996
Source: U.S. Department of Commerce, Bureau of the Census.

- Most identified exporting companies (58 percent) traded in only one foreign market. A small percentage of companies, 0.4 percent, shipped to 50 or more countries; these companies accounted for almost half (49 percent) of the known export value.

- About 84 percent of all identified exporting companies exported to at least one of the top 25 U.S. trading partners. The largest number of companies shipped to Canada, followed by Mexico, the United Kingdom, Germany, and Japan.

- Among the top 25 U.S. trading partners, China (12 percent), India (12 percent), and Brazil (11 percent) show the largest percentage increases in the number of identified exporting companies. Taiwan (−4 percent) and Japan (−3 percent) show the largest declines in the number of exporters over 2004.[1]

---

1 U.S. Department of Commerce, Bureau of the Census, "A Profile of U.S. Exporting Companies, 2004–2005," press release January 10, 2007, *http://www.census.gov/foreign-trade/Press-Release/edb/2005/edbrel-0405.pdf.*

STATE AND LOCAL GOVERNMENT

Some of our most tried and true partnerships are with the U.S. states and local governments. In many localities, federal and state operations are integrated to leverage public resources and improve customer service and convenience. However, as we seek together to broaden the base of U.S. exporters, states and cities represent much more than merely a leveraging opportunity.

- State and local governments have an unrivaled level of understanding of the market dynamics in a locality—of the on-the-ground strengths and interests of their industries, workers, and farmers. Many states can conduct substantive counseling and market research for exporters.

- State and local governments are often the trusted first point of contact for businesses seeking export assistance. As a result, states play a critical communications role, both in listening to companies and understanding their needs, and in broadcasting to companies information on new export opportunities and services.

- Many governors and mayors have made international trade and investment a top priority, dedicating resources, staff, and their own time to the effort. This kind of personal involvement by state and local leaders provides invaluable public attention to the importance of exporting for our economic competitiveness and prosperity.

One indication that cities and states understand the importance of exporting is the large number of trade missions that they lead each year. In addition to leading many overseas events on their own, states and local governments conducted 97 overseas trips and trade missions in 2006 with the assistance of the Commercial Service (*Chart 23*).

State Models

There is no standard operating model for an effective trade promotion program. However, there are aspects of the ways certain states operate that do lead to successes for companies in their regions.

Connecticut: The state has entered into a trade partnership agreement with the Commercial Service that allows qualified small and medium-sized Connecticut firms to more easily take advantage of federal export promotion programs and services. Eligible companies can cost-effectively access market research resources, schedule appointments, and advertise through U.S. Department of Commerce services such as International Partner Search, Gold Key Service, International Company Profile, Commercial News USA, and others. The state will reimburse qualified Connecticut firms up to 50 percent of the participation fee for certain U.S. Department of Commerce export programs and services.

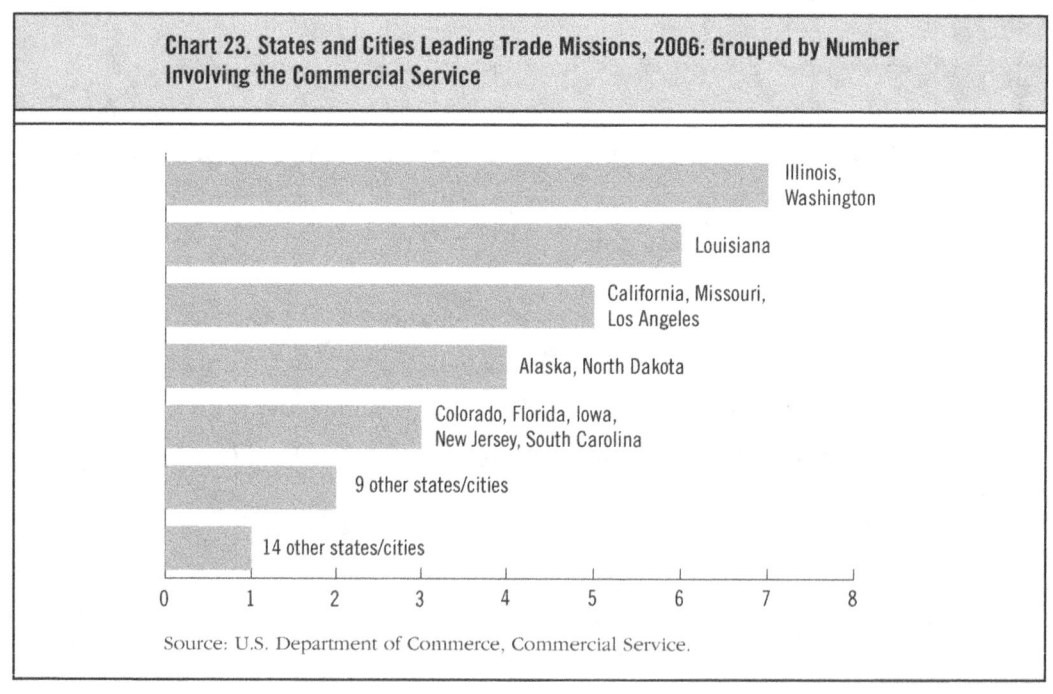

Chart 23. States and Cities Leading Trade Missions, 2006: Grouped by Number Involving the Commercial Service

Source: U.S. Department of Commerce, Commercial Service.

Florida: A public–private partnership, Enterprise Florida, Inc., is responsible for leading Florida's statewide economic development efforts. It has programs to help Florida companies enter or expand in the international marketplace through services such as export counseling and inbound and outbound foreign buyer trade missions. Enterprise Florida has offices in 14 markets: Brazil, Canada, China, the Czech Republic, Germany, Israel, Japan, Mexico, South Africa, South Korea, Spain, Taiwan, the United Kingdom, and Venezuela. Enterprise Florida also offers financial assistance through the Florida Export Finance Corporation.

Georgia: The state has ten offices overseas that help Georgia companies participate in international trade shows and missions and make in-country matchmaking appointments with international buyers. Additionally, the state works with the U.S. Chamber of Commerce's TradeRoots program in Columbus, Douglas, Gainesville, Rome, Savannah, Thomasville, and Tifton to educate companies and economic developers on the benefits of free trade agreements. The state's trade specialists are also co-located in Atlanta with Department of Commerce and Small Business Administration trade specialists to help Georgia companies leverage federal trade promotion and finance programs.

North Dakota: A private–public partnership between the North Dakota Department of Commerce, the North Dakota District Export Council, and the state's business community focuses on expanding North Dakota exports through advocacy, education, and expertise. The Trade Office serves as a catalyst among the state's universities, state and federal government agencies, and private export service professionals that collectively provide North Dakota companies with the support they need to succeed in the global marketplace. Members of the Trade Office staff are located throughout the state and provide a full range of export services including market-entry research, export education and certification, trade missions, and assistance in finding reliable international distributors.

Pennsylvania: World Trade PA, a new initiative launched by Governor Edward Rendell, is working to double the number of companies seeking export assistance and to promote sales by Pennsylvania businesses, aggressively pursuing opportunities in rapidly expanding global markets. Key elements include:

- Developing a Web-based World Trade PA Operations Center to provide a one-stop-shop where businesses can assess their capacity to enter foreign markets, develop successful business plans, and tap into an extensive sales and resource referral network;

- Expanding the commonwealth's network of overseas trade representatives and increasing operations in China, India, and other emerging markets. Currently there are 18 overseas trade offices with three more to come on line this year; and

- Launching an outreach and education campaign aimed at small and medium-sized businesses to increase awareness of Pennsylvania's innovative trade-promotion programs. The Market Access Grant (MAG) is an export promotion grant program that matches grants for small businesses seeking foreign market entry and support for trade show participation, sales/buyer trips, training, translation services, and other marketing needs. Over the last four and a half years, 209 Pennsylvania exporters have received $328,000 in MAG funding. The Export Trade Finance program is used either to access working capital or accounts-receivable financing to offer more attractive payment terms to foreign buyers. During fiscal year 2004-2005, this program awarded $2.3 million to seven companies.

Washington State: Washington State funds the Export Finance Assistance Center to assist local exporters with trade finance structuring and to access working capital guarantees and export credit insurance. The Assistance Center is a longtime City/State Partner of Ex-Im Bank and works closely with the Bank's western region staff to effectively reach exporters of all sizes throughout the state. The Center's activities include active representation of Ex-Im Bank products at trade finance seminars, banking conventions, and trade center offerings. The Assistance Center is routinely in the top echelon of Ex-Im Bank's City/State Partners in exporter interaction and in delivery of appropriate financial tools, bringing exporters together with federal programs and engaged financial providers.

Conclusion

As part of the Strategic Partnership Initiative, we will deepen and broaden our cooperation with states, cities, and other regional or local government entities. As equal partners, we can better realign resources, plan joint events and training, increase companies' access to financing, and improve customer service—all leading to our common objective of getting more U.S. companies to export. Beyond these cooperative or joint activities, we encourage states and cities to make their own trade promotion initiatives more available so that more U.S. companies have opportunities to export.

U.S. Government agencies are engaged in a number of initiatives to elevate the level of communication and information sharing with state and local government officials, and to ensure that they have all the tools needed to assist export-capable companies.

U.S. Department of Agriculture Work with Legislatures and State Regional Trade Groups

The U.S. Department of Agriculture's Foreign Agricultural Service (FAS) has a long history of working with the states and other local government groups. USDA has actively reached out to states through legislator organizations such as the National Conference of State Legislators (NCSL). Through an outreach partnership with the NCSL since 1999, the FAS has sought to educate state legislators, legislative staff, and public policy makers about agricultural trade issues, policies, and programs. The NCSL provides outreach and support to state legislators and policy makers about agricultural exports, trade agreements, and the FAS. The partnership has promoted a national dialogue on agricultural trade with state legislators. The partnership supports legislators' travel on state foreign marketing trips, and provides legislatures with technical assistance, research and analysis of legislative proposals, and the tracking of state laws related to trade. The partnership also identifies and responds to critical issues and current trends in agricultural trade policies. State legislators who have participated in the trade missions have returned with an understanding of overseas export opportunities and become strong supporters of dedicating state resources to export marketing.

State Regional Trade Groups: Among USDA's most important partners in delivering agricultural services and support to farmers are the State Regional Trade Groups (SRTGs), regional nonprofit trade organizations that partner with the FAS to offer customized exporter assistance. The SRTGs have helped to expand U.S. export opportunities by creating thousands of business contacts between foreign buyers and U.S. suppliers. They have worked with hundreds of companies to promote value-added products in over 75 countries, sponsoring hundreds of promotional and exporter assistance events with USDA support. The SRTGs offer a wide range of similar services to facilitate trade between local food companies and importers, including export promotion, customized export assistance, and technical assistance at international tradeshows. FAS supports U.S. industry efforts to build, maintain, and expand overseas markets for U.S. food and agricultural products in a variety of ways. FAS administers several export development programs including the Foreign Market Development (Cooperator) Program, Market Access Program, Technical Assistance for Specialty Crops Program, Quality Samples Program, and Emerging Markets Program. These programs provide funds to U.S. organizations to conduct a wide range of activities, such as market research, consumer promotion, trade servicing, capacity building, and market access support. Working with the SRTGs and other industry organizations, FAS encourages outreach efforts that focus on improving the export readiness of U.S. exporters.

U.S. Department of Commerce, Commercial Service Outreach

The Commercial Service has worked in partnership with many states and cities for as long as 20 to 30 years. Engagement with other states and cities has been sporadic, sometimes suffering from resource issues or from occasional differences and misunderstandings. At some levels of local government, such as the municipal or county levels, there is tremendous untapped potential for a greater focus on trade promotion—potential that some of our private and public partners are already successfully pursuing (for example, see the U.S. Chamber of Commerce's TradeRoots Program below).

In 2007, the Commercial Service will seek to strengthen partnerships in all of these regards through initiatives that ensure that we are raising the quality and availability of export services, tending to partner relationships both new and old, and sharing information.

Professional Development: Both within the Federal Government and between federal, state, and local governments, there is a growing appreciation that professional development is critical to ensuring that exporters have access to high-quality counseling and assistance. Proper training of our respective trade and business development staffs can also ensure that companies are quickly referred to the best information or assistance regardless of their initial point of contact. The Commercial Service, in coordination with states and state Chambers of Commerce, will develop new joint internal education and training programs for field staff, and recommit ourselves to ongoing joint training programs. This year, we have expanded the participation of state trade promotion staff in the TPCC Interagency Trade Officer Training Program (see text box).

We will seek greater cooperation with the State International Development Organizations (SIDO) and individual states in terms of participants, curriculum development, and speakers. The Commercial Service and partners will explore opportunities for including states in training in other areas of special interest, such as export regulation, trade financing, and e-commerce.

TPCC Trade Officer Training Program

The Program, now in its fifth year, focuses on the real-world application of federal government assistance to drive successful export marketing campaigns for American companies, especially small and medium-sized enterprises (SMEs). Trade officers completing the Program are able to more accurately gauge their customers' real needs and export objectives. Participants learn how to package and seamlessly deliver more effective, customized solutions that integrate services from throughout the Federal Government. The program is supported by interagency cost sharing and is conducted by the Business Council for International Understanding (BCIU). To date, over 400 participants from ten federal agencies and two states have completed the four-day curriculum. In 2007, several more states will participate, and states and SIDO will begin developing ways to expand state participation.

Outreach: The Commercial Service has launched an effort to increase significantly its visibility with governors, mayors, and legislators, reaching out through letters, meetings, and speaking engagements. The Commercial Service participates in national conferences of state and local officials, such as the U.S. Conference of Mayors and the National Council of Mayors. We are partnering with SIDO to reach out to more companies, including through Commercial Service-developed Webinars promoted by the states. We are developing joint promotions with the states and more actively promoting Commercial Service trade mission opportunities to the states, including opportunities to jointly develop trade missions with SIDO. We are also exploring opportunities to involve more members of Congress in raising public awareness of trade.

Information Sharing: While Commercial Service relationships with many cities and states are both strong and stable, the level of cooperation and communication is less consistent with others. The Commercial Service is sharing client information and trade statistics with governors and mayors, and updating all states with regard to clients counseled, export successes, and total dollar amounts exported from each state. Both to facilitate information sharing and to improve public service, we will expand the practice of joint calls and visits to business clients by federal and state trade specialists.

Building and Tending to Relationships: Whether a federal–state partnership is old or new, several things can challenge a previously strong relationship, including resource issues (e.g., budget changes, fee increases, cost-sharing), information sharing (e.g., clients), and other differences and misunderstandings. When these issues arise, it is critical for all parties to remain focused on our mutual interest in continuing to serve the businesses in a particular state as well as possible. In 2007, the Commercial Service will more deliberately evaluate the health of its partnerships with states and develop a strategy for resolving issues that sometimes strain these partnerships.

Ex-Im Bank City/State Partners Program

One of Ex-Im Bank's most important partnerships is the City/State Partners Program, a national marketing initiative that brings export financing services to more SMEs through closer cooperation with state and local governments and private sector organizations. Ex-Im Bank now has 45 City/State partners in 36 states and the Commonwealth of Puerto Rico. Ex-Im Bank staff have quantitative goals for adding new partner relationships, including City/State Partners. Seven new partners, representing a 10 percent increase, have been added in recent months in Utah, Hawaii, California, Idaho, Michigan, Delaware, and West Virginia. This program adds to the rolls of the SME exporters that Ex-Im Bank supports each year and greatly enhances Ex-Im Bank's reach nationwide.

Partner training and supply of marketing materials and displays are routine components of the City/State initiative. Ex-Im Bank develops state-specific direct mail campaigns with select interested partners, using targeted mail lists provided by the City/State Partner. Nearly 25,000 pieces were mailed during fiscal year 2006. The City/State Partners, including Ex-Im Bank's regional business development staff, promptly follow up with respondents. City/State Partners also identify exporters and organize solo or joint marketing meetings with Ex-Im Bank business development officers to ensure that partners are aware of financial tools that are available to support international sales.

Overseas Private Investment Corporation Partners Program and Women-Owned/Minority-Owned Workshops

The Overseas Private Investment Corporation (OPIC) continues to expand its Partners Program, working with 15 trade and investment support organizations across the country to increase business awareness of OPIC financing and insurance capabilities. In partnership with the Department of Commerce, OPIC has also initiated a series of on-the-road workshops across the United States, targeting women- and minority-owned businesses, to provide practical "how-to" information for U.S. companies about programs available in the U.S. Government to support investment and exports.

U.S. Trade and Development Agency Outreach

The U.S. Trade and Development Agency (USTDA) has aggressively expanded its outreach to small and medium-sized enterprises over the past year and intends to continue this outreach in the coming year. Working with state export promotion agencies around the country, USTDA has effectively expanded the number of companies that are well-informed about U.S. foreign assistance programs and the export markets that await their goods and services. This coming year will bring greater opportunities to expand USTDA's message to states across the country, with events already planned for Minnesota, Virginia, Maryland, Florida, and the District of Columbia.

TRADE ASSOCIATIONS AND OTHER BUSINESS GROUPS

As with cities and states, the Federal Government is working to deepen relationships with current association partners, taking advantage of not only their reach into the business community, but also their expertise on sectors, foreign markets, and issues. We are also working to broaden our contacts to new U.S. associations and business groups. With both current and future partners, we are encouraging associations to bolster the trade promotion activities in their member services portfolios, including leading foreign trade missions and conferences.

There are over 30,000 trade and professional associations in the United States. The Federal Government has long-established trade promotion partnerships with many associations and business groups. Associations have highly sophisticated knowledge of the sectors and business issues they represent, and often offer input to the Federal Government on policy and regulatory matters. On the trade front, associations help the Government identify new market access issues and develop U.S. trade policy positions that will benefit the United States.

Associations also provide a wide range of member services, including participation in domestic trade shows and exhibits. Although relatively few associations have branched into export promotion activities, there are many examples of associations successfully leading foreign trade missions, organizing foreign trade show pavilions, sponsoring foreign business conferences and symposia, and cultivating expertise and relationships with key foreign governments and buyers.

Conclusions

In the year ahead, the Federal Government will seek to deepen (with current partners) and widen (to new partners) its outreach to associations as part of the Strategic Partnership Initiative. Our goal is to encourage associations to join us in raising their members' awareness of exporting opportunities. We need associations to help us broadcast market research and trade leads, and to make export promotion programs and services more available to their members. We are also encouraging associations to lead more trade missions and events themselves so that members have more opportunities to enter foreign markets.

By engaging in more export promotion activities, associations can help their members view the global marketplace not only as a growing competitiveness challenge, but as a growing business opportunity. In the process, associations will discover that trade promotion activities also draw attention to their issues and are an effective complement to their policy agendas.

The U.S. Chamber of Commerce's TradeRoots Program

TradeRoots is the only continuous national trade education program dedicated to raising grassroots support and public awareness about the importance of international trade to local communities. Through strong partnerships with associations, local chambers of commerce, economic development groups, and the business community, TradeRoots takes the Chamber's message of promoting free enterprise and individual opportunity to local communities across the country.

- **Builds and sustains bipartisan pro-trade coalitions at the grassroots level.** TradeRoots has successfully built coalitions for past pro-trade legislation opening lucrative markets to U.S. business, and stands ready to act in support of pending pro-business trade legislation.

- **Identifies and mobilizes local leaders as pro-trade advocates in each district.** TradeRoots has trained hundreds of local chamber of commerce executives on how to build strong international support in their communities and help their member companies be strong trade advocates.

continued next page

> ■ **Facilitates international trade education programs to educate the U.S. small business community**. Using a strong and extensive partner network, TradeRoots has successfully held more than 500 international trade education grassroots programs across the United States to educate the small business community about market opportunities overseas.
>
> ■ **Partners with governors and state leaders to communicate the local benefits of trade**. TradeRoots partners with governors and economic development offices to help small and medium-size companies understand international opportunities—and how to use current, pending, and future international trade agreements.
>
> ■ **Tells trade success stories through the local media, using a vigorous communications campaign**. TradeRoots publishes a series called Faces of Trade, featuring success stories of small businesses that expanded by entering new international markets.
>
> When TradeRoots started, only 40 chambers were actively promoting international trade; now over 800 have made international trade issues a priority for their members.

U.S. Department of Agriculture Work with Trade Organizations

FAS annually partners with over 75 trade organizations to stimulate demand for U.S. agricultural products in over 100 countries. This partnership has resulted in agricultural export sales of over $68 billion in 2006, which in turn has supported an estimated one million American jobs.

For nearly five decades, FAS has partnered with food and agricultural industry organizations to develop markets overseas. Overseas markets remain vitally important to U.S. farmers and ranchers, and are an important source of income for food processing companies, transportation, and other related industries. USDA export assistance programs support the efforts of U.S. companies and industries to build and maintain commercial markets in over 100 countries for hundreds of food and agricultural products. Programs like the Market Access Program have fostered an effective trade promotion partnership between the USDA and agricultural producers and processors who are represented by nonprofit commodity or trade associations. That partnership is focused on capitalizing on opportunities to access new markets and reach new customers around the world. FAS' 80 offices overseas also support industry efforts, especially in developing markets, by providing market intelligence and by helping to introduce U.S. exporters to potential foreign customers.

U.S. Agricultural Export Development Council: The U.S. Agricultural Export Development Council (USAEDC) is a nonprofit private-sector trade association with approximately 80 members comprised of U.S. commodity trade associations, farmer cooperatives, and state regional trade groups from around the country. They represent the interest of growers and processors of a variety of U.S. agricultural products. While privately funded, the members cooperate closely with FAS in developing overseas markets for U.S. agricultural exports. These activities focus on increasing the knowledge of, and demand for, U.S. agricultural exports. Promotional and development activities include market research, trade missions, reverse trade teams, literature, trade shows, in-store promotions, and ongoing evaluations. Members of USAEDC work with foreign governments; farm, manufacturing, and importing organizations; and end users in various USDA programs that directly benefit both U.S. farmers and foreign consumers of U.S. agricultural exports.

Trade Shows: The FAS has successfully completed the process of transferring management of U.S. pavilions at international food shows to private-sector partners, allowing FAS to scale back significantly its own staff and financial commitments while still supporting high-quality and effective trade events. In fiscal year 2006, over 935 U.S. companies participated in 31 FAS-endorsed trade shows and missions overseas, making nearly 9,400 serious contacts, reporting sales totaling $210.2 million on site, and projecting estimated sales of $728 million over the following 12 months. More than 2,500 new products were introduced in various markets.

Cochran Fellowship Program: The Program provided short-term training in the United States for 551 international participants from 67 countries in fiscal year 2006. Since its inception in 1984, the Program has provided training to 12,202 participants from over 100 countries. Cochran participants meet with U.S. agribusiness, attend policy and food safety seminars, and receive technical training related to short-and long-term market development and trade capacity building.

U.S. Department of Commerce, International Trade Administration Outreach

Partnerships between the International Trade Administration (ITA) and trade associations to foster, promote, and facilitate the expansion of U.S. business abroad have provided many mutual benefits. Trade associations can be an important force multiplier toward the Commercial Service's goal of identifying new potential exporters. From the associations' perspective, the partnerships allow the associations to provide an increased level of assistance by offering an international component to their membership services portfolios.

Partnerships may use any or all of ITA's resources, including exporting seminars and events, trade missions, market research, and articles in newsletters and other publications specific to an association's industry and ITA initiatives.

Association for Manufacturing Technology Tech Center in China

The Association for Manufacturing Technology (AMT) conducts a variety of trade promotion activities, including sponsorship of a major biennial international trade show, trade missions, and representation offices in major foreign markets. One of AMT's most visible trade promotion activities is its Shanghai Technology and Service Center. The Tech Center has two primary activities: to serve as an incubator for AMT members entering the Chinese market for the first time, and to facilitate the expansion and growth of member companies already doing business there. The Tech Center enables AMT members to demonstrate machine tools in operation, provides classroom space for training and technical presentations, and offers numerous other services on a fee basis. AMT leveraged funds from a 2001 Market Development Cooperator Program grant from ITA to establish the Tech Center, which the association now operates entirely from its own resources.

The Commercial Service is currently exploring joint projects with a wide range of associations, including: the U.S.–Indian American Chamber of Commerce; the American Arbitration Association; the Accountants Global Network; the National U.S.–Arab Chamber of Commerce; the Small Business and Entrepreneurs Council; the Association for Corporate Growth; and the National Association of Women Business Owners.

District Export Councils

District Export Councils (DECs) are organizations of leaders from the local business community, appointed by successive Secretaries of Commerce, whose knowledge of international business provides a source of professional advice for local firms. The DECs are closely affiliated with the Commercial Service's Export Assistance Centers. The 56 DECs combine the energies of more than 1,500 exporters and private and public export service providers throughout the United States. This year, the DECs have divided into subcommittees including one on policy. This subcommittee has three priorities: K–12 education—getting international trade subjects into public school curriculums; large company mentoring—involving large companies' international marketing staff to help new export companies get into their first market; and IPR—outreach to new exporters on how to protect intellectual property.

State Department Partnership with the Business Council for International Understanding

Since its creation in 1955 at the initiative of President Dwight Eisenhower, the Business Council for International Understanding (BCIU) has partnered with the State Department and other agencies to explore how business and government can best work together around the world. In so doing, BCIU has been at the forefront of transforming how the Federal Government interacts with the business community, including offering the following:

- **Training**: The BCIU Commercial Diplomacy Training Program enhances the trade literacy of the U.S. Foreign Service and the efficacy of officers in other key U.S. Government trade promotion agencies by conducting year-round training programs at the Foreign Service Institute. BCIU also conducts the TPCC Interagency Trade Officer Training Program for the Commerce Department and several other partner agencies including the State Department. The Program helps both federal and state business development staff to better gauge their customers' needs, deliver customized solutions, and leverage the resources of other agencies.

- **Consultations for Ambassadors**: BCIU organizes consultations with U.S. businesses for outgoing Ambassadors to brief them on the leading business and commercial matters in their respective countries.

- **Business practicums**: BCIU organizes a unique program that places Foreign Service Officers with companies for two to three months of practical, real-world experience after they complete the Foreign Service Institute's economic and commercial training course.

BCIU also cosponsors Chiefs of Mission Conferences, business conferences overseas, and regional conferences in the United States that bring together U.S. and foreign dignitaries and business communities. These gatherings are important tools in helping to promote cooperation across governments and industries.

Ex-Im Bank Partnership with the Packaging Machinery Manufacturers Institute

For many years, Ex-Im Bank has partnered with the Packaging Machinery Manufacturers Institute (PMMI) to reach their members and foreign customers with information to improve their ability to compete in global markets. Ex-Im Bank interaction with PMMI includes participation in domestic and international trade shows as well as contributions to internal member publications of PMMI. Ex-Im Bank has also actively referred PMMI members to financial institutions that have a strong interest in the term financing required by the members' foreign buyers.

CORPORATE PARTNERS

A critical part of the Strategic Partnership Initiative is working with U.S. corporations that specialize in offering exporting services (such as shipping, financing, and e-business services). Corporate partners offer the greatest potential for achieving the Federal Government's goal of broadening the base of companies that export. Private business services providers conduct millions of contacts daily with their business clients throughout the U.S. business community—clients that could represent tens of thousands of potential exporters. Because many of these service providers share the Federal Government's interest in seeing small and medium-sized U.S. companies succeed as exporters, they can make excellent strategic partners.

Another reason to partner with private business services providers is that their innovative business solutions have knocked down many of the logistical and transactional hurdles to trade that once discouraged would-be exporters. Many U.S. companies are unaware that these services have helped to make exporting easier than ever. Strategic partnerships help to raise awareness that these world-class services are now available and can be used to enhance U.S. export competitiveness.

U.S. Department of Commerce, Commercial Service Corporate Partners Program

Commercial Service outreach to corporate partners over the past few years is proving very successful. Before the partnership program, the Commercial Service engaged companies on a one-on-one basis in a way that lacked focus and direction. The corporate partnership program is a strategic initiative that is based on a "force multiplier effect" to reach as many SMEs, in the aggregate, as possible in a focused and planned manner.

We are using the following metrics to determine the efficacy of the partnership program:

- Number of domestic outreach/seminar opportunities supported by partners;

- Number of foreign-based outreach/seminar opportunities supported by partners;

- Volume of direct mail/direct email distribution;

- Number of client referrals; and

- Number of Web site referrals.

"Export success metrics" will be developed once a baseline has been established for the above metrics and once the Commercial Service and the partners have developed their own internal processes and metrics. Preliminary data from FedEx and PNC, two of the Commercial Service's corporate partners, are positive, and FedEx's decision to reapply to the program for an additional five years is an affirmation of the value of the program to FedEx and the Commercial Service.

Another positive outcome of the partnership program is that the Commercial Service is working directly with senior management in sales and marketing of firms such as FedEx, UPS, eBay, Google, PNC Bank, M&T Bank, and City National Bank, to name a few, to further the goal of broadening the base of U.S. companies that export. This increased focus on the sales and transactional aspects of the public/private relationship is enabling the Federal Government to understand in greater depth the real market issues faced by both large and small exporters. As a result, the Commercial Service is empowered to be more responsive to the business community and, therefore, can more effectively assist SMEs to participate in the international marketplace.

Improved effectiveness is the result of a wide range of joint marketing and referral initiatives, including hundreds of local outreach events, Internet links and referrals, and advanced market segmentation initiatives. Tactics pursued by the Commercial Service with each of its corporate partners include:

■ Target marketing: partners' use of their client databases to effectively target middle-market companies with the appropriate export message and resources;

■ Seminars: export education and opportunity meetings sponsored by the Commercial Service and partners. Topics include export basics and industry, market, or opportunity-specific matters, such as U.S. free trade agreement information;

■ Webinars: Internet-based seminars that allow attendees to participate without leaving their offices. Topics include export controls, IPR protection, export opportunities in China, and export opportunities in India;

■ Internet Marketing: Internet-based marketing campaigns using email or Web presence;

■ Knowledge sharing: educating sales and marketing personnel of the corporate partner about U.S. Government export promotion resources available to enhance partner client sales and marketing efforts to generate international sales;

■ Co-branding of Trade Publications/Newsletters: enabling partners to provide an important information resource to existing or potential new customers using Commercial Service content;

- Dissemination of articles enabling partners to provide new and existing audiences with information on export promotion events and business opportunities; and

- Client Referral Program: enabling corporate partners to leverage Commercial Service expertise in the sales cycle and provides an additional source of new clients.

Case Study of Partner Activities

This past year, the Commercial Service expanded its corporate partnership outreach by creating tiered partners. Tier 1 partners have been awarded "no-cost" contracts through a competitive acquisition process and based upon their response to a formal solicitation. Awardees include industry leaders in shipping and logistics (FedEx and UPS), banking (PNC Bank and M&T Bank), and e-business (eBay and Google). Tier 2 partners, while not having participated in a procurement, are working with the Commercial Service in a coordinated manner to promote exporting; this includes companies like City National Bank and The Business Council for International Understanding. The Commercial Service intends to engage new partners each year through the competitive acquisition process. The Commercial Service is reaching out to all U.S. companies conducting significant international business to find innovative ways to jointly promote exporting.

These partners have incredible expertise and insights to share, gained through their close contact with businesses and on-the-ground experience with making exports profitable for their clients. For its part, the Federal Government has unique government capabilities and a global network of trade experts. A look at the current activities and plans under the program illustrate how both parties benefit from the partnership.

FedEx

- Joint FedEx-Commercial Service sales meetings and sales calls to FedEx clients.

- Outreach activities in the United States to promote exports, and educational events in worldwide regions to promote import growth from companies sourcing from the United States. More than 70 FedEx-Commercial Service events held around the world in 2006.

- Monthly customer newsletter promotes potential markets and regulatory updates. This electronic publication reaches more than 100,000 subscribers—and promotes a link to *www.export.gov* in each issue.

- Targeted marketing plans for SMEs, with special focus placed on developing new-to-market exporters and new-to-exporting businesses.

- Placement of Commercial Service logo within FedEx Global Trade Manager site.

- External site located at *www.export.fedex.com* enables companies to request specific information about the benefits, resources, and opportunities that exporting can offer.

- Joint media relations plan to provide opportunities for interviews and articles.

- Internal FedEx communications to promote the partnership and its benefits.

UPS

- Education of salespeople on the customer benefits of using Commercial Service programs to help grow their export sales.

- Communication of the value of Commercial Service programs in UPS customer newsletters.

- Establishment and nurturing of relationships with Commercial Service offices throughout the world.

- Jointly conducted seminars on international trade in coordination with Commercial Service experts. Examples of prior joint seminars are "Exporting to the Americas" and "Navigating the Trade Winds—U.S. and European Trade: an Opportunity for Growth".

- UPS Global Advisor, a *UPS.com* Web site, links to the Commercial Service (*www.export.gov*) and other U.S. Government Web sites to facilitate U.S. exports.

PNC Bank

- Expanded support of PNC marketing and education programs on international business to SMEs nationwide and to offshore buyers.

- Value-added and in-depth practical information through a series of jointly-conducted, scheduled, and targeted in-market seminars. Topics: trade services, export financing and foreign exchange risk management, winning export strategies, and supply chain management.

- Emerging market roadshows across the PNC network, coordinated with various U.S. Export Assistance Centers and Commercial Services overseas offices.

- Web-based conference series on "in-demand" topics, highlighting Commercial Service expertise to customers and prospects.

- Regular dissemination to PNC's client base of marketing content and access to the Commercial Service Web site.

- Sponsorships and active participation in Commercial Service events and industry trade shows both nationwide and overseas.

- Coordinated planning and sponsorship of events and activities with one other Commercial Service corporate partner.

M&T Bank

- Half-day seminars in major cities covering letters of credit, documentary collections, working capital, export credit insurance, buyer financing, foreign exchange, and Commercial Service programs. Full day seminars covering marketing, logistics, and legal issues related to an international transaction.

- Web site, Web-based conferencing, direct mail using M&T and Commercial Service databases.

- Joint advertising, brochures, internal training of M&T staff, and training for Commercial Service staff.

eBay

- eBay has the same focus as the Federal Government on small and medium-sized businesses and export activities, working with the Commercial Service to provide education, trade leads, market information, advice, and trade resources to SMEs.

- Education seminars, conferences, and other outreach programs organized by the Commercial Service.

- Direct mail, email and other direct marketing activities by the Commercial Service.

- eBay University, eBay Live!, Town Hall Meetings, and other educational conferences and online discussions sponsored by eBay.

- Coordination of information for PowerSeller Newsletters, Seller Monthly Newsletters, and other direct mail and email campaigns sponsored by eBay.

- Customer Outreach campaigns sponsored by eBay.

Google

- Joint seminars to highlight how to use Web tools such as AdSense and the free Web analytics programs. Google speakers will instruct SMEs how to get their Web site seen by search engines.

- Co-authoring content for the Commercial Service Web site under the E-Commerce Toolbox *http://www.export.gov/sellingonline/*.

- Educational Webinars on Google Video where users can search, preview, and play various topics related to exporting and international trade.

- Possible addition of a white paper to the Conversion University section of the Analytics page. The white paper could detail how international expansion can be done strategically through understanding where foreign visitors to a Web site are coming from and what products are of interest to them.

As these corporate partnerships mature, all of the parties are beginning to realize that we may have only seen the tip of the iceberg. The initial focus on mass-marketing events and exporting basics has evolved into more sophisticated and targeted marketing strategies. As interaction between partners intensifies, a corporate dialogue on improving the efficiencies of exporting is growing. This dialogue could lead to real improvements in the export process. And as the Government realizes the untapped expertise these partners have in accessing foreign markets, partners can better inform the Government of the market and competitive issues they and their clients face.

Ex-Im Bank's Network of Partners

Ex-Im Bank has incorporated extensive use of partners into its strategy to reach the broadest possible universe of U.S. exporters. Specifically, the Bank's SME strategy not only employs partnership, but also features an active effort to expand the partner groups. Ex-Im Bank's financial products, designed to expand U.S. exporting activity, fit into the business model of many financial institutions, export credit insurance brokers, City/State Partners, industry associations, and the U.S. Export Assistance Centers of the Department of Commerce. Ex-Im Bank has developed close working relationships with these partners to make its trade finance products more widely known and available. Long-time key lender partners include Comerica Bank, Silicon Valley Bank, PNC, Bank of America, UPS Capital, and M&T Bank.

Fiscal year 2006 marked a record (nearly $3.2 billion) in direct financial support for SMEs, representing 26 percent of total Ex-Im Bank authorizations—also a record. Key to this success was the continuing growth of Ex-Im Bank's Working Capital Guarantee Program, largely administered by delegating authority to the lending banks to achieve faster approval. During fiscal year 2006, due to the concentrated efforts of the Bank's Business Development Division, the multiplier network of financial institutions, brokers, and City/State Partners increased over 10 percent to more than 300 enterprises nationwide.

Supplementing this success has been the continuing excellent interagency cooperation within the U.S. Export Assistance Centers. Ex-Im Bank/SBA collaboration on working capital transactions was renewed and extended for another five years during fiscal year 2006. Over $45 million of U.S. exports were supported by Ex-Im Bank/SBA co-guaranteed transactions during the most recent year of activity. Ex-Im Bank and SBA also agreed to a joint marketing arrangement that will feature shared use of customer databases as a means of expanding, through collaboration, the universe of financial institutions offering programs from both agencies.

OPIC's Enterprise Development Network

Increased demand for OPIC services has maximized OPIC's staff resources. While deal flow has increased, it remains essential to provide tailored services and support to SME sponsors, particularly those who may be pursuing their first international investment transaction. To expand the number of small businesses it can assist, OPIC has launched the Enterprise Development Network (EDN). EDN is a strategic alliance among private-sector financial institutions, small business consultants, and law firms that is designed to expand efficient delivery of OPIC services to SMEs. EDN's structure is twofold: first, it supports selected financial institutions, called designated lenders, in facilitating greater access of capital to American SMEs, and enabling OPIC to make better use of its staff resources. Second, a network of OPIC-approved U.S. private sector financial consultants, called loan originators, advise SMEs in documenting and arranging international projects, which the loan originators submit to the designated lender for financing.

To date, the private sector has responded with significant interest. OPIC's board of directors has approved the first designated lending facility with a leading American bank that will finance more than $100 million of U.S. small business projects in emerging markets. The selection of the designated lender and 15 loan originators was based on a competitive selection process.

SBA's Private Sector and Educational Community Partners

SBA provides several critical services that SME exporters need in order to get started and succeed in trade. SBA supports a network of resource partners representing a wide range of private sector know-how, from retired business executives to lawyers to business instructors at universities and other education centers.

Private Lending Institutions: Local banks are critical to SBA's ability to reach more firms. SBA can delegate loan approval, closing, and most servicing and liquidation authority and responsibility to carefully selected lenders under the Preferred Lenders Program (PLP). A major goal for SBA in fiscal year 2007 is to approve more PLP–delegated international lenders.

Small Business Development Centers (SBDCs): This training resource is a cooperative effort of the private sector, the educational community, and federal, state, and local governments. SBDCs provide small businesses with management and technical assistance. There are more than 1,000 SBDCs nationwide. Some 35 of these centers are designated as International Trade Centers.

Service Corps of Retired Executives (SCORE): The SCORE Association's 11,500 volunteers nationwide provide counseling and training. SCORE operates an online counseling program that refers questions related to international business to retired executives.

Women's Business Centers (WBCs): The WBC network of 80 educational centers helps women start and grow small businesses.

Export Legal Assistance Network (E-LAN): Through E-LAN, international trade attorneys from the Federal Bar Association provide free initial consultations to small businesses interested in starting export operations.

State Department Economic Empowerment in Strategic Regions

On March 13, the State Department held a conference attended by over 100 senior businesspeople, government officials, and academics to discuss the Economic Empowerment in Strategic Regions Initiative (EESR). The EESR Initiative seeks to add a private-sector economic dimension to the Administration's military and political engagement in the global war on terror. We are working to promote private-sector engagement in unstable regions, such as Pakistan's border region, through this initiative. Ultimately, the goal of the EESR Initiative is to provide jobs and economic opportunity to people whose impoverishment and despair might otherwise make them vulnerable to exploitation by extremists.

Strategic Initiatives in Priority Markets

Over the past three years, the National Export Strategy has included a focus on a short list of priority markets. U.S. exporters are succeeding in many markets—large and small, developed and developing—around the world. However, a few markets are identified each year because they are large economies with high rates of growth. These are also markets where U.S. exporters benefit the most from U.S. Government assistance in navigating significant hurdles to doing business. For these reasons, the priority markets serve as a guide for where U.S. Government trade promotion agencies are focusing their resources and activities and where U.S. businesses and our public–private partners will find good export opportunities.

This year, the priority markets include the fast-growing economies of China, India, and Brazil. As a demonstration of the importance of these markets and of their overall relations with the United States, either the President has visited each of these countries or that country's leader has visited the United States at least once since March 2006. U.S. exports to these markets grew a combined 30 percent in 2006. Recent trade missions, especially Commerce Secretary Gutierrez's mission to China and Under Secretary of Commerce for International Trade Frank Lavin's mission to India, have promoted U.S. exports and helped hundreds of American firms successfully pursue opportunities in those markets. We have already identified approximately $8 billion in business that came out of the Secretary's mission to China, and continue to register new results coming out of both of these missions. Jim Lambright, Chairman of Ex-Im Bank, traveled twice to both India and China in 2006. USTDA supported more projects in China and India than anywhere else. In June 2006, Commerce

Secretary Gutierrez led a policy mission to Brazil that included OPIC President and CEO Rob Mosbacher, and a number of USTDA staff. In addition, Ex-Im Chairman Lambright traveled to Brazil in 2006 in connection with aircraft and project finance transactions. An important goal of these trips is to elevate the bilateral commercial dialogue with each country.

CHINA

Many U.S. companies were originally drawn to China to source industrial inputs or to contract for manufacturing services. U.S. companies are now looking at China's growing consumer market and burgeoning middle class as an opportunity for selling everything we make. Since China joined the WTO at the end of 2001, U.S. exports have grown from $19 billion to $55 billion (*Chart 24*). China has moved from our ninth largest export market to our fourth largest.

Chart 24. U.S.-China Merchandise Trade, 1990–2006

Source: U.S. Department of Commerce, Bureau of the Census.

2006 was a particularly good year for U.S. exports to China in a number of sectors. Higher value-added products like machine tools showed strong growth (131 percent), for example. U.S. agricultural, fishery, and forestry exports to China are at the highest level in history and forecasted to reach $7.8 billion in 2007. The U.S.–China Business Council reports that 81 percent of members surveyed claimed their Chinese operations are profitable, with more than half saying that profitability rates for their China operations meet or exceed global profit margins. Ninety-seven percent of respondents say that they are optimistic about prospects for their China business over the next five years. All of this points to a Chinese economy that is more open to U.S. exports than in previous years. Highlights that show this openness include Citibank's acquisition of a stake in Guangdong Development Bank and the selection of Westinghouse for a $5–8 billion nuclear power contract.

Despite these positive signs, China continues to be one of the most challenging markets in the world for U.S. companies. U.S. businesses tend to underestimate the challenges of market entry in China. Encouraged by a Chinese Government eager for foreign capital and technology, and attracted by the prospect of 1.3 billion consumers, thousands of foreign firms have charged into the Chinese market. These companies often do not sufficiently investigate the market situation in advance. The challenges of doing business in China can be grouped into four general categories:

- China's business environment lacks predictability. A transparent and consistent body of laws and regulations would make the Chinese market more predictable. However, China's current legal and regulatory system can be opaque, inconsistent, and arbitrary. Enforcement of the law is inconsistent.

- The lack of effective Chinese Government protection and enforcement of intellectual property rights (IPR) is of particular concern for many American companies. This becomes a problem because approximately 85 percent of U.S. SMEs exporting abroad do not know that their U.S. patents and trademarks do not protect them abroad, according to a 2005 study by the U.S. Patent and Trademark Office.

- China's Government still practices or allows some mercantilist-style policies. China has made significant progress toward a market-oriented economy, but parts of its central, provincial, and local bureaucracies unfairly protect local firms, especially state-owned firms, from imports, while encouraging exports.

- China retains much of the apparatus of a planned economy. A five-year program sets economic goals, strategies, and targets. The State and the Communist Party directly manage the only legal labor union. In many sectors of the Chinese business community, there is an incomplete understanding of the importance of free enterprise and fair competition.

Conclusions

Recognizing these and other challenges on the economic front, the Chinese and U.S. Governments created the Strategic Economic Dialogue (SED) in 2006. Under the SED, we agreed to conduct discussions on the development of efficient, innovative service sectors and on ways to improve health care. We have launched a bilateral investment dialogue and are enhancing cooperation on transparency issues. The Chinese Government agreed to invigorate ongoing work within the U.S.–China Joint Commission on Commerce and Trade (JCCT) on high-tech trade, IPR, and structural economic issues. Both sides agreed to increase bilateral cooperation on more efficient and environmentally sustainable energy use, facilitation of personal and business travel, development assistance, and multilateral development bank lending. We also concluded an agreement to facilitate financing to support U.S. exports to China and agreed to relaunch bilateral air services negotiations.

IPR: The United States continues to work on many fronts to engage China as part of the Bush Administration's larger IPR strategy, which includes the *Stopfakes.gov* Web site, education programs, a hotline, and training. China-specific initiatives include:

- U.S.–China Intellectual Property Rights Training Program: In May 2006, USTDA began a technical assistance program with China's General Administration of Customs (GAC) that included training for GAC management and front-line officers on customs regulations and methods to improve enforcement capabilities. Working with IPR specialists from the U.S. Government, including U.S. Customs and Border Protection and the U.S. Patent and Trademark Office, the program provides for a series of seminars at the Shanghai Customs College on the role of customs inspection and enforcement in protecting IPR. In addition, the training will provide U.S. private-sector representatives with an opportunity to provide company- and product-specific information to GAC's officers, so that they will be able to more effectively identify goods that violate IPR. The program consists of three separate two-week sessions. Sessions will review IPR law and international conventions and the role of customs administrations in IPR protection, including trademark, patent, and copyright protections, and IPR enforcement.

- A China IPR Advisory Program: the program provides U.S. companies with a one-hour free legal consultation with a volunteer attorney to learn how to protect and enforce their IPR in China. Over 47 companies have used the free service.

- IPR-related domestic outreach programs, and one-on-one consultations: There have been 11 outreach events in 2006 and hundreds of consultations.

- A monthly China IPR Webinar Series for U.S. industry: Twelve Webinars have occurred to date with over 600 online participants. Each Webinar is available for downloading at *www.stopfakes.gov*.

Trade Promotion Infrastructure: In addition to cooperating with the Chinese to make their market more open, Federal Government agencies are helping U.S. companies take advantage of the enormous economic growth in China. Much of this effort is occurring through the continued development of U.S.

Violations of Intellectual Property Rights

According to the World Intellectual Property Organization (WIPO),[1] counterfeiting and piracy cost the global economy at least $100 billion per year.

In fiscal year 2006, China was the top source country for seizures of infringing products at U.S. borders, accounting for 81 percent of the total domestic value seized, or $126 million out of a total $155 million seized by the U.S. Department of Homeland Security (DHS). Footwear was the top commodity seized, accounting for 41 percent of the total domestic value.[2] Seizures by DHS increased by 67 percent in fiscal year 2006, involving more than 14,000 seizures. These numbers are in part a result of new techniques DHS is employing to target and intercept pirated goods from overseas at all of the 326 ports of entry and mail facilities in the United States.

Operation Spring, the first U.S.–Sino joint undercover law enforcement operation in the People's Republic of China, resulted in the arrest of a U.S. citizen in Shanghai and the forfeiture of 160,000 counterfeit DVDs.[3]

Government agencies' trade promotion infrastructure in China. These agencies help U.S. companies directly and assist our public- and private-sector multipliers in their support of U.S. companies. China is the largest post in the world for both the Foreign Agricultural Service (five offices and 49 staff) and the Department of Commerce (six offices and 113 staff). In addition, the Commercial Service has American Trading Centers in 14 fast-growing secondary cities around China. Highlights of last year's trade promotion effort include:

---

1   World Intellectual Property Organization, "WIPO to Host Global Anti Counterfeiting and Piracy Meeting," press release, January 19, 2007, *http://www.wipo.int/pressroom/en/articles/2007/article_0002.html*.

2   U.S. Department of Homeland Security, "FY 2006 Top Trading Partners for IPR Seizures," press release, November 7, 2006, *http://www.cbp.gov/xp/cgov/import/commercial_enforcement/ipr/seizure/trading/*.

3   U.S. Department of Homeland Security, "Counterfeit Goods Seizures Up 83% in FY 2006," press release, January 11, 2007, *http://www.cbp.gov/xp/cgov/newsroom/news_releases/012007/01112007_1.xml*.

- Commerce Secretary Gutierrez's trade mission to Shanghai and Beijing in October/November 2006 included 22 senior executives from U.S. companies and resulted in projects valued at $8 billion.

- The U.S. Departments of Commerce and State, in association with the Department of Education, launched the U.S. Electronic Education Fair initiative, in partnership with 41 U.S. educational institutions from 27 states and the District of Columbia, to promote American higher education opportunities to students in China using multimedia. To date, information on the initiative has reached over 180 million people on television and over 500,000 through the Internet.

- Our Embassy in China hosted 10 state-led and three city-led trade missions.

- Under the auspices of the SED with China, Ex-Im Bank completed negotiations pursuant to a Framework Agreement with the Ministry of Finance and the Export-Import Bank of China and other banks to facilitate the sale of medium-term financing for U.S. capital goods and services exports to China.

- USTDA and the Department of Transportation hosted the U.S.–China Aviation Summit to help strengthen the technical and commercial relationship between the U.S. and Chinese aviation sectors.

- Ongoing USDA promotion efforts in China focus on areas of potential export growth. U.S. food and agriculture exports to China have risen dramatically over the past five years to reach $6.7 billion in fiscal year 2006. At the May 2006 Sial–China trade show in Shanghai, the USA Pavilion hosted 25 U.S. companies and agricultural trade organizations. More than 19,000 food trade visitors attended the show, resulting in $1.2 million of actual on-site sales.

Focus on Second-Tier Cities and Key Sectors: In 2007, agencies will continue to focus on China's second-tier cities. These cities account for 53.5 percent of the country's imports, 19 percent of total output, and 8 percent of total population. Cities like Tainjin import more foreign goods than larger cities like Beijing. In addition, the agencies are focusing on many of the high-growth sectors like agriculture-related products, aviation equipment, safety and security, pollution control and energy effiency, health care, and construction. Key events and activities include:

- Commerce Assistant Secretary David Bohigian led the Clean Energy Technologies Trade Mission to India and Beijing and Nanjing, China, with support from the Department of State. The mission helped U.S. providers of energy efficiency equipment and services identify opportunities in the China market.

- The third annual U.S. Health Care Forum will take place this year to encourage improvements in the Chinese regulatory environment and promote U.S healthcare equipment, services, and pharmaceuticals.

- Federal Government trade promotion agencies will continue to support the growing number of U.S. states that are organizing and leading trade missions to China.

- FAS provided critical input and support to several market access requests in 2006 through the utilization of bilateral working groups and fora like the Agricultural Working Group (JCCT-AWG) and SPS Working Group (JCCT-SPSWG). Issues included access for U.S. citrus and grapes to the seaport of Shenzhen; the relisting of 13 meat and poultry processing establishments; recognition of the U.S. national fruit fly trapping program; and the easing of requirements for orchard and packing-house lists for exports of horticultural products to China. Each of these issues had been previously addressed in technical fora, but in most cases required a political-level intervention in order for China to reach an agreement. Engagement at the technical level by USDA also led to a market access agreement for California plums, as well as resumption of the Alaska seed potato program.

INDIA

With a GDP currently growing at more than 9 percent a year, India is one of the fastest growing economies in the world. India has over one billion people and presents increasingly lucrative and diverse opportunities for U.S. exporters with the right products, services, and commitment. These trends have made India a market of growing strategic importance to U.S. exporters. In 2006, U.S. goods exports to India reached over $10 billion, an increase of more than 27 percent over 2005, and more than double U.S. exports in 2003 (*Chart 25*). As India's economy globalizes and expands in the medium term, its demand for goods and services in sectors such as infrastructure, transportation, energy, environment, health care, high technology, and defense is expected to exceed tens of billions of dollars.

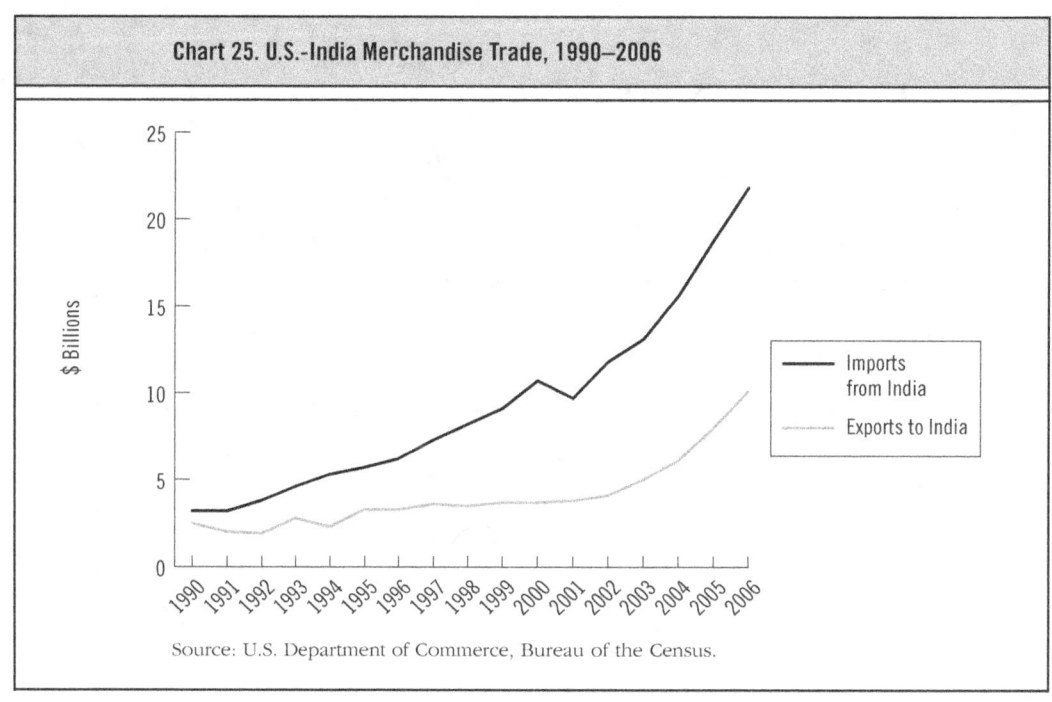

Chart 25. U.S.-India Merchandise Trade, 1990–2006

Source: U.S. Department of Commerce, Bureau of the Census.

The U.S.–India commercial relationship has improved significantly over the past few years. However, much bureaucratic reform in India is needed, and extensive tariff barriers to trade still remain. Although India has progressively reduced tariff rates since the early 1990s, much progress still needs to be made. U.S. companies experience problems with tariff and non-tariff barriers, the protection and enforcement of IPR, transparency, and poor infrastructure. At the same time, India's pressing infrastructure requirements present trade and investment opportunities. Key factors for successfully doing business in India include: finding good partners who have knowledge of the local market as well as legal, policy, and procedural issues; early planning; due diligence and follow-up; and perhaps most importantly, patience and commitment.

Conclusions

Bilateral Dialogues: To increase opportunities for U.S. companies and therefore boost bilateral trade and investment flows, the United States and India established the U.S.–India Economic Dialogue during Prime Minister Manmohan Singh's July 2005 visit to Washington, D.C. Under the Dialogue, a host of bilateral exchanges take place. The U.S.–India Trade Policy Forum (TPF), led by the Office of the U.S. Trade Representative to undertake strategic trade policy concerns, already has resolved several trade-related concerns. The TPF continues to pursue outstanding issues through five focus groups—agriculture, innovation and creativity (IPR), investment, services, and tariff and non-tariff barriers—chaired by senior economic officials on each side. The Department of the Treasury leads U.S. Government discussion with India on financial sector issues via the Financial and Economic Forum. The U.S. Department of Agriculture leads the Agricultural Knowledge Initiative (see below), and the U.S. Department of Commerce chairs the Commercial Dialogue and the High-Technology Working Group (see below). Other efforts include an environmental dialogue led by the Environmental Protection Agency and an energy dialogue led by the U.S. Department of Energy.

One of the most important opportunities for discussion between the United States and India is led by the private sector. President Bush and Prime Minister Singh established the **U.S.–India CEO Forum** in July 2005 as a mechanism for soliciting private sector input to energize the Economic Dialogue. The CEO Forum presented its initial set of recommendations during President Bush's visit to India in March 2006: 16 recommendations for the U.S. Government on a range of economic, defense, immigration, and scientific issues; and 13 recommendations for the Indian Government that included proposed liberalization in the financial services sector and steps to improve the overall business climate. The CEO Forum continues to meet and offer guidance to both governments on how to enhance bilateral trade and investment through policy initiatives to be undertaken by both countries.

The **U.S.–India Agricultural Knowledge Initiative (AKI)** announced by President Bush and Prime Minister Singh in July 2005 brings the U.S. and Indian private and public sectors together to work on innovative projects that will increase Indian agricultural productivity, help Indian farmers prosper, and strengthen trade. In November 2006, USDA Secretary Mike Johanns met in India with government and private-sector leadership in support of the AKI. Since meeting in November, the AKI Board has announced several new initiatives, including a multimillion-dollar agricultural market information system project. Bilateral agreement with the Government of India to collaborate on transfer of biotechnology research into production applications has enabled farmers and local markets to reap the benefits offered from biotechnology. In addition, other USDA projects are promoting a more functional regulatory and policy environment for agricultural biotechnology in India.

The two dialogues led by the Commerce Department seek to improve commercial relations and address trade barriers. The goal is to bring about the easing of governmental regulations on trade to benefit both U.S. and Indian companies.

■ The **Commercial Dialogue** serves as a forum for U.S. and Indian companies to develop common interests and present their views to the two Governments. In 2006, there were three major meetings of the Commercial Dialogue in addition to a number of smaller events. Topics addressed this past year include:

☐ Dialogue on Standards (a series of videoconferences)

☐ Roundtable on Pharmaceuticals (New York City)

☐ Financial Services Roundtable (Mumbai)

☐ IPR/Entertainment Industry Roundtable (Mumbai)

☐ Medical Device and Harmonization Roundtable (New Delhi)

☐ Pharmaceuticals Seminar on Anti-Counterfeiting (New Delhi).

In the year ahead, the Commercial Dialogue will focus on investment caps and retail trade.

■ The **U.S.–India High-Technology Cooperation Group (HTCG)** has helped increase bilateral trade by effectively identifying and removing trade barriers. In addition to governmental meetings, the HTCG provides a forum for business executives to discuss high-technology issues and present trade-facilitating recommendations to government. The HTCG contributed to regulatory changes that reduced the percentage of exports to India requiring a license. From 1999 to 2006, the percent of U.S. exports to India controlled by the Commerce Department plummeted from 24 percent to one percent. In 2006, 91 percent of license applications were approved, and average processing times for India are now in line with those of key U.S. partners. In the coming year, the HTCG plans to focus on the biotechnology, information technology, defense trade, and nanotechnology sectors.

India Business Development Mission, major milestone in U.S.–India trade, took place in December 2006. The mission stemmed from the mandate to increase commercial ties as a result of President Bush's visit to India in March 2006. In response, the Department of Commerce developed a mega-mission—the largest trade mission in U.S. Government history. This mission included a business summit, spin-off missions to six cities throughout India, four Commercial Dialogue events, and policy meetings on the sidelines of the trade mission to discuss U.S.–India civilian nuclear trade. Over 258 executives from 194 U.S. companies participated in the mission. Over half of the participants reported that this event was their first trip to India. Almost 70 percent of the companies represented were small businesses. Over 600 Indian business-people participated in meetings with the U.S. mission participants.

Much of the Federal Government's trade promotion activity in the coming year stems from this mission:

- Representatives from eight U.S. states and cities participated in the mission. Four of these are now planning trade missions of their own in the coming year: Florida, Mississippi, California, and the City of Dallas. In addition, the Governor of Minnesota is planning a mission to India.

- As India's economy grows, so does its need for energy. The mission opened a dialogue between U.S. companies and Indian civil nuclear officials in the context of a possible U.S.–India Civil Nuclear Cooperation Agreement. U.S. companies are not yet allowed to sell nuclear power products and services to India, but in 2007, they will continue to work with the Federal Government to make sure they are in a position to take advantage of commercial opportunities when an agreement is reached.

- In addition to the nuclear sector, the Departments of Commerce and State supported the Clean Energy Technologies Trade Mission to India led by Assistant Secretary of Commerce Bohigian. The trade mission targeted a broad range of clean energy technologies such as renewable energy, energy efficiency, clean coal, and distributed generation.

- A key element in the success of the mega-mission was the assistance of private partners, who helped to support the summit and recruit participants from among their clients in the United States. Based on this success, the Commercial Service in India has developed the Gateway to India Program, focused on the tremendous growth in demand for U.S. consumer goods in India. Large Indian retail companies plan to purchase as much as $6 billion in consumer goods in 2007. The Commercial Service in India is working with our private partners to connect U.S. companies with major Indian purchasers like Reliance.

Other Priorities: In addition to follow-on activities from the mission, there are two other major areas of focus for the Federal Government.

- The **Aviation Cooperation Program** (ACP) is a public-private partnership established to provide a forum for unified communication between the Government of India and U.S. public and private sector entities in India. Participants include USTDA, the U.S. Department of Transportation's Federal Aviation Administration (FAA), the Department of Commerce, Ex-Im Bank, and U.S. aviation companies. The ACP is designed to work directly with the Indian Government to identify and support India's civil aviation sector modernization priorities, which include major airport developments and traffic control systems.

- The Commercial Service is developing partnerships with U.S. companies that have production facilities in India to bring potential U.S. suppliers on trade missions to India for possible integration into the facilities' supply chains.

BRAZIL

While Brazil is growing at a less torrid pace than China or India, its economy registered a strong 3.7 percent growth in 2006 and is forecast to grow more than 4 percent a year through 2008[4], well above its 2.5 percent historical average. Domestic demand is expected to be the principal driver of growth during this period. Lower inflation and real interest rates will foster continued steady growth of real income, investment, and employment. Targeted tax breaks and other measures announced in January 2007 may help stimulate investments in infrastructure and certain information technology, if approved by the Brazilian Congress.

U.S. exports to Brazil grew 25 percent from 2005 to 2006. The United States continues to be Brazil's single largest trading partner, with $19.2 billion in exports in 2006 (*Chart 26*). Promising sectors for U.S. exports and investment include: agricultural equipment, agriculture, aircraft and parts, airports, computer software, e-commerce, highways, insurance, iron and steel, IT hardware, medical equipment, mining, oil and gas, pharmaceuticals, pollution equipment, ports, railroads, safety equipment, telecommunications, and tourism.

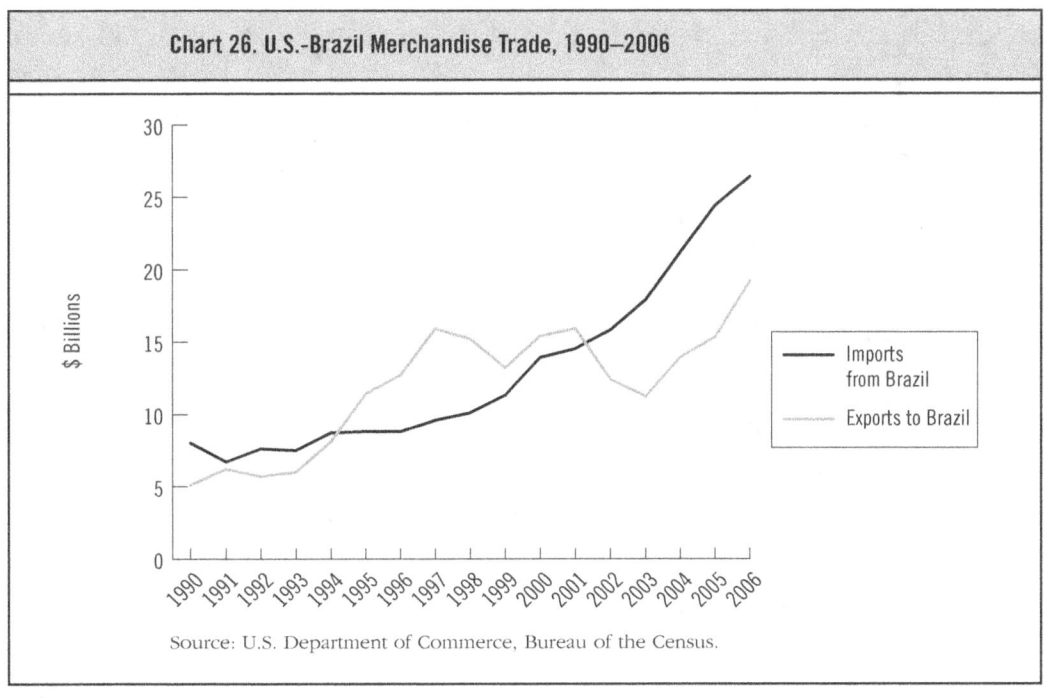

Chart 26. U.S.-Brazil Merchandise Trade, 1990–2006

Source: U.S. Department of Commerce, Bureau of the Census.

---

4   International Monetary Fund, *World Economic Outlook*, p. 2, April 2007.

U.S. exporters to Brazil continue to face a number of challenges. One of the most common complaints of U.S. companies is that the high tax burden, when combined with import taxes, can result in a doubling of the price of goods shipped to Brazil. U.S. companies are also hampered by an array of government regulations and red tape, as well as a confusing product standards process.

Conclusions

Bilateral Dialogues: To help address many of these issues, the U.S. and Brazilian Governments have developed two new bilateral fora.

- Commerce Secretary Gutierrez and Brazilian Commerce Minister Furlan launched the **U.S.–Brazil Commercial Dialogue** in June 2006. The Dialogue came out of commitments made in the joint declaration issued during President Bush's visit to Brazil in November 2005. The Dialogue's four groups cover trade facilitation, standards, intellectual property, and export and investment promotion. The initiatives are all designed to address issues in our bilateral commercial relationship by increasing commerce and competitiveness.

- The United States and Brazil have also agreed to establish a **U.S.–Brazil CEO Forum**, consisting of both private- and public-sector members. The CEO Forum aims to bring together leaders of the U.S. and Brazilian business communities to discuss issues of mutual interest, including ways to strengthen economic and commercial ties.

- SBA is also actively engaged in dialogue with Brazil's Ministry of Development, Industry, and Trade to increase cooperation on small business development and facilitate trade relationships between U.S. and Brazilian small businesses. SBA continues to work closely with Brazil's quasi-governmental small-business service agency SEBRAE on advancing the SME Congress of the Americas on International Trade, a network to promote and facilitate small-business participation in the global marketplace.

These initiatives are still new; however, the discussions are encouraging and have already yielded progress in some areas such as express delivery services.

Business Opportunities in Brazil: On the trade promotion side, the Commercial Service recorded over 1,265 export successes in 2006—confirmed instances where Commercial Service assistance directly contributed to sales for a U.S. firm. A highlight was the sale of 50 General Electric locomotives produced in Pennsylvania, with the help of a USTDA orientation visit.

- USTDA helped with other transportation projects like the Rio Traffic Control and Management Systems Upgrade to develop an intelligent transportation system architecture plan for Rio. USTDA is supporting activities under the Commercial Dialogue through training and the development of intelligent port logistics and supply chains; these will help with trade facilitation issues.

- In addition to promoting U.S. participation in major trade shows in Brazil, the Department of Commerce is organizing several U.S. trade missions to Brazil in the aerospace, healthcare technologies, and energy efficiency sectors.

Americas Competitiveness Forum

Secretary Gutierrez will host the inaugural Americas Competitiveness Forum on June 11–12, 2007, in Atlanta, Georgia. The heads of several Federal Government trade agencies will also participate. The Forum will provide a venue for government ministers from Brazil and other parts of the Western Hemisphere to come together with private-sector and academic leaders to explore cutting-edge ideas and best practices in several key areas of competitiveness. The four main tracks include: innovation, education and workforce development, supporting small businesses, and global supply-chain strategies.

Appendix A
TPCC Agencies' Accomplishments in FY 2006

Strategy:

- Open and expand foreign markets for U.S. goods and services and improve the nation's export performance.

- Promote U.S. export growth through the implementation of the National Export Strategy by:

  - Expanding and enhancing cooperation with partnership organizations,

  - Ensuring that U.S. businesses benefit from global business through free market trade negotiations and through identified priority markets, and

  - Ensuring that U.S. small and medium-sized enterprises (SME) and manufacturers can compete and win in the global economy.

- Ensure that export controls do not place U.S. firms at a competitive disadvantage in world markets, by eliminating outdated controls and streamlining the process for obtaining export licenses for products that remain under export controls.

Results:

- The Department of Commerce continues to advance U.S.-negotiated trade positions and expand trade through FTAs including recently negotiated, but pending, FTAs with Colombia, Peru, Panama, and South Korea.

- The Department of Commerce continued to advance U.S. commercial relationships with key emerging markets. Commerce Secretary Gutierrez's trade mission to Shanghai and Beijing in October/November 2006 included 22 senior executives from U.S. companies and resulted in projects valued at $8 billion. Since China joined the WTO at the end of 2001, U.S. exports have grown from $19 billion to $55 billion in 2006. In December 2006, Under Secretary of Commerce for International Trade Frank Lavin led a mega-mission of 258 executives from 194 U.S. companies to India and elevated the U.S.–India Commercial Dialogue launched in spring 2006. U.S. exports to India nearly doubled from $4.1 billion in 2002 to over $8 billion in 2006.

- In 2006, the Commercial Service expanded its corporate partnership outreach by creating tiered partners. Tier 1 partners have been awarded "no-cost" contracts through a competitive acquisition process and based upon their response to a formal solicitation. Awardees include: FedEx, UPS, PNC Bank, M&T Bank, and eBay. Tier 2 partners, while not having participated in a procurement, are working with the Commercial Service in a coordinated manner to promote exporting; this tier includes companies and business groups like City National Bank and the Business Council for International Understanding. The Commerce Department is also engaging state and city partners to cooperate more closely on training, outreach, and trade events.

- In 2006, the Department of Commerce helped complete 11,919 export successes that directly assisted U.S. firms to (a) export for the first time, (b) enter a new market, or (c) increase their market share in an existing market.

- The Mexican Cement Agreement was a mutually acceptable bilateral agreement that has resolved a long-standing trade dispute between the United States and Mexico over imports of cement. The Agreement is in accordance with U.S. trade laws and provides improved market access for U.S. cement producers into the Mexican market.

- The Department continued to ensure the timely review of all export license applications, with an average processing time of 33 days. The Department processed 18,934 export license applications in FY 2006, an increase of 13 percent from FY 2005 and the highest number of applications processed since FY 1993.

- The Department of Commerce opened 51 compliance/market access cases on behalf of SMEs, exceeded its goal by initiating 178 cases, and resolved 140 cases. Of these cases, 46 percent were resolved successfully.

EXPORT–IMPORT BANK OF THE UNITED STATES

Strategy:

- Increased attention to the needs of small business exporters. Creation in 2006 of the Small Business Division to further Ex-Im's outreach and business development efforts. Designated specialists throughout the Bank's operating units who devote their attention and expertise to the processing of small-business transactions.

- Making it easier for our customers to do business with the Bank is of primary importance. Ex-Im Online, the Bank's new Web-based application and transaction-management system, is now available. Usage is expected to grow as we expand its capabilities. Ex-Im will develop this system further to maximize efficiency and to reduce paperwork and processing times while increasing the transparency of our operations.

- Adapting to meet the needs of a dynamic global marketplace. Some export credit agencies (ECAs) are taking on the characteristics of the private sector, while others in emerging markets are growing rapidly, unconstrained by the export-credit guidelines of the Organization for Economic Cooperation and Development (OECD). To keep pace with the changing marketplace, Ex-Im Bank will deepen existing relationships with OECD member ECAs and build new relationships with rising ECAs.

- Special focus on expansion of partner network of financial institutions, export credit insurance brokers, City/State Partners, and industry associations.

- A concerted commitment to increasing its financing support for sales of U.S. goods and services to the countries in sub-Saharan Africa.

Results:

- In FY 2006, more than $12 billion in new authorizations to over 80 countries.

- Over $3 billion in small-business transactions authorized, accounting for 26 percent of total authorizations and 84 percent of total transactions.

- Establishment of a working relationship with the Export–Import Bank of China, as a result, the two ECAs have created a framework agreement to facilitate the financing of U.S. exports of medium-term goods and services to China. Discussions are ongoing regarding other areas of cooperation.

- Partner network growth of greater than 10 percent was achieved in FY 2006. Included within the over $3 billion in small business authorizations was a record of nearly $1.2 billion in working capital guarantee authorizations, with over 78 percent supporting small business exporters.

- For every taxpayer dollar used in FY 2006, Ex-Im Bank facilitated an estimated $61 of U.S. exports, compared to $57 of U.S. exports in FY 2005 and $51 the year before.

- In FY 2006 as compared to FY 2005, Ex-Im Bank's authorizations for sub-Saharan Africa increased 22 percent from 115 to 140 transactions. Amounts authorized also rose 15 percent from $462 million in 20 countries to $532 million in 23 countries.

OVERSEAS PRIVATE INVESTMENT CORPORATION

Strategy:

- By working in closer collaboration with other U.S. Government agencies to bring economic development to emerging or underserved markets, OPIC better focused its resources and efforts.

- By focusing on access to credit, small business, and housing, OPIC is developing dynamic and efficient catalysts for growth.

- By enhancing transparency and fighting corruption, OPIC worked to level the playing field for U.S. businesses as they participate in international commerce.

- By reaching out in more ways to U.S. small businesses and minority- and women-owned enterprises, OPIC ensured greater access to opportunity for more U.S. businesses.

- By identifying and supporting projects that extend significant developmental benefits to the widest possible audiences, OPIC fulfilled its mission throughout the world.

- By charging market-based fees for its products, OPIC continued to meet these responsibilities as a self-sustaining agency, operating at no net cost to taxpayers and returning money to the U.S. Treasury.

Results:

- OPIC announced support for new Central American private equity investment funds and signed agreements for over $300 million in finance and insurance for housing, energy, microfinance, and small business projects.

- Working with financial institutions, OPIC has improved access to credit for SMEs and microfinance entities to promote effective development.

- The OPIC Anti-Corruption and Transparency Initiative, announced in September 2006, builds on the agency's efforts over the past five years to combat corruption in host countries, create a level playing field for lawful business activities, and improve information-sharing and the transparency of OPIC's own operations.

- OPIC expanded its outreach to both the U.S. business community and to governments, organizations, and entrepreneurs in developing nations around the world through its annual international conferences.

U.S. TRADE AND DEVELOPMENT AGENCY

Strategy:

- Continue to target programs that open markets for U.S. industry while supporting economic development in foreign markets.

- Focus attention on building the infrastructure for development; supporting U.S. trade policy; enhancing global energy security; and strengthening transportation safety and security.

- Expand the agency's outreach to the U.S. business community with a particular focus on small and medium-sized enterprises that may be able to take advantage of USTDA's programs while increasing their international exposure.

Results:

- USTDA implemented its CAFTA–DR Trade Integration Initiative through ongoing support for greater transportation linkages with its regional neighbors and the United States.

- Over the last ten-year period, USTDA has identified over $42 in U.S. exports associated with every dollar invested in projects around the world.

- USTDA expanded its outreach to U.S. industry through an increase in site visits and participation in business briefings with foreign delegates who traveled to the United States to see the world's best manufacturing base.

U.S. SMALL BUSINESS ADMINISTRATION

Strategy:

- Structure and service delivery improvements resulting in record loan numbers to small businesses.

- SME Congress of the Americas: SBA's noted support of the Summit of the Americas Process.

- SBA/Ex-Im Bank Co-guarantee (thinking outside the box and being a good U.S. Government partner).

Results:

- SBA made a record number of export loans in FY 2006 and surpassed the $1 billion mark for the first time in the history of the program. U.S. Export Assistance Center (USEAC) realignment and changes in reporting made service delivery more efficient. SBA's USEAC representatives and District Offices facilitated 3,304 loans to small business exporters, supporting $2.2 billion dollars in export sales. USEACs also provided counseling and training to more than 10,000 small businesses.

- The SME Congress of the Americas is a hemispheric network promoting and facilitating the participation of small business in trade. SBA spearheaded and leads this initiative. Support for the SME Congress and small business trade was specifically included in the November 2005 Summit of the Americas Declaration and Action Plan (signed by President Bush). SBA and SME Congress counterparts played an important role in the strong inclusion of small business issues in the Summit dialogue. More than 150 representatives from 17 countries participated in the Second SME Congress in Mexico in May 2006. SBA and its Argentine counterparts coordinated a successful pilot small-business matchmaking event as part of the Second SME Congress. Approximately 50 information and communications technologies companies from seven countries participated in this event.

- SBA's Office of International Trade (OIT) worked extensively with Ex-Im Bank to develop a joint marketing plan to support SMEs and to harmonize SBA/Ex-Im Bank credit and insurance products. This marketing plan was created to enhance service and delivery, through outreach and collaboration with U.S. banks, and to facilitate the cross-selling of each agency's programs and products for small business exporters. USEAC staff have made more than 20 loans using this procedure. OIT also worked to convert Ex-Im Bank's Delegated Lenders to SBA Export PLP Lenders and represented SBA at Ex-Im Bank training.

Strategy:

- Expand and maintain international export opportunities.

- Support international economic development and trade capacity building.

- Improve SPS system to facilitate agricultural trade.

Result:

- U.S. agricultural exports rose on broad-based gains for many products to a record $68.7 billion in FY 2006, up $6.2 billion from FY 2005. This included a $1.8 billion increase in horticultural exports, corn exports rising $1.5 billion, livestock exports rising $1.2 billion, and cotton exports jumping $800 million. U.S. agricultural exports to NAFTA partners continue to set records. Canada remains our largest market and the largest market for U.S. fresh and processed fruits and vegetables, snack foods, juices, and wine. At a record $10.4 billion in FY 2006, Mexico remains the second largest market for U.S. agricultural exports having overtaken Japan in 2005. U.S. exports to China, the fifth largest market, reached a record $6.7 billion in FY 2006. USDA's industry partners promote trade and outreach activities to educate producers, processors, and exporters on emerging market opportunities that result from trade agreements.

- FAS increased access to the global market for U.S. agricultural producers and exporters by preserving trade opportunities through monitoring and compliance enforcement, overseas advocacy and negotiation of technical protocols. The two most important successes were the European Union's indefinite postponement of new requirements on wood-packaging material that exceeds the agreed-upon international standard, and the reopening of the Japanese market for U.S. beef.

- FAS improved the ability of developing countries to sustain economic growth and benefit from international trade through food assistance, trade and development programs, and trade capacity building. USDA provided technical assistance and training to improve agricultural statistics programs in ten countries. Short-term assignments supported work in Armenia,

Brazil, China, Costa Rica, El Salvador, Georgia, Mexico, Mongolia, Russia, and Ukraine. The Department also coordinated and/or conducted briefings and/or training programs in the United States for 158 visitors representing 17 countries. FAS' improved analysis supported trade and the more efficient marketing of U.S. agricultural products. The McGovern-Dole International Food for Education and Child Nutrition Program provides for the donation of U.S. agricultural commodities and associated financial and technical assistance for pre-school and school-based feeding programs in developing countries, and in FY 2006 supported the feeding of 3.3 million women, infants, and children.

■ FAS fostered an improved global SPS system for facilitating agricultural trade by addressing SPS measures and other technical barriers to trade, and by monitoring international regulatory activities. In FY 2006, USDA reopened or expanded restricted beef markets in Japan, Mexico, CAFTA–DR countries, Peru, Malaysia, Taiwan, and Singapore. USDA staff in more than 90 countries help open, retain, and expand international markets for U.S. food and agricultural products.

U.S. DEPARTMENT OF STATE

Strategy:

■ Promote international support for a "total economic engagement" approach to poverty reduction and sustainable economic growth by leading cooperative efforts with multilateral financial and assistance organizations, with the Millennium Challenge Corporation, and other U.S. aid agencies. Support international financial institutions' efforts to encourage pro-market economic reforms and financial sector development.

■ Advance the Doha Round and bilateral efforts to conclude FTAs by supporting U.S. Government efforts, including protection and enforcement of U.S. intellectual property rights overseas and reducing trade barriers for agricultural exports.

■ Develop international communications policies that are vital for our economic and military security, trade in goods and services, e-commerce, intellectual property protection, and fostering of democratic societies. Ensure market access, freedom of technology choice, the integrity of the Internet, and adherence to international standards by leading multilateral and bilateral efforts.

- Promote transparent and open energy investment regimes and markets, strategic petroleum stockholding, diverse and secure energy supplies and sources, and development of clean alternative energy technologies that are vital to long-term U.S. energy security.

- Negotiate air services agreements, seeking to foster competition among airlines by removing restrictions on the number of carriers, routes, aircraft, services, and prices.

- Improve business and investment climates abroad through the negotiation of bilateral investment treaties (State–USTR co-lead), investment, and IPR chapters of free trade agreements (USTR lead), and ongoing policy dialogues.

- Advocate for U.S. companies to ensure fair play, to assist with regulatory and investment problems (including intellectual property protection and enforcement), and to maximize commercial opportunities.

- Improve support for U.S. business overseas, particularly at those 100 Embassies that do not have a Commercial Service office ("non-Commercial Service"), at which State's economic officers are responsible for providing commercial services.

- Build the capacity of foreign police, prosecutors, border and customs officials, and judges in the fight against IP crime by funding law enforcement training and technical assistance.

Results:

- The Department of State provided advocacy services for over 350 company-specific cases and recorded 95 success stories during 2006. An increased emphasis on tracking business advocacy supports the Department's outreach efforts to Congressional offices, to the U.S. business community, and to foreign governments.

- The Department hosted over 185 business outreach programs during 2006, in an effort to promote best business practices, public diplomacy goals, and awareness and understanding of U.S. Government policy affecting American business abroad.

- The Joint Commercial Service-State Post Partnership Program has led to increased support for the existing 75 regional commercial partnership programs, established between non-Commercial Service embassies and partnered with nearby Commercial Service offices. During 2006, the Department funded trade fairs, trade capacity building seminars, and business outreach activities in more than 50 non-Commercial Service embassies to further support commercial diplomacy efforts in the host country. During 2006-2007, joint Commercial Service-State partnership training will be provided for more than 40 embassies partnered with Commercial Service offices in Bangkok, Dakar, Johannesburg, New Delhi, and Santo Domingo. IT improvements have been made on the Department's intranet to provide State Department economic officers the tools necessary to better support U.S. companies.

- Forty two IPR training and technical assistance projects totaling $8.5 million over the past three years have been funded by the Bureau of International Narcotics and Law Enforcement Affairs and the Bureau of Economic and Business Affairs.

U.S. DEPARTMENT OF TRANSPORTATION

Strategy:

- Facilitate increased trade through the planning of and facilitation and construction of increased physical capacity at and near land border ports of entry.

- Improve consistency between domestic and international standards.

- Explore and develop market opportunities for the U.S. transportation industry.

Results:

- Federal Highway Administration (FHWA) activities in 2006 to increase capacity and planning along the borders with Canada and Mexico include: a new approach near the Pacific Highway Border Crossing; planning for new border crossing capacity in the Detroit, Michigan/Windsor, Ontario area; additional bridge capacity at the Peace Bridge in New York and Otay Mesa in California; planning for new plaza capacity at the Blue Water Bridge in Michigan; Champlain, New York Phase 2 construction; and new FAST lanes at the Mariposa, Arizona crossing. FHWA also developed border information flow architecture to enhance interoperability of technologies used at or near the border and led an initiative to establish border crossing delay measures.

- Standards: In 2006, DOT's Pipeline and Hazardous Material Safety Administration led the development of international standards for UN pressure receptacles (i.e. gas cylinders) and for fuel cell technologies. Also in 2006, FHWA established the Technology Exchange Center (TEC) in Iraq to be the focal point for the introduction of information on U.S. standards, new technologies, and best practices. This will serve in the long run to institutionalize the use of U.S. standards in road building, which will in turn open the Iraqi market to U.S. products.

- South Africa World Cup Infrastructure: In April 2006, representatives of FHWA and the Federal Transit Administration (FTA) visited South Africa to develop market opportunities in preparation for the 2010 World Cup in South Africa. FHWA, in partnership with FTA, coordinated a USTDA-funded orientation visit to expose South African Government officials to U.S. technologies, companies, policies, and practices. FTA and the Commercial Service have assisted U.S. companies in their bids on railroad signaling equipment, software, and services to the urban passenger rail systems and the national freight systems.

- China Bus Transmissions: The Allison Transmission Division of General Motors participated in the FTA's first trade mission to China in 2004. In 2006, Allison won contracts to supply 3,435 automatic transmissions to Beijing Public Transport Holdings Ltd., to be installed in the Chinese capital's city buses.

- Egypt Rail Safety: Since September 2006, the Federal Railroad Administration (FRA) has provided technical assistance to the Egyptian National Railway (ENR), and USTDA has approved funding for a $600,000 grant to the Ministry of Transport for development of a Traffic Management System for the ENR. FRA is also working with U.S. rail component suppliers to help them present their proposals to the Egyptian Ministry of Transport.

Appendix B
TPCC Program Budget Authority

TPCC Program Budget Authority, In Millions of Dollars			
	FY 2006	FY 2007	FY 2008
	Acutal	Enacted	Request
Department of Agriculture	819	693	588
Department of Commerce	352	335	346
Department of Energy	9	9	9
Department of State*	170	174	191
Department of the Treasury	3	3	3
Export-Import Bank**	98	55	1
Overseas Private Investment Corporation***	(161)	(113)	(160)
Small Business Administration	4	6	5
U.S. Trade and Development Agency	50	50	50
U.S. Trade Reprentative	44	44	44
Total	1,549	1,369	1,237

Note: Amounts may be restated in the future to reflect new data or definitions.
Figures may include administrative expenses, transfers, or other adjustments.
     * Dollars are cumulative of all business and economic activities in the State Department
    ** The FY 2008 budget estimates that the Bank's export credit support will total
       $18.7 billion in lending activity, and will be funded entirely by receipts collected
       from the Bank's customers. The Bank expects to collect $146 million in receipts in
       excess of estimated losses in FY 2008. These receipts will be used to cover both the
       $68 million for credit programs as well as the $78 million for administrative expenses.
    *** Totals do not include OPIC.

Appendix C
FTA Country-by-Country Profiles

The United States–Australia FTA was signed on May 18, 2004, and entered into force January 1, 2005. Its goals were to strengthen commercial ties between the United States and Australia and address barriers to U.S. exports.

The successful conclusion of the United States–Australia FTA expands market access opportunities for U.S. companies by over 20 million consumers and $456 billion in GDP (2005). In the year prior to entry into force of the FTA (2004), the United States exported $14.2 billion in goods to Australia. By 2006, annual exports had grown to $17.8 billion—a 25 percent increase. Australia's exports to the United States increased to $8.2 billion in 2006 for total trade of $26 billion. Services exports from the United States also increased by 7 percent to $7.4 billion in 2005 (latest available).

Major accomplishments include:

Tariffs: The FTA eliminated duties on over 99 percent of tariff lines covering industrial and consumer goods. This brought immediate benefits to key U.S. manufacturing sectors, including autos and auto parts; aircraft; chemicals, plastics, and soda ash; construction equipment; electrical equipment and appliances; fabricated metal products; furniture and fixtures; information technology products; medical and optical equipment; non-electrical machinery; and paper and wood products.

Government Procurement: Under the FTA, Australia has agreed to provide U.S. firms with non-discriminatory rights to bid on procurements of 80 central government entities, including key ministries and government enterprises. These commitments are particularly significant since Australia is one of the only developed countries that is not a signatory to the plurilateral WTO

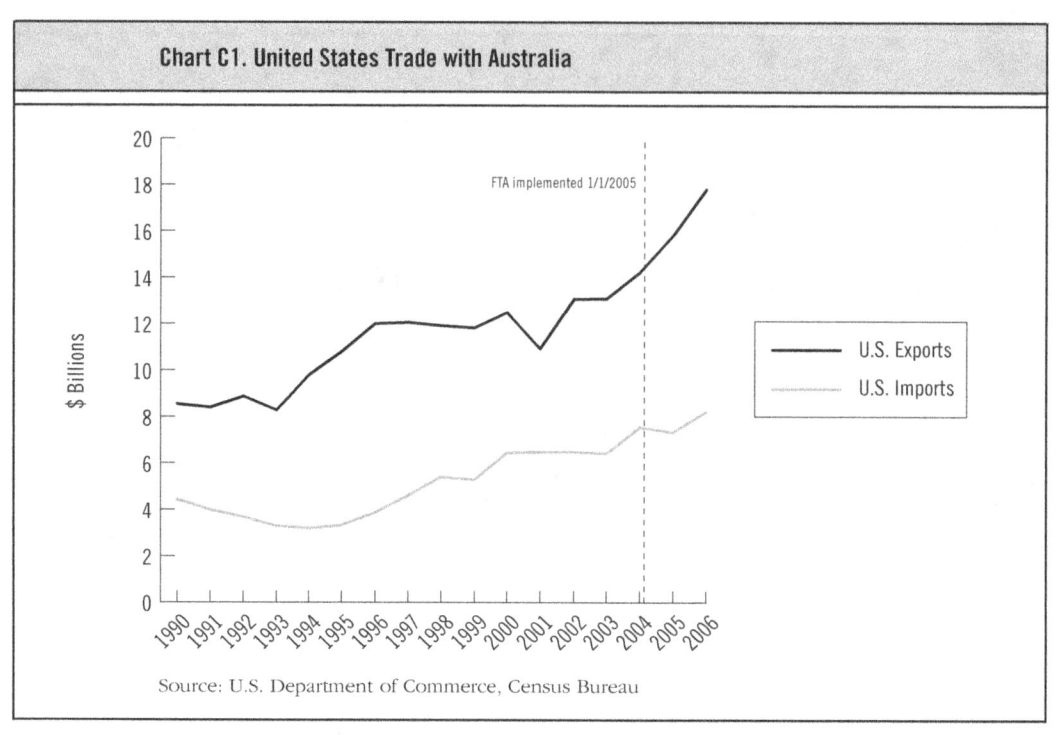

Chart C1. United States Trade with Australia

FTA implemented 1/1/2005

— U.S. Exports
— U.S. Imports

Source: U.S. Department of Commerce, Census Bureau

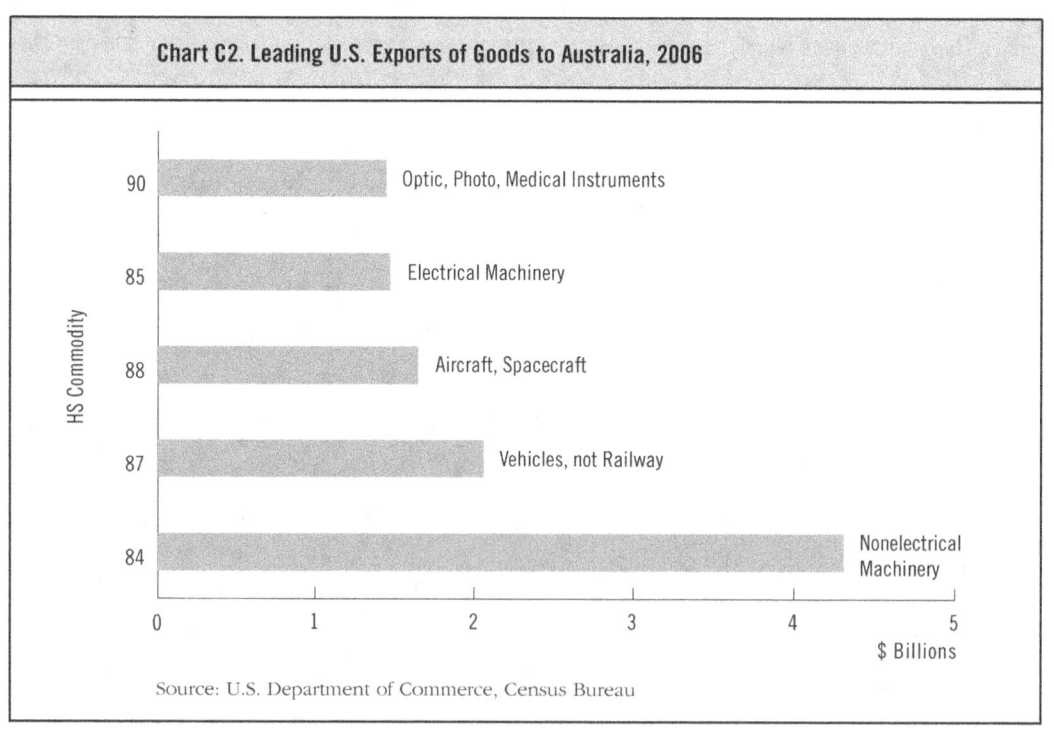

Chart C2. Leading U.S. Exports of Goods to Australia, 2006

90 — Optic, Photo, Medical Instruments

85 — Electrical Machinery

88 — Aircraft, Spacecraft

87 — Vehicles, not Railway

84 — Nonelectrical Machinery

HS Commodity

$ Billions

Source: U.S. Department of Commerce, Census Bureau

Government Procurement Agreement (GPA). The FTA also requires the use of fair and transparent procurement procedures, including advance notice of purchases for procurement covered by the Agreement. Under the FTA, Australia agreed to eliminate its industry development programs, which required suppliers to provide various types of offsets.

Intellectual Property Rights: Under the FTA, U.S. producers of creative material and innovative products benefit from higher standards for protecting intellectual property rights such as copyrights, patents, trademarks, and trade secrets and enhanced means for enforcing those rights. Licensing fees and royalties from Australia grew from $800 million in 2002 to $1.2 billion in 2006.

THE UNITED STATES–BAHRAIN FTA

The United States–Bahrain FTA was signed in September 2004, and entered into force on August 1, 2006. The United States–Bahrain FTA is an important step in implementing the President's economic reforms in the Middle East and pursuing his goal of a Middle East Free Trade Area by 2013.

The United States–Bahrain FTA expands market access opportunities for U.S. companies by roughly 725,000 consumers and $13 billion in GDP (2005). In the year prior to entry into force of the FTA (2005), the United States exported $350.8 million in goods to Bahrain. In 2006, U.S. exports totaled $491 million—a 40 percent increase over the previous year. Bahrain's exports to the United States totaled $632 million for total trade of $1.1 billion in 2006.

Major accomplishments include:

Tariffs: The United States–Bahrain FTA is the first FTA with a Persian Gulf state and the third with an Arab state. On the first day the United States–Bahrain FTA went into effect, 100 percent of two-way trade in industrial and consumer products became duty-free, with Bahrain providing duty-free access for 98 percent of U.S. agricultural tariff lines.

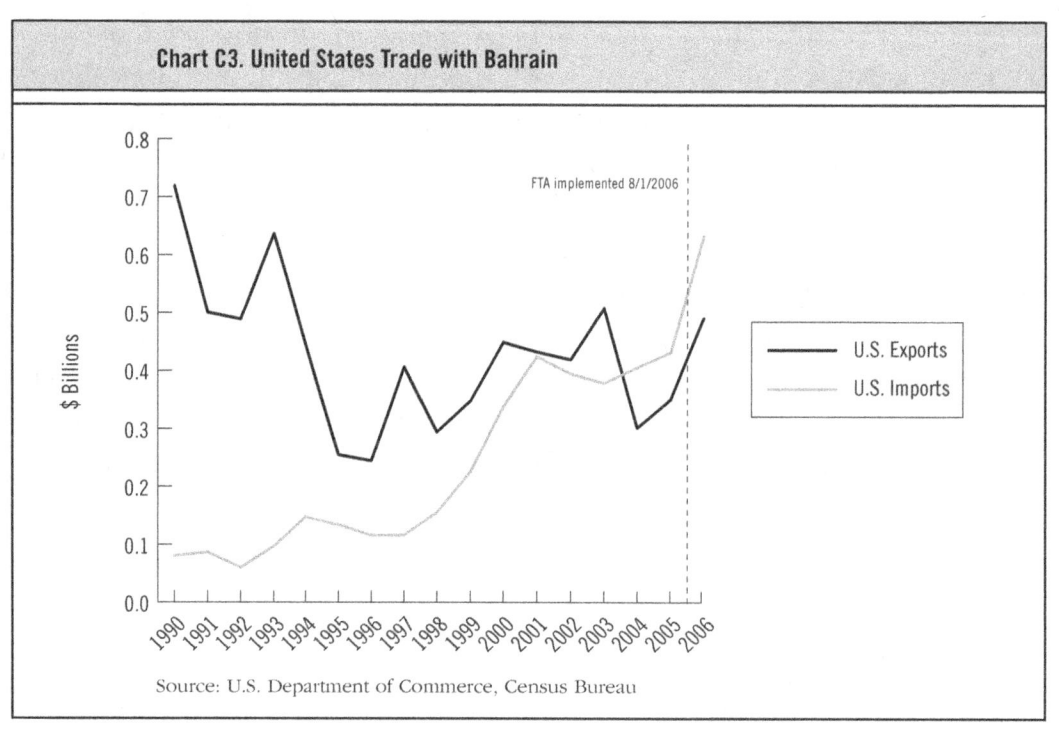

Chart C3. United States Trade with Bahrain

FTA implemented 8/1/2006

U.S. Exports
U.S. Imports

Source: U.S. Department of Commerce, Census Bureau

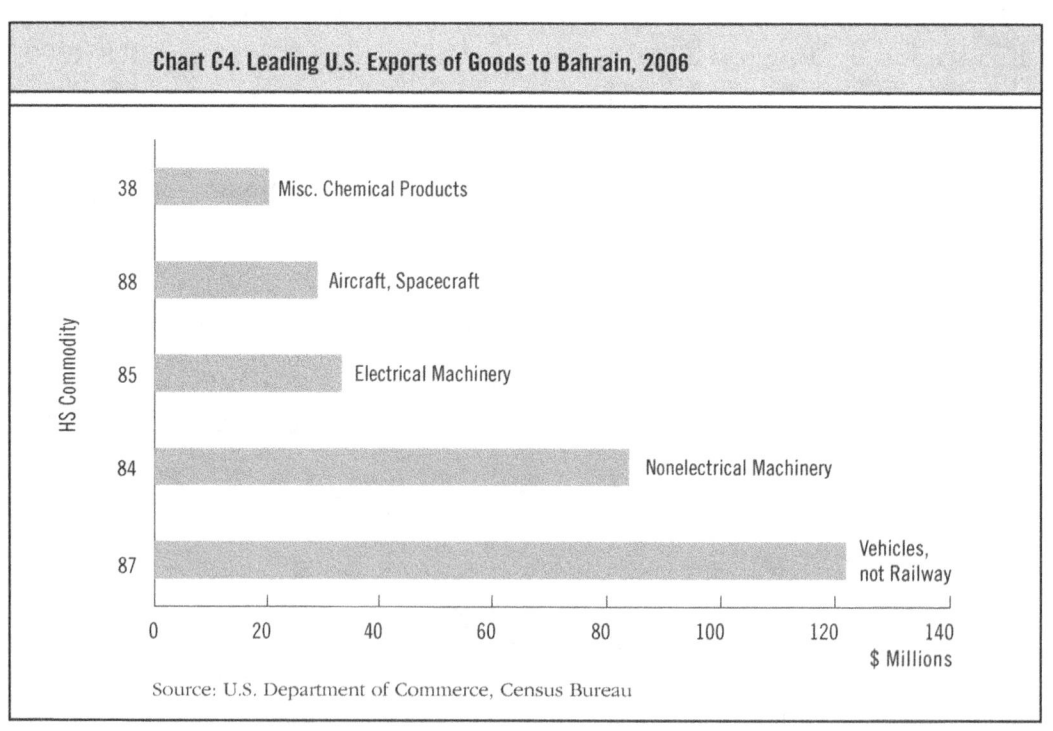

Chart C4. Leading U.S. Exports of Goods to Bahrain, 2006

HS Commodity	
38	Misc. Chemical Products
88	Aircraft, Spacecraft
85	Electrical Machinery
84	Nonelectrical Machinery
87	Vehicles, not Railway

$ Millions

Source: U.S. Department of Commerce, Census Bureau

Services: Bahrain's services sector accounts for roughly 50 percent of its GDP. Bahrain is a leading financial center in the Middle East and a large provider of various services to the surrounding region. U.S. financial, insurance, legal, and medical service providers stand to reap large gains from the United States–Bahrain FTA as barriers to entry are removed.

Government Procurement: The FTA includes disciplines on procurement by most Bahraini Government agencies. These include not discriminating against U.S. firms or in favor of Bahraini firms when making government purchases in excess of agreed monetary thresholds. The FTA's strong government procurement disciplines set a precedent for the Gulf. Each government must maintain criminal and other penalties for bribery in government procurement.

Intellectual Property Rights: Under the FTA, U.S. producers of creative material and innovative products benefit from higher standards for protecting intellectual property rights such as copyrights, patents, trademarks, and trade secrets and enhanced means for enforcing those rights. In order to come into compliance with its obligations under the FTA, Bahrain passed several key pieces of intellectual property legislation to improve protections and criminalize various intellectual property rights violations, which then permitted the Bahraini Ministry of Information to set up enforcement raids of IT resellers distributing illegal software.

DOMINICAN REPUBLIC-CENTRAL AMERICA-UNITED STATES FTA (CAFTA-DR)

The United States, the five countries of Central America (Costa Rica, El Salvador, Guatemala, Honduras, and Nicaragua), and the Dominican Republic signed the Dominican Republic–Central America–United States Free Trade Agreement (CAFTA–DR) on August 5, 2004. The FTA creates new commercial opportunities for the United States, while promoting regional stability, economic integration, stronger democratic institutions, and economic development for an important group of U.S. neighbors. The agreement is entering into force on a rolling basis for each country as it takes the steps to complete its domestic procedures for approval and implementation of its commitments under the agreement. The agreement entered into force during 2006 for El Salvador, Guatemala, Honduras, and Nicaragua. In addition, the agreement entered into force for the Dominican Republic on March 1, 2007.

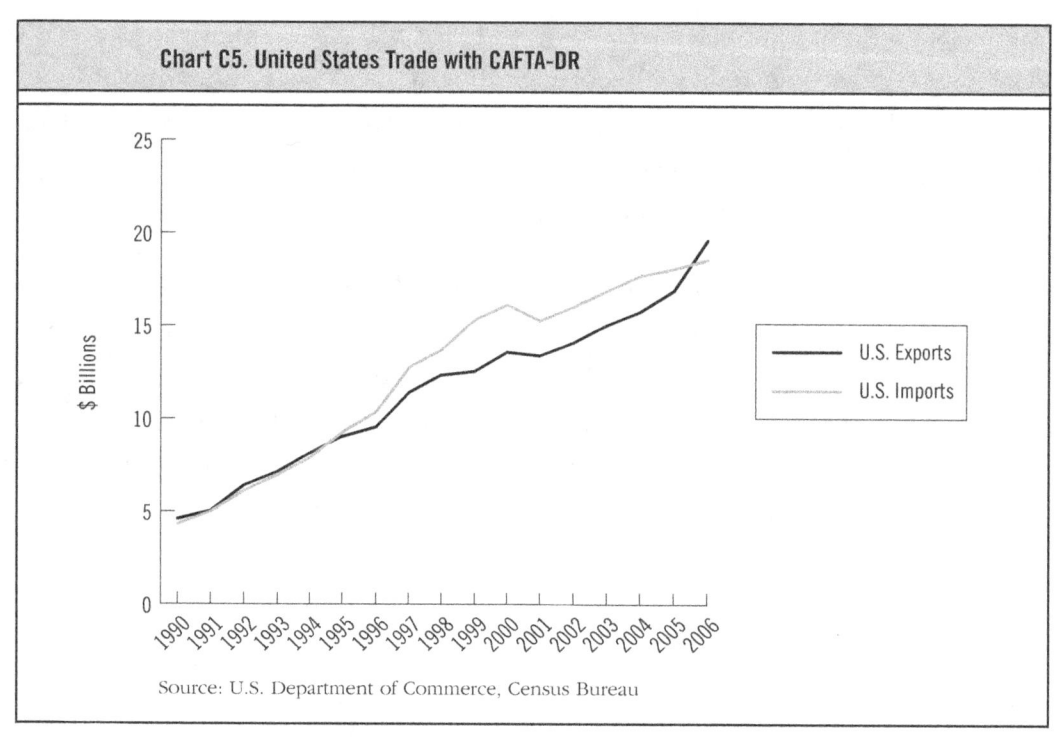

Chart C5. United States Trade with CAFTA-DR

Source: U.S. Department of Commerce, Census Bureau

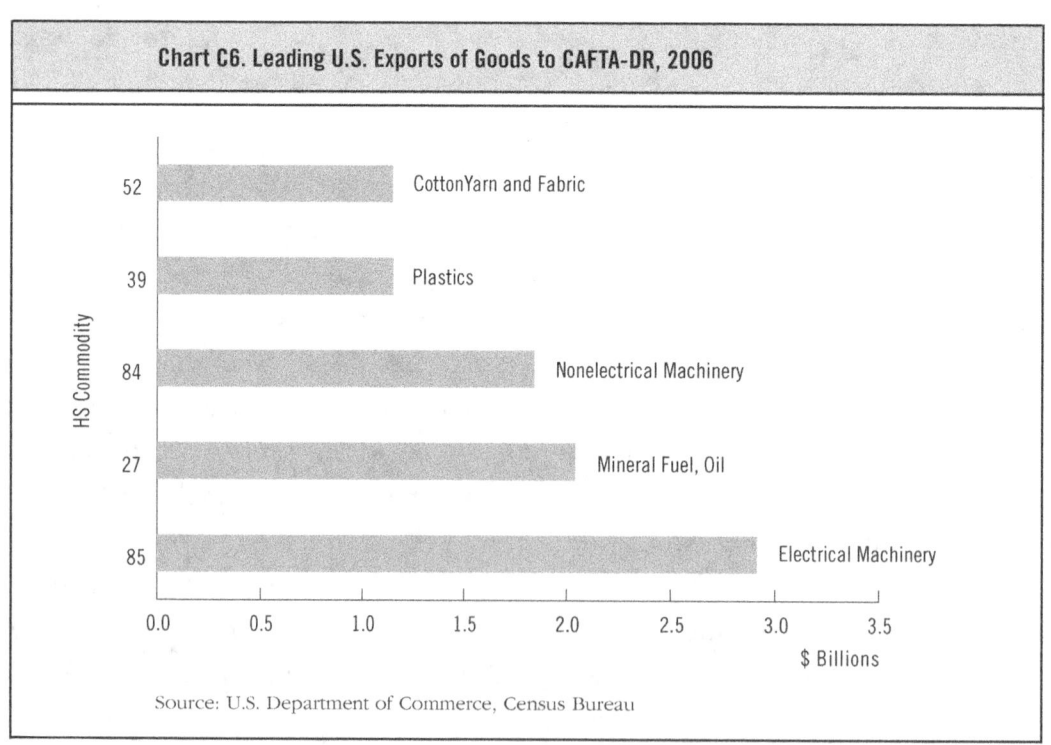

Chart C6. Leading U.S. Exports of Goods to CAFTA-DR, 2006

Source: U.S. Department of Commerce, Census Bureau

The CAFTA–DR levels the playing field for U.S. manufacturers, service providers, farmers, and ranchers that sell to Central America and the Dominican Republic. In 2004, over 80 percent of the CAFTA–DR countries' goods exports to the United States came in duty-free under unilateral U.S. trade preference programs or under zero Most Favored Nation tariffs. The CAFTA–DR opens mutual trade benefits, eliminating tariffs and reducing barriers to U.S. exports. In addition, the FTA eliminates the competitive disadvantage U.S. commercial interests in these countries faced because of the preferential treatment accorded under Central American and Dominican Republic free trade agreements with other countries, including Canada, Mexico, and Chile.

Note: Both charts (*Charts C5* and *C6)* include trade data through 2006 with all countries that signed the CAFTA-DR in 2004.

CAFTA–DR FTA: EL SALVADOR

The CAFTA–DR agreement entered into force between the United States and El Salvador on March 1, 2006. The FTA expands market access opportunities for U.S. companies by about 7 million consumers and approximately $17 billion in GDP (2005). In the last full year prior to entry into force of the FTA (2005), the United States exported $1.9 billion in goods to El Salvador. In 2006, U.S. exports totaled $2.2 billion—a 16.3 percent increase over the previous year. El Salvador's exports to the United States decreased 6.7 percent to $1.9 billion for total trade of $4.1 billion in 2006.

Major accomplishments include:

Tariffs: About 80 percent of U.S. exports of consumer and industrial goods became duty-free into El Salvador immediately, with remaining tariffs phased out over 10 years. Key U.S. export sectors will benefit, such as information technology products, agricultural and construction equipment, paper products, chemicals, and medical and scientific equipment.

Investment: The agreement establishes a more secure and predictable legal framework for U.S. investors operating in El Salvador. All forms of investment are protected under the FTA, including real property, enterprises, debt, concessions, and other similar contracts, and intellectual property. U.S. investors enjoy in most circumstances the right to establish, acquire, and operate investments in

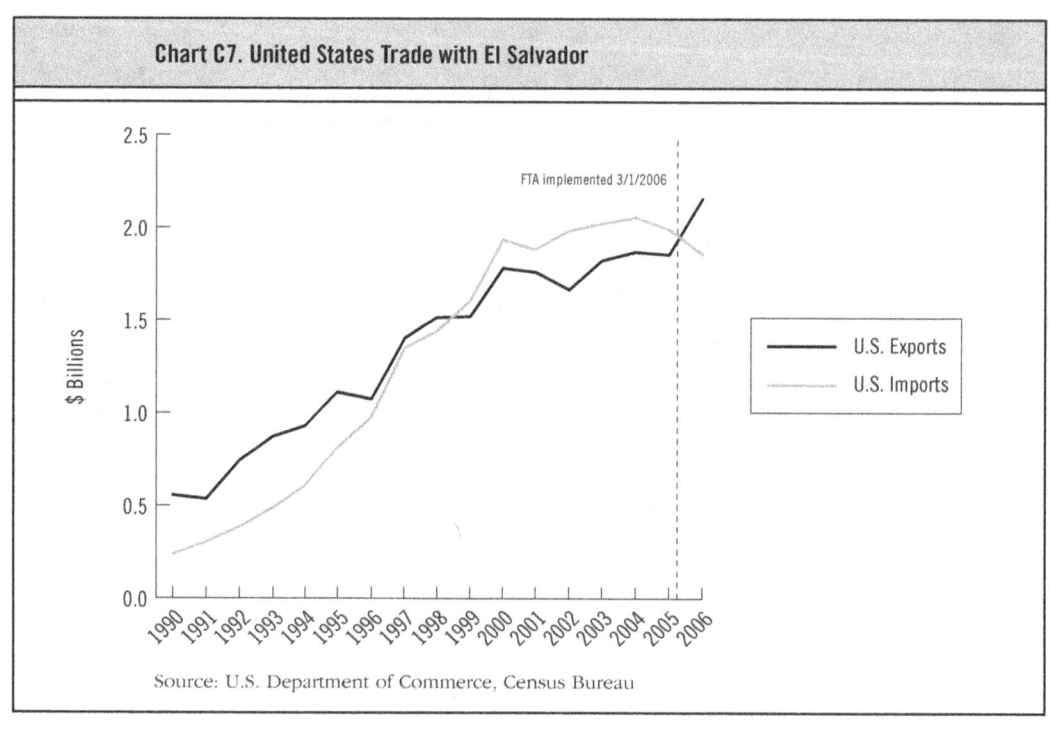

Chart C7. United States Trade with El Salvador

FTA implemented 3/1/2006

$ Billions

— U.S. Exports
— U.S. Imports

Source: U.S. Department of Commerce, Census Bureau

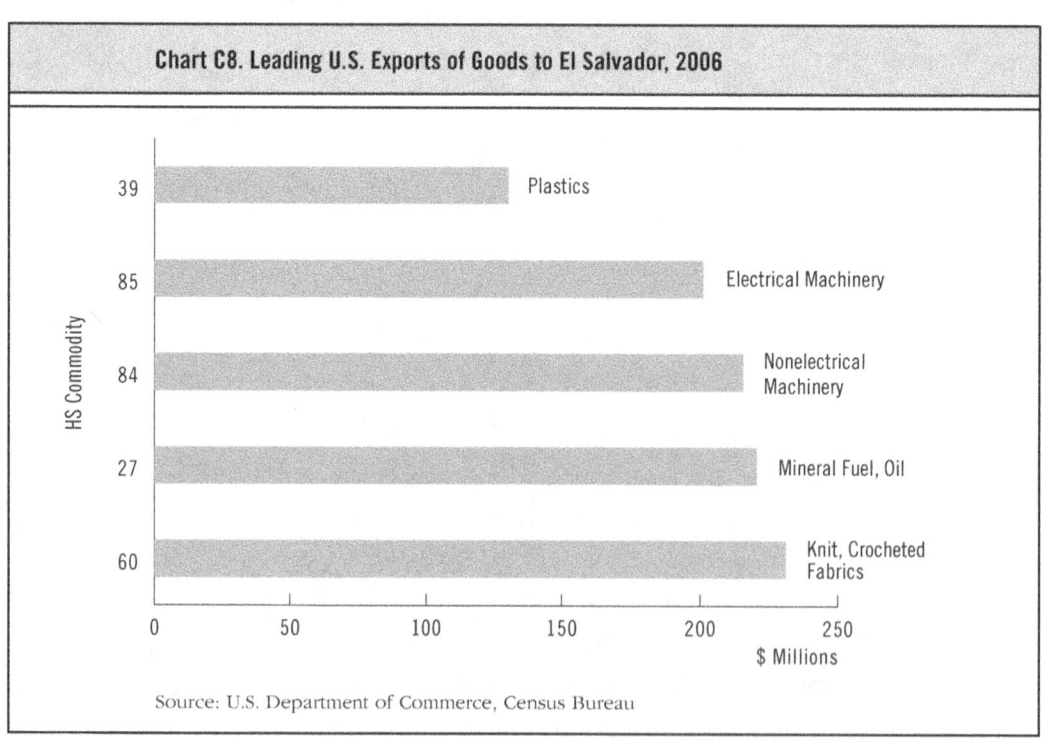

Chart C8. Leading U.S. Exports of Goods to El Salvador, 2006

HS Commodity

39 — Plastics
85 — Electrical Machinery
84 — Nonelectrical Machinery
27 — Mineral Fuel, Oil
60 — Knit, Crocheted Fabrics

$ Millions

Source: U.S. Department of Commerce, Census Bureau

El Salvador on an equal footing with local investors, and with investors of other countries. In the construction sector, for example, the FTA reduces the percentage of Salvadoran ownership required for a construction project.

Services: Under the FTA, El Salvador accords substantial market access across its entire services regime. El Salvador provided no market access commitments in the environmental services sector under the WTO General Agreement on Trade in Services, but allows full market access to that sector under the FTA. This will allow U.S. service suppliers to participate in the growing recycling and solid waste treatment industry in El Salvador.

Intellectual Property Rights: Under the FTA, U.S. producers of creative material and innovative products benefit from higher standards for protecting intellectual property rights such as copyrights, patents, trademarks, and trade secrets and enhanced means for enforcing those rights. In El Salvador, the government has taken significant steps to legitimize and modernize its software systems.

CAFTA-DR FTA: GUATEMALA

The CAFTA-DR agreement entered into force between the United States and Guatemala on July 1, 2006. The FTA expands market access opportunities for U.S. companies by about 13 million consumers and approximately $32 billion in GDP (2005). In the last full year prior to entry into force of the FTA (2005), the United States exported $2.8 billion in goods to Guatemala. In 2006, U.S. exports totaled $3.5 billion—a 24.1 percent increase over the previous year. Guatemala's exports to the United States fell 1.2 percent to 3.1 billion for total trade of $6.6 billion in 2006.

Major accomplishments include:

Tariffs: About 80 percent of U.S. exports of consumer and industrial goods became duty-free into Guatemala immediately, with remaining tariffs phased out over 10 years. Key U.S. export sectors will benefit, such as information technology products, agricultural and construction equipment, paper products, chemicals, and medical and scientific equipment.

Investment: The agreement establishes a more secure and predictable legal framework for U.S. investors operating in Guatemala. All forms of investment are protected under the FTA, including real property, enterprises, debt, concessions,

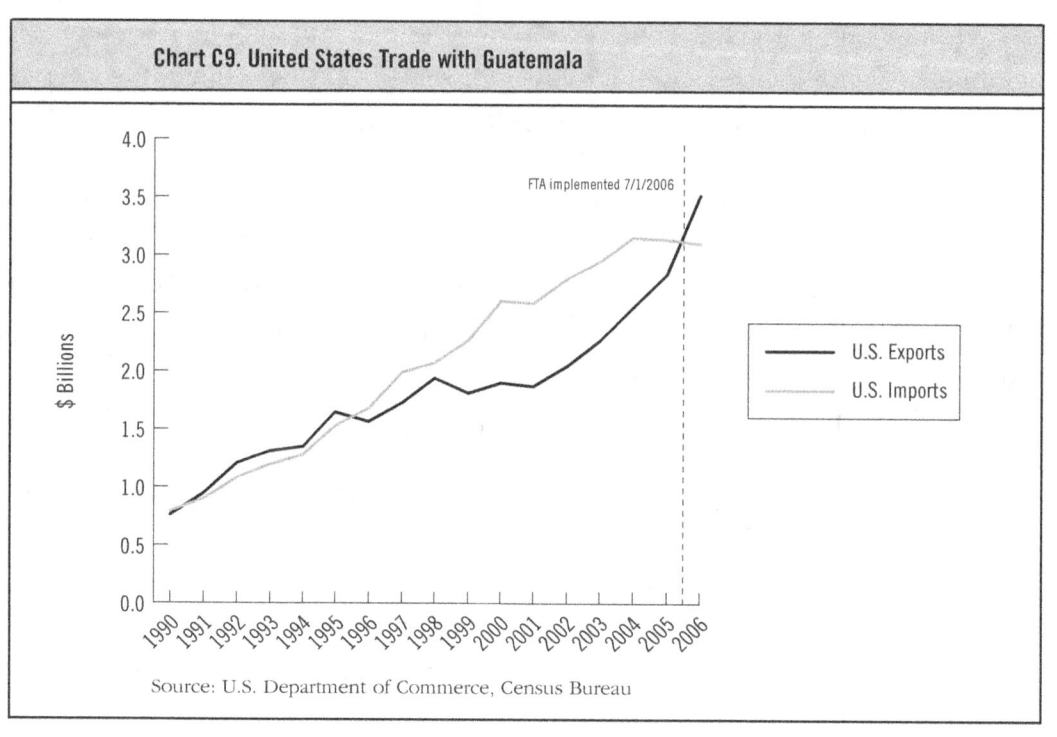

Chart C9. United States Trade with Guatemala

FTA implemented 7/1/2006

U.S. Exports
U.S. Imports

Source: U.S. Department of Commerce, Census Bureau

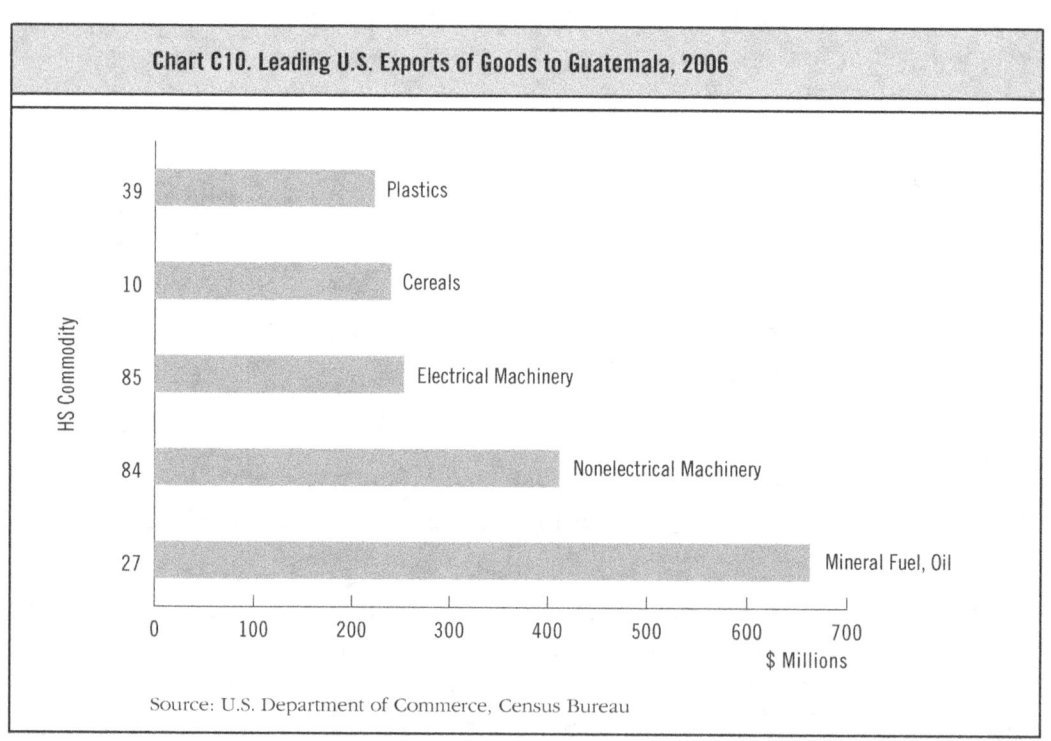

Chart C10. Leading U.S. Exports of Goods to Guatemala, 2006

39 — Plastics
10 — Cereals
85 — Electrical Machinery
84 — Nonelectrical Machinery
27 — Mineral Fuel, Oil

HS Commodity

$ Millions

Source: U.S. Department of Commerce, Census Bureau

and other similar contracts, and intellectual property. U.S. investors enjoy in most circumstances the right to establish, acquire, and operate investments in Guatemala on an equal footing with local investors, and with investors of other countries. In Guatemala, for example, the government has stated that it is looking to private investors to take the lead in expanding the services sector. The investment protections will help foster an environment that will allow U.S. investors to participate in that expansion in virtually all sectors.

Services: Under the FTA, Guatemala accords substantial market access across its entire services regime. In addition, restrictive "dealer protection" regimes are disciplined that have locked U.S. firms into exclusive or inefficient distributor arrangements. The FTA also resulted in the removal of a number of Guatemalan restrictions on U.S. suppliers of construction and engineering services.

Intellectual Property Rights: Under the FTA, U.S. producers of creative material and innovative products benefit from higher standards for protecting intellectual property rights such as copyrights, patents, trademarks, and trade secrets and enhanced means for enforcing those rights. In Guatemala, the Ministry of Economy, which oversees the national IPR registry, committed to catalogue and properly license software in his ministry and will promote similar action by his cabinet colleagues.

CAFTA-DR FTA: HONDURAS

The CAFTA–DR agreement entered into force between the United States and Honduras on April 1, 2006. The FTA expands market access opportunities for U.S. companies in Honduras by over 7 million consumers and approximately $8 billion in GDP (2005). In the last full year prior to entry into force (2005), the United States exported $3.3 billion in goods to Honduras. In 2006, U.S. exports totaled $3.7 billion—a 13.5 percent increase over the prior year. Honduran exports to the United States decreased 0.8 percent to $3.7 billion for total trade of 7.4 billion in 2006.

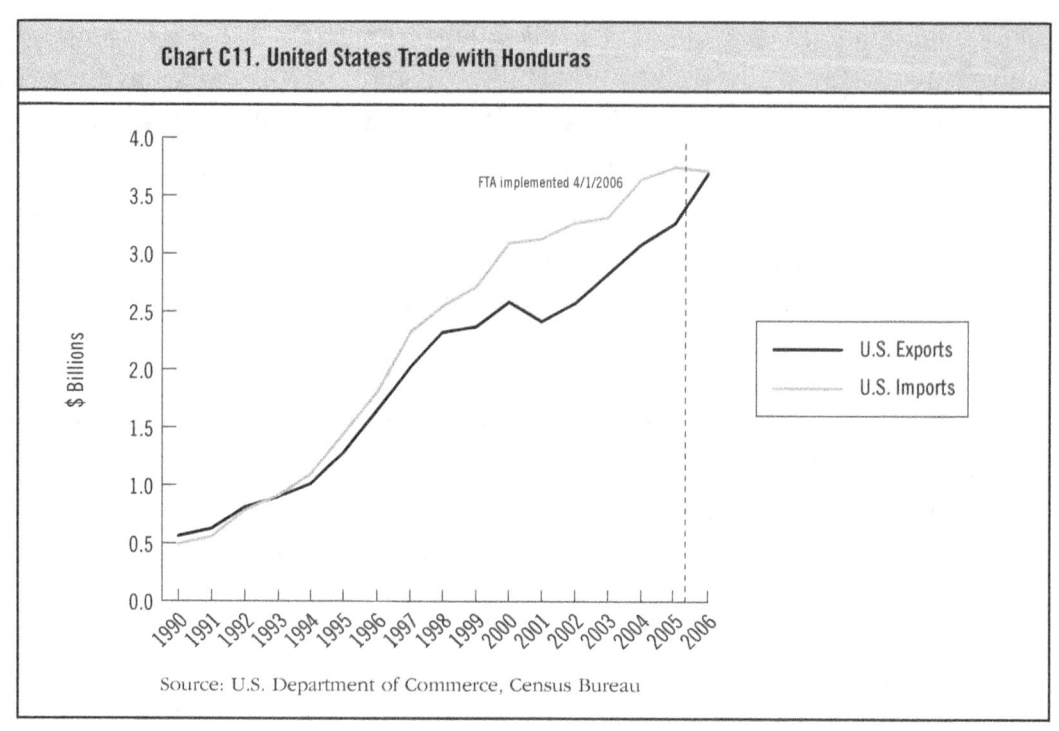

Chart C11. United States Trade with Honduras

FTA implemented 4/1/2006

U.S. Exports
U.S. Imports

Source: U.S. Department of Commerce, Census Bureau

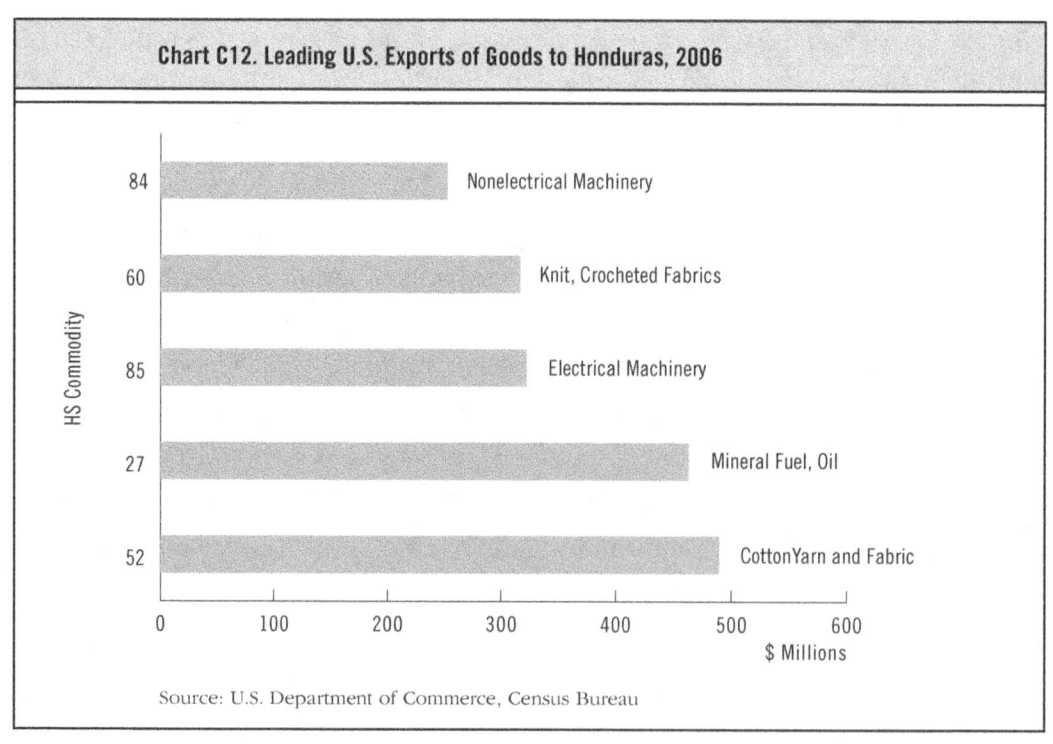

Chart C12. Leading U.S. Exports of Goods to Honduras, 2006

HS Commodity	
84	Nonelectrical Machinery
60	Knit, Crocheted Fabrics
85	Electrical Machinery
27	Mineral Fuel, Oil
52	Cotton Yarn and Fabric

$ Millions

Source: U.S. Department of Commerce, Census Bureau

Major accomplishments include:

Tariffs: About 80 percent of U.S. exports of consumer and industrial goods became duty-free into Honduras immediately, with remaining tariffs phased out over 10 years. Key U.S. export sectors will benefit, such as information technology products, agricultural and construction equipment, paper products, chemicals, and medical and scientific equipment.

Investment: The agreement builds upon the existing bilateral investment treaty in establishing a more secure and predictable legal framework for U.S. investors operating in Honduras. All forms of investment are protected under the FTA, including real property, enterprises, debt, concessions, and other similar contracts, and intellectual property. U.S. investors enjoy in most circumstances the right to establish, acquire, and operate investments in Honduras on an equal footing with local investors, and with investors of other countries.

Services: Under the FTA, Honduras accords substantial market access across its entire services regime. In addition, restrictive "dealer protection" regimes are disciplined that have locked U.S. firms into exclusive or inefficient distributor arrangements. Under the 1997 GATS Financial Services Agreement, Honduras made no commitments in asset management. However, the FTA provides legal certainty that U.S. asset management firms will be afforded national treatment, non-discrimination, and the right of establishment in Honduras.

Intellectual Property Rights: Under the FTA, U.S. producers of creative material and innovative products benefit from higher standards for protecting intellectual property rights such as copyrights, patents, trademarks, and trade secrets and enhanced means for enforcing those rights. In anticipation of the FTA, Honduras introduced legislation to provide patent protection for plant varieties and the design of integrated circuits.

CAFTA–DR FTA: NICARAGUA

The CAFTA–DR agreement entered into force between the United States and Nicaragua on April 1, 2006. The FTA expands market access opportunities for U.S. companies in Nicaragua by about 6 million consumers and approximately $5 billion in GDP (2005). In the last full year prior to entry into force (2005), the

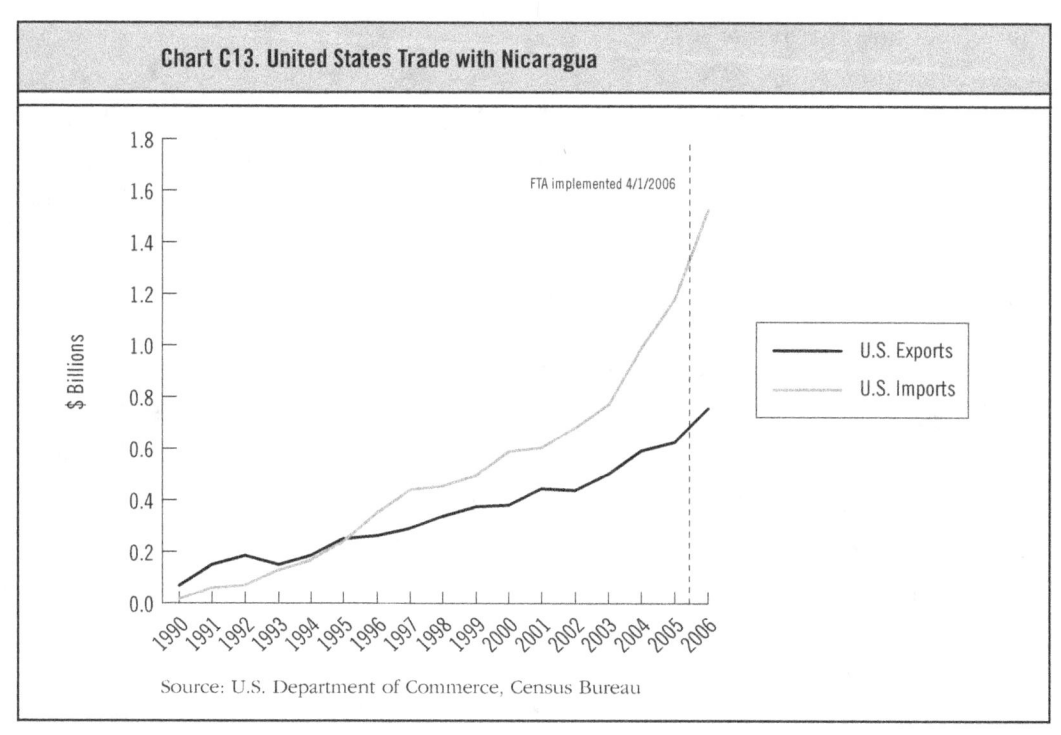

Chart C13. United States Trade with Nicaragua

FTA implemented 4/1/2006

U.S. Exports
U.S. Imports

Source: U.S. Department of Commerce, Census Bureau

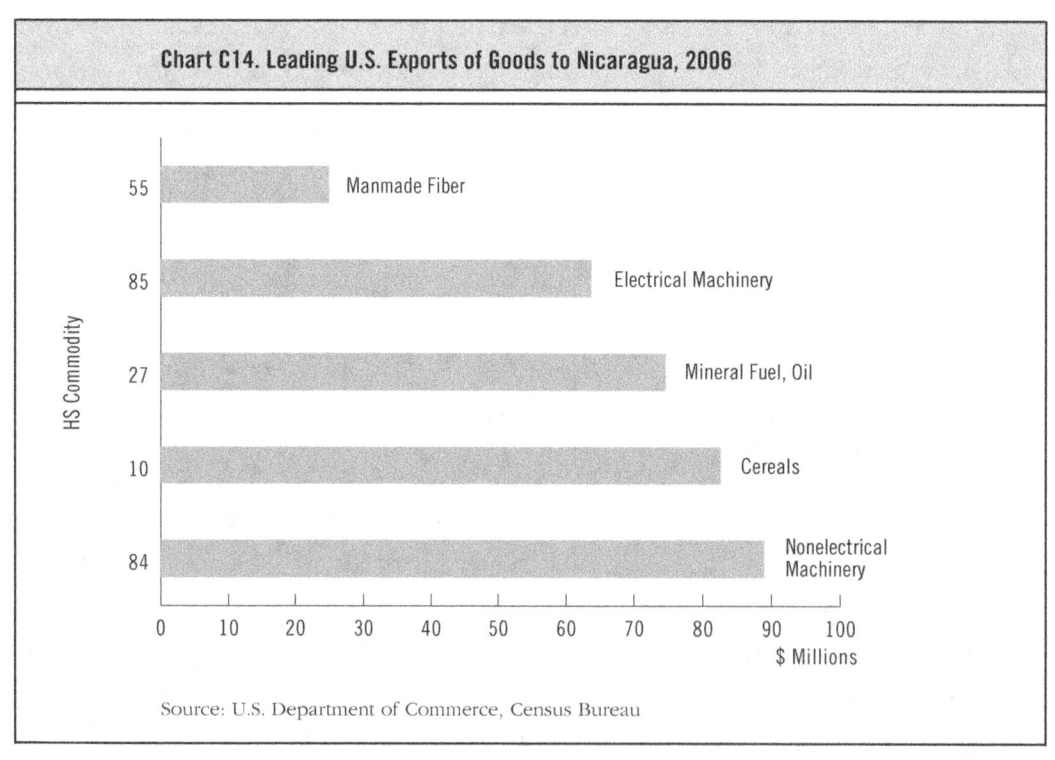

Chart C14. Leading U.S. Exports of Goods to Nicaragua, 2006

55 — Manmade Fiber
85 — Electrical Machinery
27 — Mineral Fuel, Oil
10 — Cereals
84 — Nonelectrical Machinery

Source: U.S. Department of Commerce, Census Bureau

United States exported $625 million in goods to Nicaragua. In 2006, U.S. exports totaled $755 million—a 20.8 percent increase over the prior year. Nicaragua's exports to the United States increased 29.2 percent to $1.526 billion for total trade of $2.3 billion in 2006.

Major accomplishments include:

Tariffs: About 80 percent of U.S. exports of consumer and industrial goods became duty-free into Nicaragua immediately, with remaining tariffs phased out over 10 years. Key U.S. export sectors will benefit, such as information technology products, agricultural and construction equipment, paper products, chemicals, and medical and scientific equipment.

Investment: The agreement establishes a more secure and predictable legal framework for U.S. investors operating in Nicaragua. All forms of investment are protected under the FTA, including real property, enterprises, debt, concessions, and other similar contracts, and intellectual property. U.S. investors enjoy in most circumstances the right to establish, acquire, and operate investments in Nicaragua on an equal footing with local investors, and with investors of other countries. As a result of the FTA, Nicaragua reports at least $235 million in new investments.

Services: Under the FTA, Nicaragua accords substantial market access across its entire services regime,. In addition, restrictive "dealer protection" regimes are disciplined that have locked U.S. firms into exclusive or inefficient distributor arrangements. Under the FTA, Nicaragua committed to completely opening its market for advertising, a significant improvement over its WTO General Agreement on Trade in Services schedule, where no market access was guaranteed.

Intellectual Property Rights: Under the FTA, U.S. producers of creative material and innovative products benefit from higher standards for protecting intellectual property rights such as copyrights, patents, trademarks, and trade secrets and enhanced means for enforcing those rights. Just six months after Nicaragua adopted stronger intellectual property laws in preparation for entry into force of the FTA, Nicaraguan prosecutors scored a major victory with the country's first intellectual property conviction.

The United States–Chile FTA was signed on June 6, 2003, and entered into force January 1, 2004. The FTA leveled the playing field for U.S. businesses and increased choice and value for American consumers.

The successful conclusion of the U.S.–Chile FTA expands market access opportunities for U.S. companies by over 16 million consumers and $115.3 billion in GDP (2005). In the year prior to entry into force of the FTA (2003), the United States exported $2.7 billion in goods to Chile. By 2006, annual exports had increased to $6.8 billion—a 152 percent increase. Chile's exports to the U.S. increased to $9.6 billion in 2006 for total trade of $16.4 billion. Services exports from the United States also increased by 24 percent to $1.35 billion in 2005 (latest available).

Major accomplishments include:

Tariffs: More than 85 percent of bilateral trade in consumer and industrial products became tariff-free immediately, with most remaining tariffs eliminated within four years. Key U.S. export sectors benefit, such as agricultural

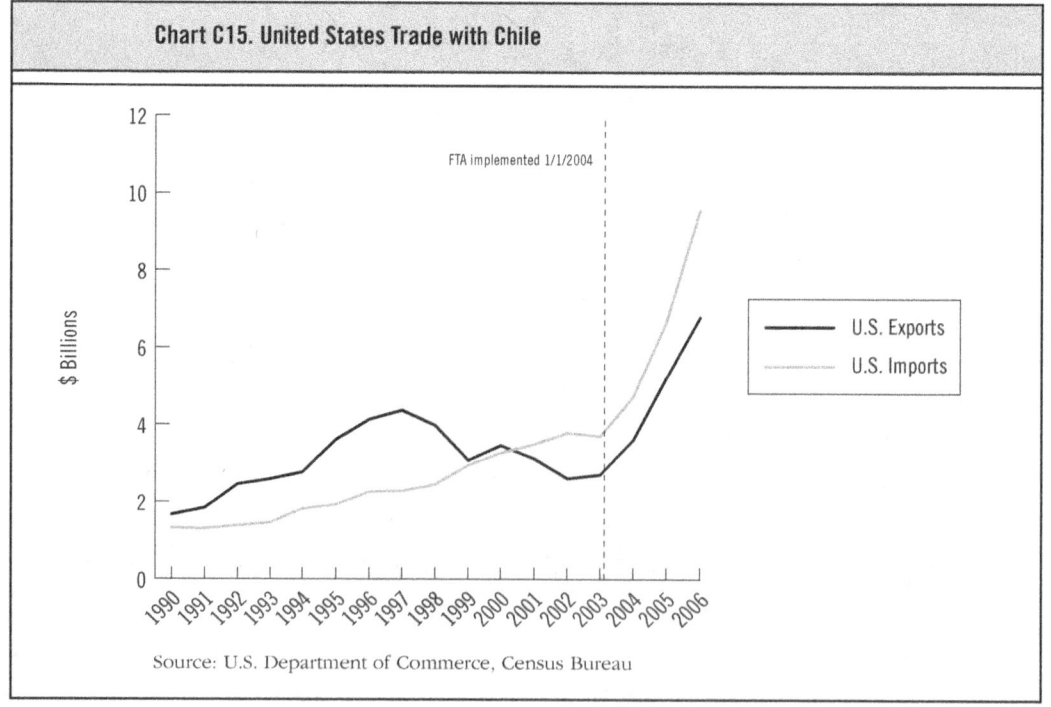

Chart C15. United States Trade with Chile

FTA implemented 1/1/2004

U.S. Exports
U.S. Imports

Source: U.S. Department of Commerce, Census Bureau

and construction equipment, autos and auto parts, computers and other information technology products, medical equipment, and paper products. For example, U.S. exports of automotive parts to Chile increased from $103 million in 2003 to $207 million in 2006, an increase of 100 percent.

Services: The agreement also offers new access for U.S. banks, insurance companies, telecommunications companies, securities firms, express delivery companies, and professionals. U.S. firms may now offer financial services to participants in Chile's highly successful privatized pension system.

Government Procurement: U.S. firms are guaranteed a fair and transparent process to sell goods and services to a wide range of Chilean government entities. A Government of Chile procurement Web site (*www.chilecompra.cl*) was established to increase transparency, enhance opportunities, and reduce government procurement costs. The site serves as a central source for all Chilean government procurement.

Non-Tariff Barriers: The U.S.–Chile FTA included an agreement to eliminate Chile's 85 percent luxury tax on imported autos valued at more than $15,835.

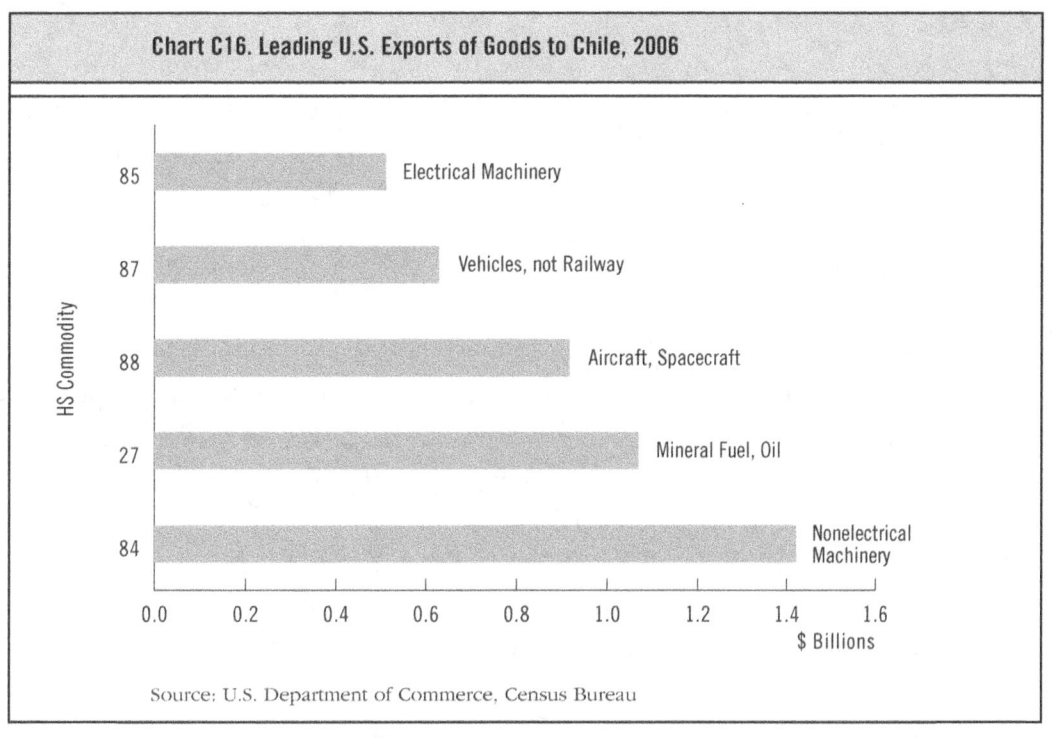

Chart C16. Leading U.S. Exports of Goods to Chile, 2006

Source: U.S. Department of Commerce, Census Bureau

Under the terms of the FTA, this luxury tax was reduced by 25 percent annually over a four-year period. In tandem with the annual tax reduction, the threshold value at which the tax was imposed on imported autos increased annually by $2,500 over the four-year period. As of January 1, 2007, the four-year period has ended and the auto luxury tax is completely phased out.

UNITED STATES–ISRAEL FTA

The United States–Israel FTA took effect September 1, 1985. The FTA eliminated duties in manufactured goods as of January 1, 1995. It also allowed the United States and Israel to protect sensitive agricultural sub-sectors with non-tariff barriers, including import bans, quotas, and fees. An agriculture agreement was signed in 2004. The United States–Israel FTA differs from modern U.S. FTAs because it has detailed obligations only on merchandise trade. The FTAs the United States signs today include detailed obligations on issues including agriculture, services, investment, intellectual property rights, standards, transparency, and the rule of law.

The successful conclusion of the United States–Israel FTA expands market access opportunities for U.S. companies by 7 million consumers and $127 billion in GDP (2005). In the year prior to entry into force of the FTA (1984), the United States exported $1.8 billion in goods to Israel. By 2006, exports had grown to $11 billion. Israel's exports to the United States increased to $19.1 billion in 2006 for total trade of $30.1 billion. U.S. services exports to Israel totaled $2.7 billion, while Israel services exports to the U.S. totaled $2.4 billion in 2005 (latest available).

Major accomplishments include:

Tariffs: Over a 10-year period ending January 1, 1995, the FTA eliminated nearly all customs duties between the countries, except for those on certain agricultural products. It also eliminated virtually all other restrictions on trade in goods for those products meeting the rule of origin and certification requirements.

Other Issues: The United States-Israel FTA also contained provisions on government procurement, trade-related performance requirements, services, import licensing, and intellectual property. However, for the most part, the subsequent WTO Uruguay Round Agreements have effectively supplanted those commitments with stronger, more detailed obligations.

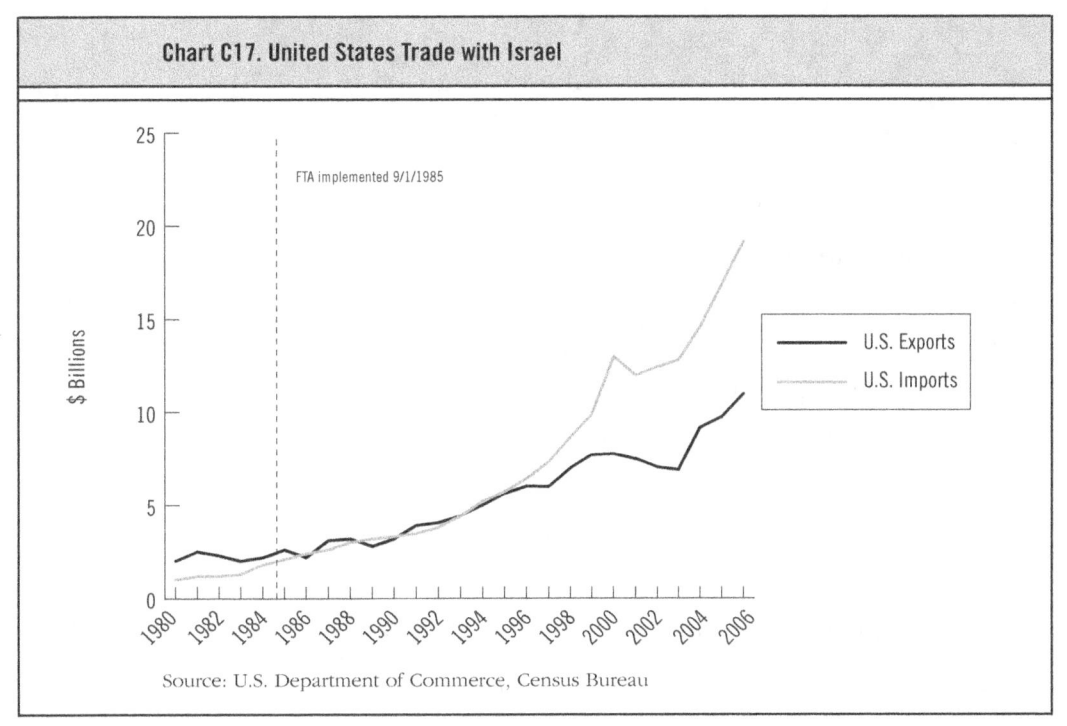

Chart C17. United States Trade with Israel

FTA implemented 9/1/1985

$ Billions

— U.S. Exports
— U.S. Imports

Source: U.S. Department of Commerce, Census Bureau

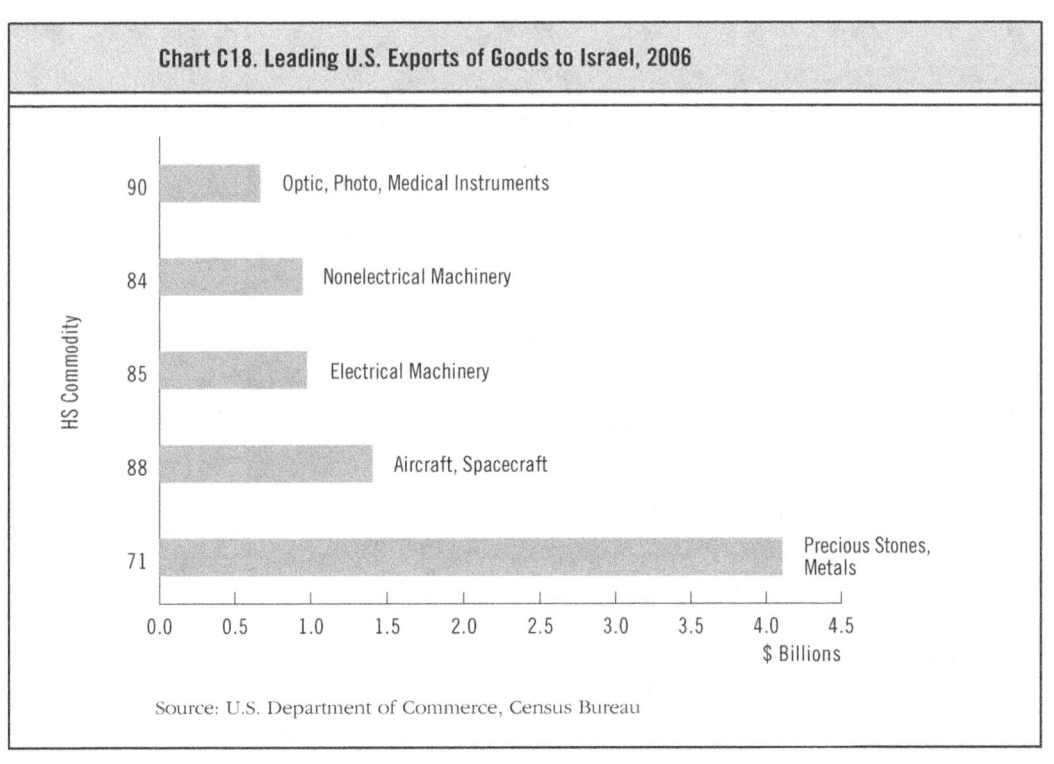

Chart C18. Leading U.S. Exports of Goods to Israel, 2006

HS Commodity

90 — Optic, Photo, Medical Instruments
84 — Nonelectrical Machinery
85 — Electrical Machinery
88 — Aircraft, Spacecraft
71 — Precious Stones, Metals

$ Billions

Source: U.S. Department of Commerce, Census Bureau

The United States–Jordan FTA was signed on October 24, 2000, and entered into force on December 17, 2001.

The successful conclusion of the United States–Jordan FTA expands market access opportunities for U.S. companies by 5.4 million consumers and $11.3 billion in GDP (2005). During 2001, the United States exported $339 million in goods to Jordan. By 2006, exports had increased to $650 million—for 92 percent growth since implementation. Jordan's exports to the U.S. increased to $1.4 billion in 2006 for total trade of $2.1 billion.

Major accomplishments include:

Services: The FTA opened up trade in services, giving American service providers excellent opportunities in Jordan's financial, education, audio-visual, courier, and other services.

E-commerce: For the first time in a free trade agreement, Jordan and the United States each committed to promoting free trade in electronic commerce. Both countries agreed to avoid imposing customs duties on electronic transmissions, imposing unnecessary barriers to market access for digital products, and impeding the ability to electronically deliver services.

Environment: Since the entry into force of the United States–Jordan FTA in December 2001, Jordan has made major strides in strengthening environmental protection, attributing their success in part to the FTA and the resulting Environmental Cooperation efforts. The Ministry of Environment was created as a standalone department in 2003. The new Ministry has reorganized to strengthen environmental enforcement and outreach, and Jordan's Parliament passed a permanent environmental law only days before the FTA Joint Committee meeting. This law institutionalized the Ministry's role as a regulator and gave it new enforcement and compliance tools. The Minister especially credits the Environmental Protection Agency's help through the Embassy Science Fellows Program on addressing particular environmental problems, such as the Al-Ekeder Waste Disposal site, and the Russeifa Landfill. He has also complimented the U.S. Agency for International Development's work on wastewater re-use and treatment, and on the manifest system to track solid and liquid waste.

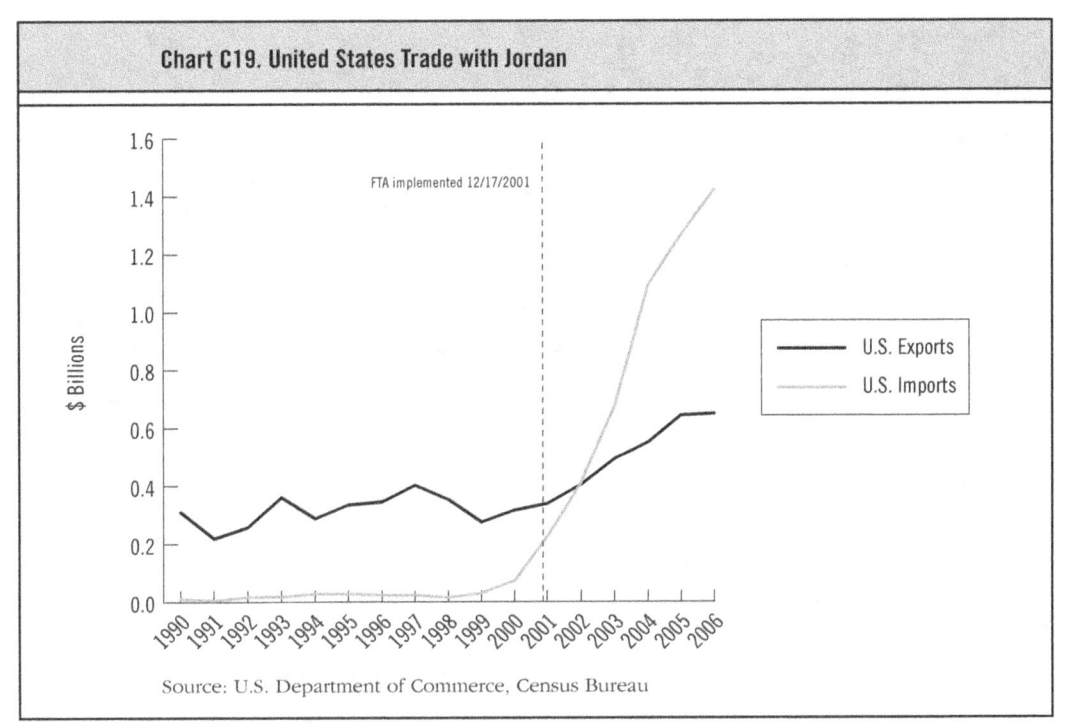

Chart C19. United States Trade with Jordan

FTA implemented 12/17/2001

U.S. Exports
U.S. Imports

Source: U.S. Department of Commerce, Census Bureau

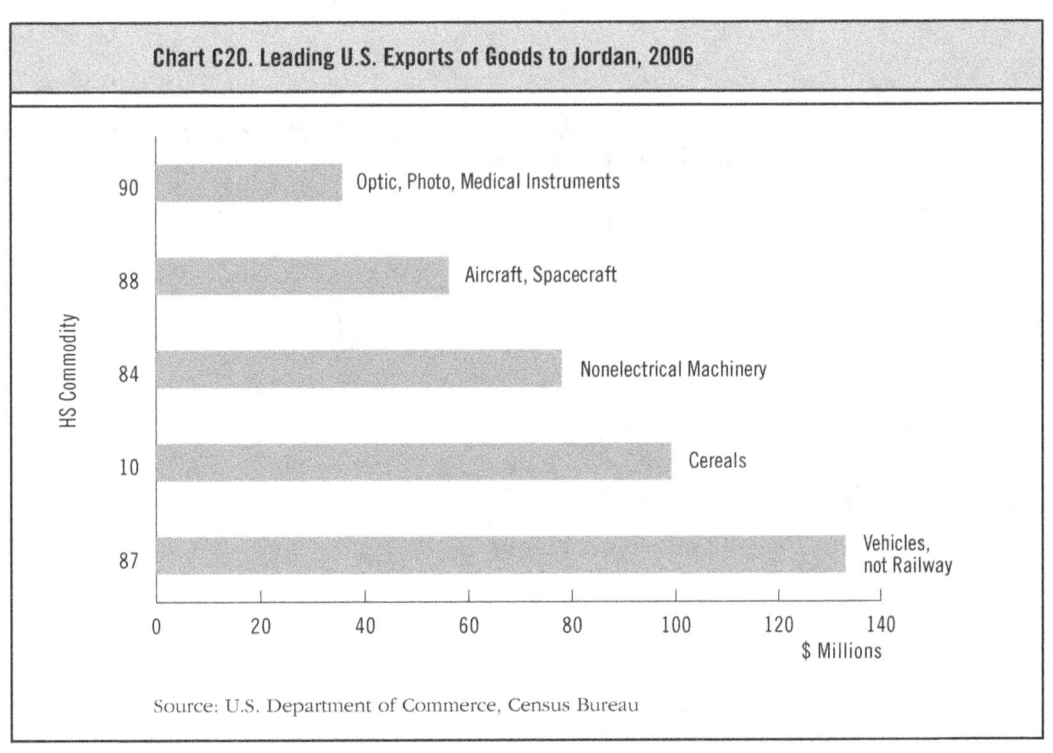

Chart C20. Leading U.S. Exports of Goods to Jordan, 2006

90 — Optic, Photo, Medical Instruments
88 — Aircraft, Spacecraft
84 — Nonelectrical Machinery
10 — Cereals
87 — Vehicles, not Railway

HS Commodity

$ Millions

Source: U.S. Department of Commerce, Census Bureau

The United States–Morocco FTA was signed on June 15, 2004, and entered into force January 1, 2006.

The successful conclusion of the United States–Morocco FTA expands market access opportunities for U.S. companies by over 30 million consumers and $52 billion in GDP (2005). In the year prior to entry into force of the FTA (2005), the United States exported $525 million in goods to Morocco. In 2006, exports increased to over $876 million—for 67 percent growth since implementation. Morocco exports to the U.S. increased to over $521 million in 2006 for total trade of more than $1.4 billion.

Major accomplishments include:

Tariffs: The agreement, which covers all agricultural products, opens Morocco's market for many U.S. farm products. More than 95 percent of bilateral trade in consumer and industrial products became duty-free immediately upon entry into force of the agreement, with all remaining tariffs to be eliminated within nine years. Textiles and apparel trade will be duty-free if imports meet the agreement's

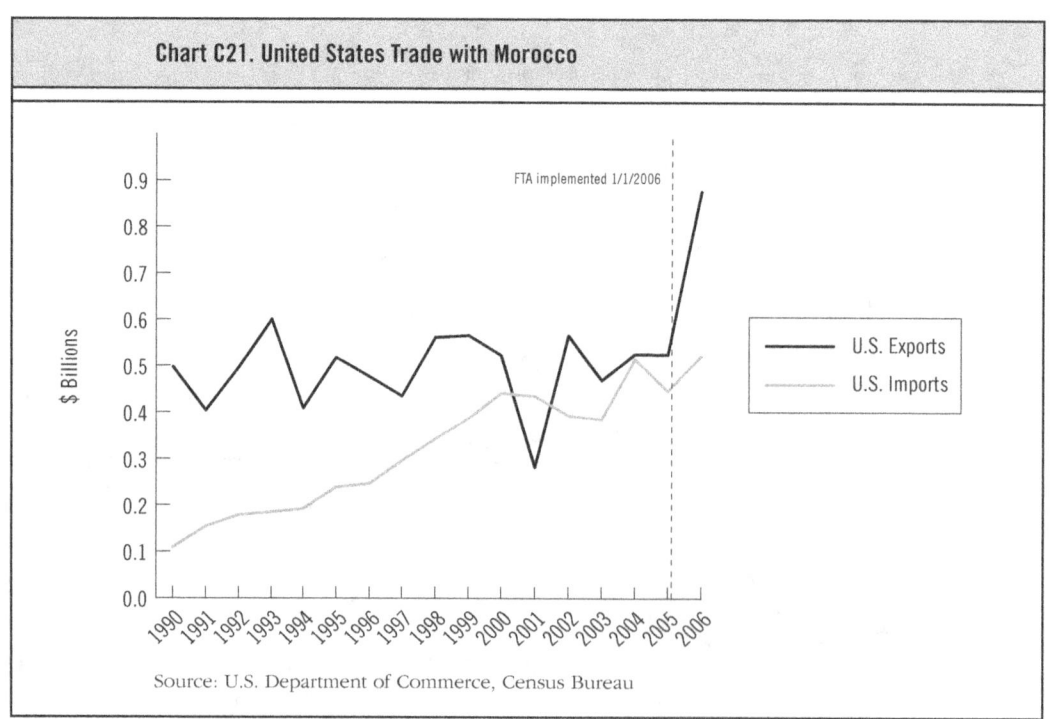

Chart C21. United States Trade with Morocco

FTA implemented 1/1/2006

U.S. Exports
U.S. Imports

Source: U.S. Department of Commerce, Census Bureau

rule of origin requirements, promoting new opportunities for U.S. and Moroccan fiber, yarn, fabric, and apparel manufacturing. The agreement requires qualifying apparel to contain either U.S. or Moroccan yarn and fabric and contains a temporary 30 million square meter allowance for apparel containing third country content (equals 0.2 percent of imports into the United States).

Labor: The prospect of an FTA with the United States helped to forge a domestic consensus for labor law reform in Morocco, spurring reform efforts that had been stymied for more than 20 years. A comprehensive new labor law went into effect on June 8, 2004. The new Moroccan labor law is a significant improvement addressing child labor, work hours and minimum wage, worker health and safety, and gender and disabilities. It also guarantees the rights of association and collective bargaining. In addition, Morocco has ratified seven of the eight International Labor Organization core conventions, and is currently considering ratification of the final one.

Intellectual Property Rights: Under the FTA, U.S. producers of creative material and innovative products benefit from higher standards for protecting intellectual property rights such as copyrights, patents, trademarks, and trade secrets and enhanced

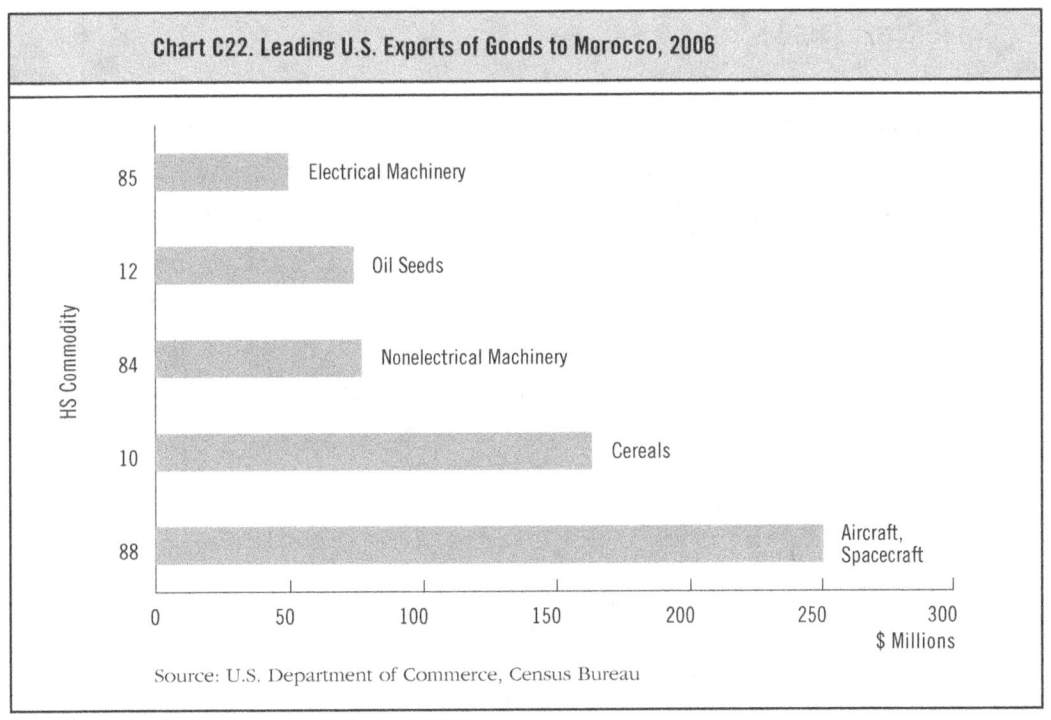

Chart C22. Leading U.S. Exports of Goods to Morocco, 2006

Source: U.S. Department of Commerce, Census Bureau

means for enforcing those rights. As part of their FTA implementation, Morocco adopted a new Industrial Property Law, which introduces an electronic trademark application system permitting trademark applications to be filed online. It also introduces the opposition system of trademarks in Morocco, creating an opportunity for third parties to challenge a trademark application. In addition, the law improved enforcement of negotiated intellectual property rights, strengthening border measures and simplifying the process of seizing counterfeit goods. The law also represents the first time Morocco recognized the registrability of sound and scent marks.

Government Procurement: The agreement includes disciplines on the purchases of most Moroccan central government agencies, as well as the vast majority of Moroccan regional and municipal governments. It requires that covered Moroccan government purchasers not discriminate against U.S. firms, or in favor of Moroccan firms, when making covered government purchases in excess of agreed monetary thresholds.

NORTH AMERICAN FREE TRADE AGREEMENT (NAFTA)

The United States, Canada, and Mexico entered into FTA negotiations in May of 1991 to eliminate trade barriers, facilitate cross-border movement of goods and services, increase investment opportunities, promote fair competition, and enforce intellectual property rights in each party's territory. The resulting North American Free Trade Agreement (NAFTA) was signed on December 17, 1992, and entered into force on January 1, 1994. With entry into force of the NAFTA, the United States–Canada FTA was suspended. The successful conclusion of the NAFTA expanded market access opportunities for U.S. companies.

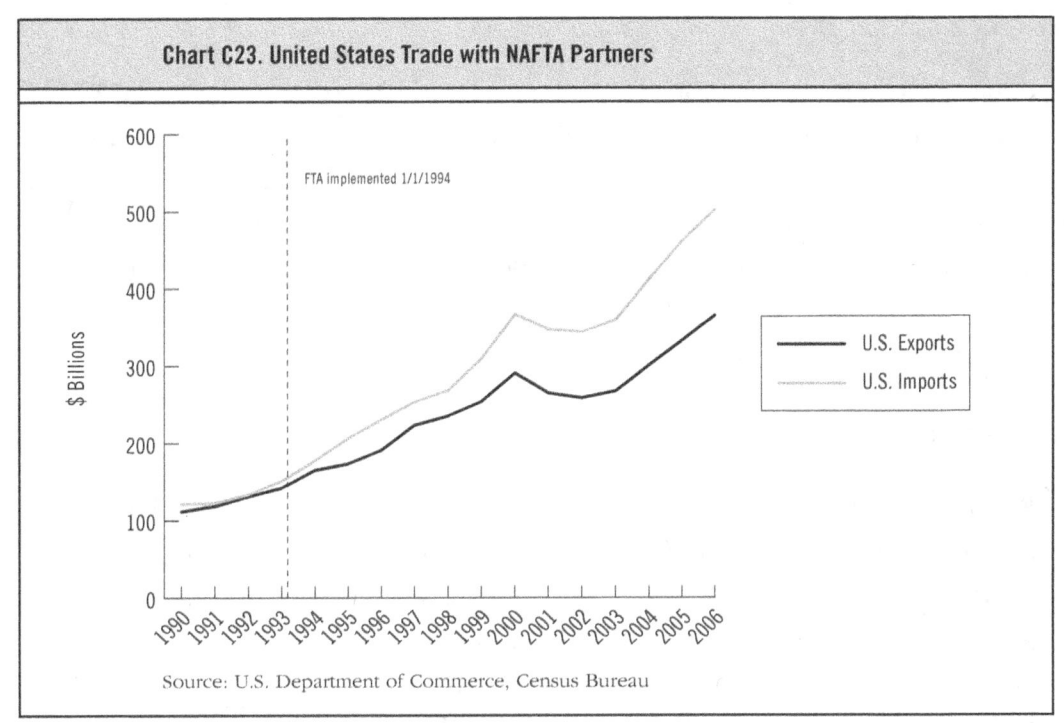

Chart C23. United States Trade with NAFTA Partners

FTA implemented 1/1/1994

$ Billions

— U.S. Exports
···· U.S. Imports

Source: U.S. Department of Commerce, Census Bureau

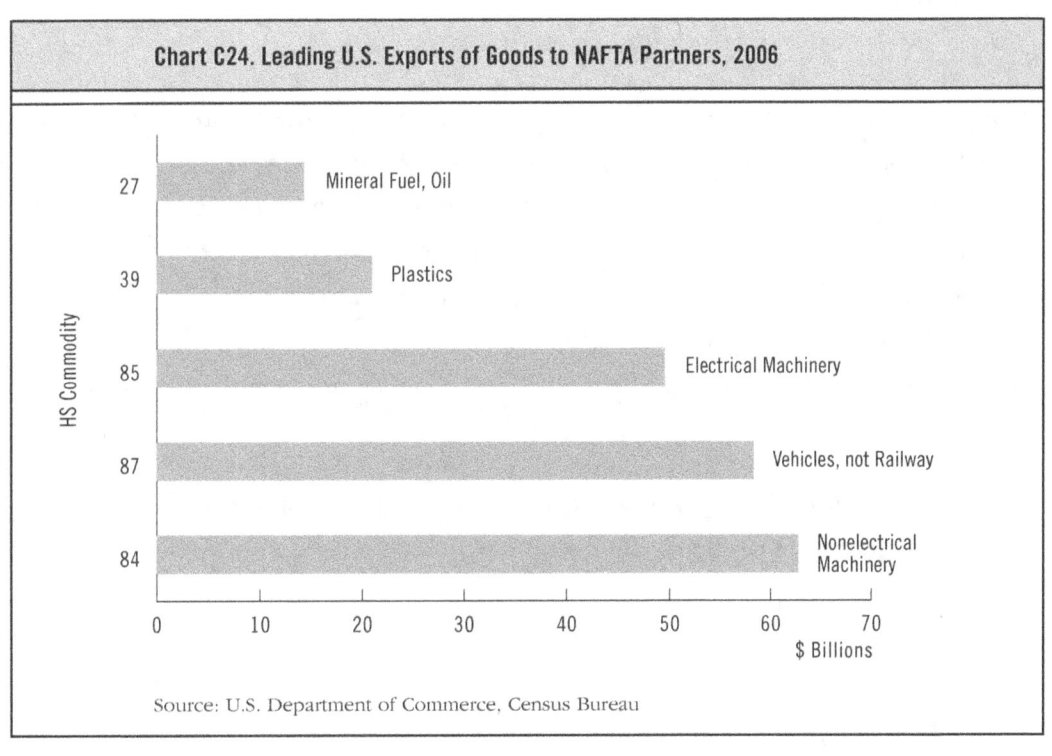

Chart C24. Leading U.S. Exports of Goods to NAFTA Partners, 2006

HS Commodity

27 — Mineral Fuel, Oil
39 — Plastics
85 — Electrical Machinery
87 — Vehicles, not Railway
84 — Nonelectrical Machinery

$ Billions

Source: U.S. Department of Commerce, Census Bureau

Canada has a population of over 32 million people and a GDP of $1.12 trillion (2005). In 1993, the United States exported $100.2 billion in goods to Canada. In the 13 years since the entry into force of the NAFTA, U.S. exports increased to $230.3 billion in 2006—a 130 percent increase. Canada's exports to the United States increased to $303.4 billion in 2006. Total trade in goods between the United States and Canada reached $534 billion in 2006. Services exports to Canada increased by 91 percent to $32.5 billion in 2005 (latest available).

Major accomplishments include:

Services: The United States–Canada Free Trade Agreement established the first comprehensive set of principles governing services trade. The NAFTA broadened these protections. Virtually all services are covered by the NAFTA with the exception of aviation transport, maritime, and basic telecommunications.

Investment: The agreement establishes a more secure and predictable legal framework for U.S. investors operating in Canada and Mexico. All forms of investment are protected under the NAFTA, including real property, enterprises, debt, concessions, and intellectual property.

Government Procurement: The government procurement provisions of the NAFTA apply to a wide range of goods and services, creating opportunities in construction, environmental and computer software and design services, oil and gas field equipment and services, heavy electrical equipment, communications and computer systems, electronics, pharmaceutical products, and medical equipment. U.S. companies have access to all significant procuring entities in the Canadian Government, including state-owned enterprises such as the Canada Post Corporation.

Tariff Reduction: With the exception of tariff rate quotas on certain supply-managed agricultural products, all Canada–U.S. trade has been duty free since 1998.

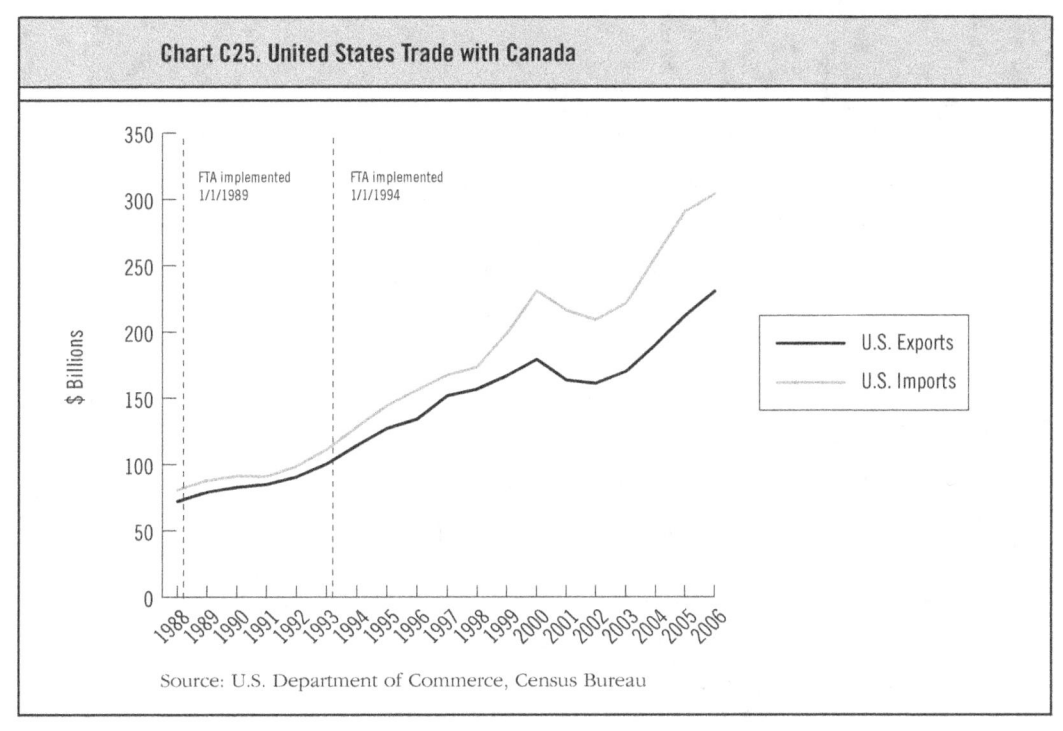

Chart C25. United States Trade with Canada

FTA implemented
1/1/1989

FTA implemented
1/1/1994

U.S. Exports
U.S. Imports

Source: U.S. Department of Commerce, Census Bureau

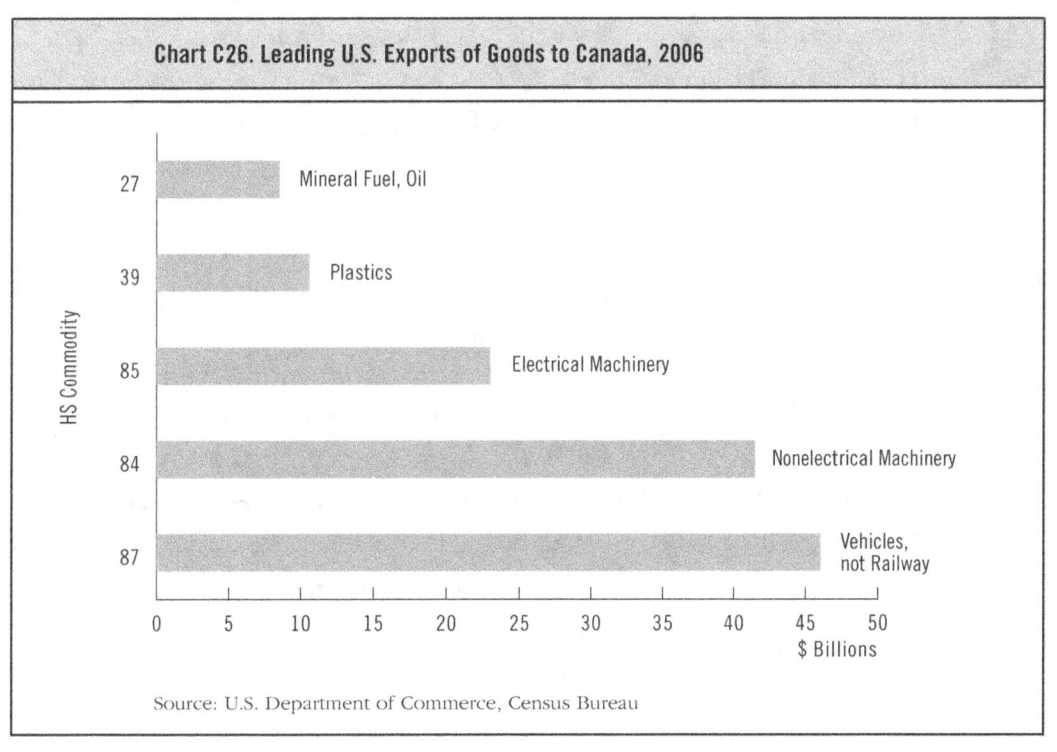

Chart C26. Leading U.S. Exports of Goods to Canada, 2006

27 Mineral Fuel, Oil

39 Plastics

85 Electrical Machinery

84 Nonelectrical Machinery

87 Vehicles, not Railway

HS Commodity

$ Billions

Source: U.S. Department of Commerce, Census Bureau

The North American Free Trade Agreement entered into force on January 1, 1994. Mexico has a population of over 103 million people and a GDP of $768 billion (2005). In 1993, the United States exported $41.6 billion in goods to Mexico. In the 13 years since the entry into force of the NAFTA, exports increased to $134.2 billion in 2006—a 223 percent increase. Mexico's exports to the United States increased to $198.3 billion in 2006. Total bilateral trade in goods reached $332.4 billion in 2006.

Major accomplishments include:

Tariff Reduction: Upon the NAFTA's entry into force on January 1, 1994, Mexico eliminated tariffs on nearly 50 percent of all industrial goods imported from the United States and removed many non-tariff barriers. All tariffs on industrial goods were eliminated by 2004. Tariffs on U.S. exports to Mexico of certain agricultural products will be phased out by 2009.

Investment: The NAFTA ensures that U.S. investments and investors will receive treatment equal to domestic investments and investors in Mexico. It also provides for prompt, adequate, and effective compensation for property expropriated for a public purpose and free transfers, into and out of a host country, of capital relating to an investment. The NAFTA gives investors access to binding international arbitration of claims that a Party has breached an obligation of the investment chapter in a manner that has damaged an investment or an investor.

Services: Virtually all services are covered by the NAFTA with the exception of aviation transport, maritime, and basic telecommunications.

Government Procurement: The government procurement provisions of the NAFTA apply to a wide range of goods and services, creating opportunities in construction, environmental and computer software and design services, oil and gas field equipment and services, heavy electrical equipment, communications and computer systems, electronics, pharmaceutical products, and medical equipment. U.S. companies have access to all significant procuring entities in the Mexican Government, including state-owned enterprises such as Mexico's oil company, PEMEX.

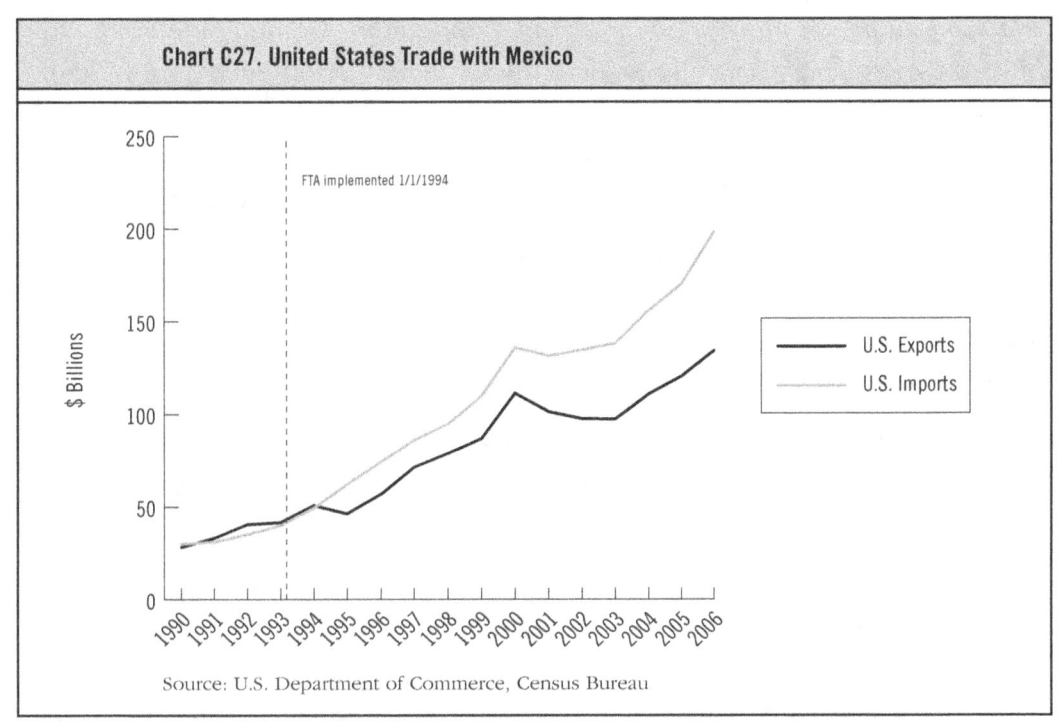

Chart C27. United States Trade with Mexico

FTA implemented 1/1/1994

U.S. Exports
U.S. Imports

Source: U.S. Department of Commerce, Census Bureau

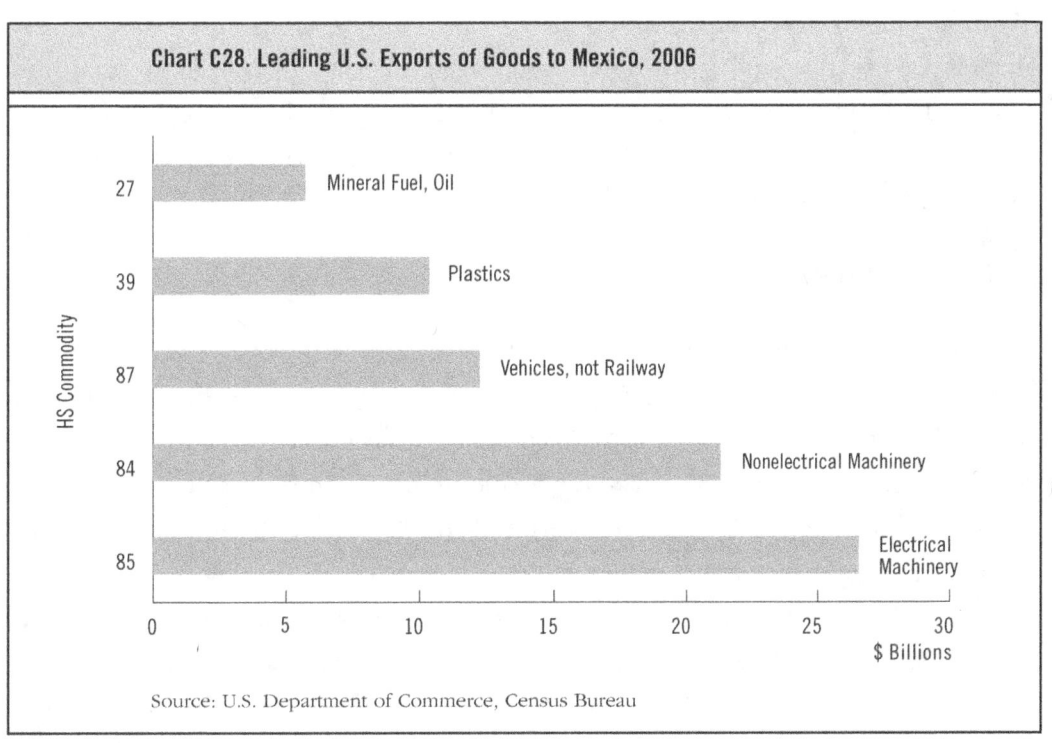

Chart C28. Leading U.S. Exports of Goods to Mexico, 2006

HS Commodity	
27	Mineral Fuel, Oil
39	Plastics
87	Vehicles, not Railway
84	Nonelectrical Machinery
85	Electrical Machinery

$ Billions

Source: U.S. Department of Commerce, Census Bureau

Environment: The Border Environment Cooperation Commission (BECC) and the North American Development Bank (NADBank) were created as part of the NAFTA. The BECC and NADBank constitute a binational approach to environmental infrastructure development and financing in the U.S.–Mexico border region. The NADBank has provided $810.4 million in loans and/or grant resources to partially finance 95 infrastructure projects estimated to cost a total of $2.5 billion to build.

UNITED STATES–SINGAPORE FTA

The United States–Singapore FTA was signed on May 6, 2003, and entered into force January 1, 2004. It was the first such agreement with an Asian country. The agreement provided for state-of-the-art protections for Internet commerce and intellectual property, and helped drive growth and innovation in the dynamic technology sectors. Resulting in immediate zero tariffs on all U.S. products, the United States–Singapore FTA, as well as the negotiations themselves, set important benchmarks upon which successive FTA negotiations have been based.

The successful conclusion of the United States–Singapore FTA expands market access opportunities for U.S. companies by over 4.2 million consumers and $116.7 billion in GDP (2005). Since the FTA came into force, exports have increased by 50 percent to $24.7 billion in 2006. Singapore's exports to the U.S. increased to $17.8 billion in 2006 for total trade of $42.5 billion.

Major accomplishments include:

Intellectual Property Rights: Under the FTA, U.S. producers of creative material and innovative products benefit from higher standards for protecting intellectual property rights such as copyrights, patents, trademarks, and trade secrets and enhanced means for enforcing those rights. In line with its FTA commitments and obligations under international treaties and conventions, Singapore has developed one of the strongest IPR regimes in Asia. Amendments to the Trademarks Act, the Patents Act, the Layout Designs of Integrated Circuits Act, and the Registered Designs Act, as well as a new Plant Varieties Protection Act, and a new Manufacture of Optical Discs Act came into effect in July 2004. The amended Copyright Act became effective in January 2005, and was further amended in August 2005.

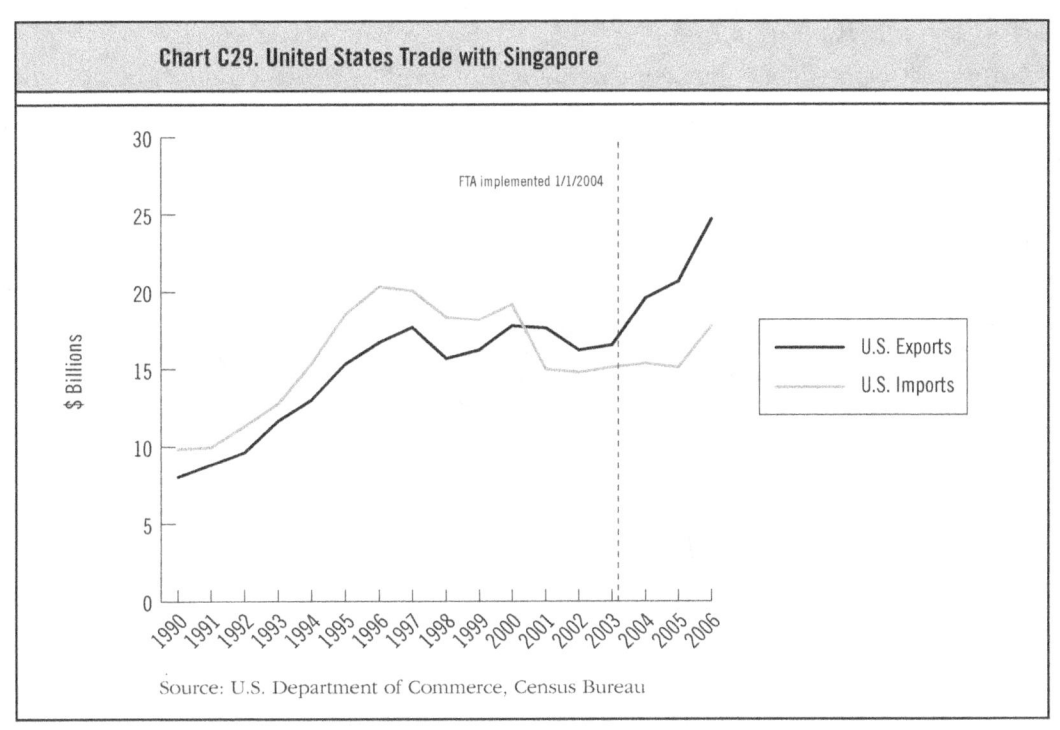

Chart C29. United States Trade with Singapore

FTA implemented 1/1/2004

U.S. Exports
U.S. Imports

Source: U.S. Department of Commerce, Census Bureau

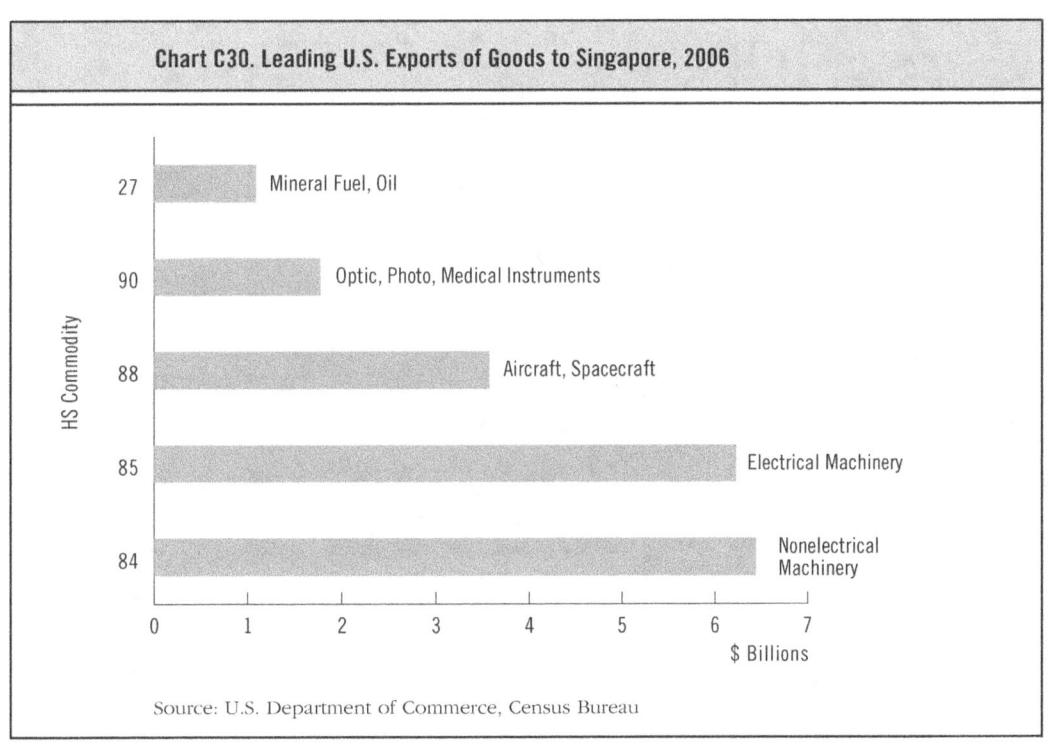

Chart C30. Leading U.S. Exports of Goods to Singapore, 2006

27 Mineral Fuel, Oil

90 Optic, Photo, Medical Instruments

88 Aircraft, Spacecraft

85 Electrical Machinery

84 Nonelectrical Machinery

$ Billions

Source: U.S. Department of Commerce, Census Bureau

Government Procurement: The FTA expands on the access of U.S. firms to Singapore government procurement by applying a threshold for central government procurement that is lower than the threshold both countries apply as GPA Parties.

Investment: The agreement establishes a more secure and predictable legal framework for U.S. investors operating in Singapore. All forms of investment are protected under the United States–Singapore FTA, including real property, enterprises, debt, concessions, and intellectual property.

Appendix D
Acronyms and Abbreviations

ACP	Aviation Cooperation Program
AKI	Agricultural Knowledge Initiative (U.S.-India)
AMT	Association for Manufacturing Technology
APP	Asia Pacific Partnership
B2B	business-to-business
B2C	business-to-consumer
B2G	business-to-Government
BCI	Business Competitiveness Initiative
BCIU	Business Council for International Understanding
BEA	Bureau of Economic Analysis (U.S. Department of Commerce)
CAFTA-DR	Central America-Dominican Republic-United States Free Trade Agreement
C.O.D.	Cash on Delivery
CS	Commercial Service (U.S. Department of Commerce)
DEC	District Export Council
DFI	Digital Freedom Initiative
DHS	Department of Homeland Security

ECA	Export Credit Agency
EDN	Enterprise Development Network (OPIC)
EESR	Economic Empowerment in Strategic Regions Initiative
EIU	Economist Intelligence Unit
ELAN	Export Legal Assistance Network
ENR	Egyptian National Railway
EU	European Union
Ex-Im Bank	Export-Import Bank of the United States
FAA	Federal Aviation Administration
FAS	Foreign Agricultural Service (USDA)
FDI	foreign direct investment
FHWA	Federal Highway Administration
FRA	Federal Rail Administration
FTA	Federal Transit Administration
FTA	Free Trade Agreement
FUSE	Featured U.S. Exporters
FY	fiscal year
G7	Group of Seven
GAC	General Administration of Customs (China)
GCI	Global Competitiveness Index
GDP	Gross Domestic Product
GII	Global Innovation Index

HTCG	High Technology Cooperation Group (U.S.-India)
ICT	information and communications technology
IDB	Inter-American Development Bank
IFA	International Franchise Association
IMF	International Monetary Fund
IP	intellectual property
IPR	intellectual property rights
IT	information technology
ITA	International Trade Administration (U.S. Department of Commerce)
JCCT	Joint Commission on Commerce and Trade (U.S.–China)
MAG	market access grant
MCC	Millennium Challenge Corporation
MEFTA	Middle East Free Trade Area Initiative
MOU	Memorandum of Understanding
NAICS	North American Industry Classification System
NAFTA	North American Free Trade Agreement
NCSL	National Council of State Legislators
OECD	Organization for Economic Cooperation and Development
OIT	Office of International Trade (SBA)
OPIC	Overseas Private Investment Corporation
PLP	Preferred Lenders Program (SBA)

PMMI	Packaging Machinery Manufacturers Institute
SBA	Small Business Administration
SBDCs	Small Business Development Centers
SCORE	Service Corps of Retired Executives
SED	Strategic Economic Dialogue
SIDO	State International Development Organizations
SMEs	small and medium-sized enterprises
SPS	sanitary/phytosanitary
SRTGs	State Regional Trade Groups
STOP	Strategy Targeting Organized Piracy
TIA	Travel Industry Association
TPA	Trade Promotion Authority
TPCC	Trade Promotion Coordinating Committee
TPF	Trade Policy Forum (U.S.–India)
TPIS	Trade Policy Information System
TRIPS	Trade-Related Aspects of Intellectual Property Rights
UN	United Nations
UNCTAD	United Nations Conference on Trade and Development
USAEDC	U.S. Agricultural Export Development Council
USAID	U.S. Agency for International Development
USDA	U.S. Department of Agriculture
USEAC	U.S. Export Assistance Center

USLGE   U.S. Livestock Genetics Export, Inc.

USPTO   U.S. Patent and Trademark Office
(U.S. Department of Commerce)

USTDA   United States Trade and Development Agency

USTR   Office of the United States Trade Representative

WBCs   Women's Business Centers

WEF   World Economic Forum

WIPO   World Intellectual Property Organization

WTO   World Trade Organization

Appendix E
Federal Trade Promotion Resource Guide

GENERAL COUNSELING AND ASSISTANCE

- **Export.gov**—the U.S. Government's export assistance portal (*http://www.export.gov*)

- **Trade Information Center (TIC)**—first stop for export assistance (1-800-USA-TRADE)

- **U.S. Export Assistance Centers (USEACs)**—one-stop domestic shops for Commercial Service, SBA, and Ex-Im Bank services (for location, contact 1-800-USA-TRADE or visit *http://www.export.gov/eac/index.asp*)

- **Agricultural counseling and assistance**—local, state, and regional contacts (*http://www.fas.usda.gov/agx/counseling_advocacy/counseling_advocacy.asp*)

- **Small Business Development Centers (SBDCs)**—new-to-export counseling and training (for location, contact 1-800-USA-TRADE or *www.sba.gov/sbdc*)

- **State.gov**—for investment/expropriation disputes, contact agreements, market access, and policy advocacy assistance

- **Business Visa Center**—connects U.S. firms with the State Department's Bureau of Consular Affairs for business travel facilitation (*http://travel.state.gov/visa*)

- **Export Legal Assistance Network (ELAN)**—free initial legal assistance through a U.S. Government program with the Federal Bar Association (*www.export-legal-assistance.org/*)

- **Service Corps of Retired Executives (SCORE)**—volunteers provide real-world business expertise to new firms, including new exporters (*www.score.org*)

- **Manufacturing Extension Partnership (MEP)**—productivity and efficiency counseling for U.S. manufacturers (*http://www.mep.nist.gov*)

- **Foreign Trade Statistical Regulations**—describes exporters' reporting requirements (*www.census.gov/traderegs*)

- **Automated Export System (AES) and AESDirect**—the Census Bureau's free Internet system for filing electronic export information (*www.census.gov/aes*)

EXPORT CONTROLS AND LICENSING

- **U.S. Department of State's Directorate of Defense Trade Controls**— (*www.pmddtc.state.gov*)

- **U.S. Department of Commerce's Bureau of Industry and Security**—guidance on export licensing requirements under the Export Administration Regulations—visit *www.bis.doc.gov* or call the Office of Exporter Services– 202-482-4811 (DC) or 949-660-0144 (CA)

MARKET RESEARCH AND STATISTICS

- **Market Research Library**—Access information from our embassies and consulates (users must register) (*http://www.export.gov/mrktresearch/index.asp*)

- **TradeStats Express**—Display and graph U.S. trade by country and product (*http://tse.export.gov*)

- **U.S. Census Bureau**—foreign trade statistics (*http://www.census.gov/foreign-trade/statistics/index.html*)

- **Agricultural Trade Data**—(http://www.fas.usda.gov/data.asp)

- **Customized Market Research**—custom/fee-based responses to issues related to a client's product or service (call 1-800-USA-TRADE for nearest USEAC location)

- **Export Trading Company Affairs**—assistance in forming U.S. Export Joint Ventures (*www.ita.doc.gov/oetca*)

COUNTRY AND SECTOR-SPECIFIC ASSISTANCE

- **Commercial Service Overseas Offices**—150 offices within embassies and consulates in 80 countries worldwide (*http://www.buyusa.gov/home/world-wide_us.html*)

- **Foreign Agricultural Service Overseas Offices**—representatives in 80 embassies and trade offices worldwide (*http://www.fas.usda.gov/scriptsw/fasfield/ovs_directory_search.asp*)

- **Department of State Economic–Commercial Offices**—At the 100 Embassies and 40 Consulates where there is no Commercial Service Office, U.S. Department of State staff are responsible for providing commercial services

- **Country Desk Officers**—ITA experts on the commercial, economic, and political climates in assigned countries (call 1-800 USA-TRADE for appropriate contacts)

- **Industry Desk Officers**—ITA industry experts and economists, sector specific Web resources (*http://www.trade.gov/mas*)

- **Region-specific Business Information Centers**—China (*http://www.export.gov/china/*); Russia and the Newly Independent States (*http://www.bisnis.doc.gov/bisnis/bisnis.cfm*); Middle East and North Africa (*http://www.export.gov/middleeast/*)

INTERNATIONAL SALES AND MARKETING

Commercial Service: call 1-800-USA-TRADE for nearest USEAC location or visit *http://www.export.gov/eac/index.asp*

- **Gold Key**—for firms visiting a foreign country: orientation briefings, meetings with pre-screened potential partners, interpreters, follow-up planning

- **International Partner Search**—find qualified international buyers, partners, or agents without traveling overseas

- **Platinum Key**—long-term, custom-made assistance for firms entering a market, bidding on a contract, resolving problems or market access issues

- **International Company Profile**—checks the reputation, reliability, and financial status of a prospective trading partner

- **Commercial News USA**—product catalog promoting U.S. products and services to more than 400,000 international buyers in 145 countries

Foreign Agricultural Service:
www.fas.usda.gov/agx/partners_trade_leads/partners_trade_leads.asp

- **Foreign Buyer Lists**—more than 25,000 foreign buyers in more than 80 countries

- **U.S. Supplier Lists**— searchable database of U.S. suppliers

- **Export Directory of U.S. Food Distribution Companies**—mixed containers

FOREIGN AND DOMESTIC TRADE EVENTS
(http://www.export.gov/eac/trade_events.asp)

- **Foreign Trade Fairs and Exhibits**—U.S. Government promotes U.S. pavilions and support services in worldwide trade fairs

- **Trade Missions**—group travel to one or more foreign markets for appointments with officials and prospective business partners (Note: agricultural trade missions are managed through the State Regional Trade Groups [*http://www.srtg.org/*])

- **Product Literature and Sample Displays**—low-cost, industry-focused exhibits at trade shows where U.S. Government officials display U.S. company literature and samples

- **International Buyer Program**—groups of qualified international buyers are brought to major U.S. trade shows to meet U.S. firms

- **Orientation Visits**—foreign government visits to the United States to meet U.S. industry and government representatives (call USTDA Information Resource Center: 703-875-4357)

FINANCING AND GRANTS

■ **U.S. Small Business Administration (SBA)**—business development and working capital guarantees/loans for small businesses (*http://www.sba.gov/aboutsba/sbaprograms/internationaltrade/index.html*)

■ **Export-Import Bank**—export credit insurance, working capital, and foreign buyer guarantees/loans (*http://www.exim.gov/products/index.html*)

■ **Overseas Private Investment Corporation (OPIC)**—political/foreign exchange risk insurance, direct loans for direct investment in developing countries (*http://www.opic.gov/*)

■ **U.S. Department of Agriculture**—export credit guarantee programs and business development grants (*http://www.fas.usda.gov/excredits/ecgp.asp*)

■ **Multilateral Development Banks**—Commercial Service Offices at each of the five Multilateral Development Banks (*http://www.buyusa.gov/worldbank/*)

■ **U.S. Trade and Development Agency (USTDA)**—technical assistance, feasibility studies, training, orientation visits, and business workshops for infrastructure projects in developing and middle income countries (*http://www.ustda.gov/*)

■ **Market Development Cooperator Program**—competitive matching funds for non-profit export multipliers, e.g., states, associations, chambers, world trade centers (*http://www.trade.gov/mdcp/*)

HELP WITH TRADE PROBLEMS

■ **The Advocacy Center**— helps level the playing field on foreign government procurements (*http://www.export.gov/advocacy/*)

■ **Country Desk Officers**—in ITA's Market Access and Compliance unit (call 1-800 USA-TRADE for appropriate contacts)

■ **Trade Compliance Center**—Online gateway and one-stop shop for addressing foreign trade barriers or unfair practices (*http://tcc.export.gov*)

- **National Center for Standards and Certification Information**—non-agricultural foreign standards, technical regulations, conformity assessment (*http://ts.nist.gov/standards/conformity/ncsci.cfm/* or call 1-301-975-4040)

- **Strategy Targeting Organized Piracy (STOP!)**—protecting intellectual property rights (*http://www.stopfakes.gov/* or call 1-866-999-HALT)